BETWEEN OBAMA'S LINES

How We Almost Lost The Middle East, The Cold War, and The Atlantic Alliance

Franck Prissert

The Other Street
127 Dalena Way
Palm Beach Gardens
Fl. 33418
Tel: 561.714.3904

Figures 2, 3, 12, and 13 are Courtesy of the University of
Texas Libraries, The University of Texas at Austin.

ISBN: 978-1-7328326-1-9 (sc)
ISBN: 978-1-7328326-4-0 (hc)
ISBN: 978-1-7328326-3-3 (e)

Because of the dynamic nature of the Internet, any web addresses or links contained in
this book may have changed since publication and may no longer be valid. The views
expressed in this work are solely those of the author and do not necessarily reflect the
views of the publisher, and the publisher hereby disclaims any responsibility for them.

Any people depicted in stock imagery provided by Getty Images are
models, and such images are being used for illustrative purposes only.
Certain stock imagery © Getty Images.

Lulu Publishing Services rev. date: 11/09/2018

The Other Street®

"If I know this, everybody does. But if I don't tell you, who will?" – Dad, 1928-2017.

"When people don't know, they don't understand. When they don't understand, they don't care. This is when things happen. All it takes is a goon with bad intentions, and it's over before people find out what they don't know."

Contents

Foreword

It was a gorgeous morning in the Catskills this 18th of July 2013. The Delaware River was sparkling, the sun just warm enough in the morning breeze. Breakfast at Circle K was its usual funky, in the local groove. Went back to the cabin, readying for camp visiting weekend, circus time.

Then it hit me, out of the blue. A daymare. Something was decidedly wrong with our policy in the Middle East. And Russia.

The Administration was lying about Benghazi. It was condoning the Muslim Brotherhood. It was allowing Iran to become a nuclear power and befriending its new President, Rouhani. It was letting the Iraqi Kurds down, snubbing Israel and Saudi Arabia, chastising the Egyptian leader, and ineptly standing by, watching the Syrian genocide. It was creating a power vacuum, knowing full well it would be filled by al-Qaeda, or worse, by Russia.

A year later, Team Obama was still negotiating, but Russia had filled the vacuum. Adding Crimea, Yemen, and a bit of Iraq to its Grand Board of Go[1], it was on its way to unfettered access to the Arabian Sea and the Indian Ocean. The Tipping Point in its Eurasian quest, and the bell toll for Atlanticism. The Russo-Islamic Alliance it was, scripted in Putin's early days by a fellow by the name of Aleksandr Dugin[2], fully scary and deserving of his Rasputin nickname.

In 1947, President Truman had warned about the danger of communism spreading to the Middle East. President Obama had apparently decided it was time to revisit. It came down to simple questions. Who was he? Who were his advisors? What was his motivation? And how was it that Russia was about to finally win the Cold War, under his watch?

This is where we were, in mid-2014.

On the domestic side, there was a tangible move to the UNanny States of America, a combination of welfare and Other People's Money. In other countries, it was called Socialism, or Communism. In the U.S., we did not have a name for it. The CPUSA[3] was a thing of the past, but President Obama had a slogan, "Change."

On Foreign Policy, the script was a flashback to the Nineteen Thirties, in the neutralism and appeasement era of Franklin Roosevelt and Neville Chamberlain. Truman was out, Global Anything was in. The Military was out, Apologies were in.

Another flashback was anti-Semitism. A creeping vocal wave that spread from Norway to Europe to Russia to the Middle East, and even to United States' Student Campuses. Judenrein was still part of the vocabulary, eighty years later. And louder.

Because today's conflicts are rooted in the past, I decided to look back. This was not going to be just another Obama story. I will spare you the historical account of past Presidents' blunders, except for a blurb on President Eisenhower and his Special Group, when they shaped the Cold War. Instead, I thought we should focus on how we got to The Tipping Point, and try to figure out why.

The only way to do this was to connect hard-to-find dots. Because so many foreign policy decisions were not making sense, because conspiracy theory is a business, conventional media and official declarations had to be double checked, and then some. At times, it was quite difficult to discern facts from fiction which is why, in the end, this is a non-fiction fiction book, somewhat of an unfinished puzzle. And because it did not make sense in the first place, I admit to having my own theory in mind, "To Be Or Not FSB".

The FSB, short for Federal Security Service of the Russian Federation, was created in 1995. It was the successor of the FSK, short for Federal Counterintelligence Service, which itself was created after the fall of the Soviet Union in 1991. In the battle of acronyms, it was merely the KGB, renamed. First, there was Yevgeny Primakov, an apparatchik all the way back to the Khrushchev years, a spymaster by excellence, and specialist of the Middle East, who ultimately became Yieltsin's interim Prime Minister.

Then there was the man in charge of the Russian Federation since 2000, and its current President, Vladimir Putin, who had served in the KGB for sixteen years, and as Director of the FSB in 1998-1999.

Finally, there was this Aleksandr Dugin fellow who had written a little known 600-page book titled "Foundations of Geopolitics".

The book, published in 1997, instantly became the textbook of the General Staff Academy of Russian Military, the equivalent of West Point. It basically laid out the plan for Russia to conquer Eurasia, and destroy the Atlantic alliance, i.e. the world as we know it. The means was Russia's vast natural resources, and the logistical corridor was the Russo-Islamic Alliance.

Very little has been written about it, except for a few think tank analyses. No English version except for a totally obtuse computer generated translation. In his 2009 sequel, "The Fourth Political Theory[4]," Dugin concluded:

> *"The current world is unipolar, with the global West as its center and with the United States as its core. [...] The American Empire should be destroyed. And at one point, it will be. [...] Spiritually, globalization is the creation of a grand parody, the kingdom of the Antichrist. And the United States is the center of its expansion.*

This was the extreme version of the Primakov Doctrine, which only got as far as a measured counter to the Atlantic Alliance.

Bottom line, in 2014, Russia's New Order strategy was staring us in the face, carefully executed yet nowhere in the headlines, and it was no secret.

To anyone who thinks the Cold War ended with President Reagan, that the Russo-Islamic Alliance is a figment of imagination, and that Russia's buck stops in the barren lands of the Middle East, think twice. Trashing decades of history, the question is, why did the Obama Administration knowingly led Russia to the gates of Eurasia?

"Why" is a difficult question. "How" is what you are about to read. It was still making no sense in 2018, but there was a new President.

1

The End

All television networks interrupted their regular programming. In the background, the video of a large scale explosion followed by a mushroom cloud was running in a cataclysmic loop, with charred human remains scattered on streets, buildings collapsed, people running, walking to nowhere or simply standing still, or crouched in a daze. The captions, in all languages, mostly in English and Arabic, laid it simple: "Israel strikes Iran".

In the foreground, the cameras showed a still image of the United Nations pulpit. The Permanent Security Council had been called for an emergency meeting, and the leaders of China, France, the Russian Federation, the United Kingdom and the United States had been meeting since the morning. The Presidents of the United States and Russia were to hold a joint conference, scheduled for 21:00 EST.

A day earlier, Iran had fired yet another missile test from its Sharud site in the North. In response, Israel had decided the time had come. Much like a date is about to expire on a milk carton, the threat of an Iranian nuclear or electromagnetic pulse attack had been imminent for too long. It was time to throw the carton out.

It was now 21:17 EST. The commentators' voice-overs were biding time, each with their own theory and bias. "It had to happen" one asserted. As all networks were suddenly watching the same show, it felt like an open discussion. Another replied: "Sure, but did you see this? It's a carnage." "No it is not, that's Al Jazeera's coverage[5]. I am one mile away from Arak, and there is no damage here. Lights out, but no fires." "Fox, shut up, we know where you come from." One chipped in, in Arabic, "Yaumul Hisab, this is The Day of Reckoning."

One thing was sure, Israel had targeted nine sites, curiously shaping a Star of David: Darkhouin, Mo'Allem Kalayeh, Khondab, Arak, Esfahan, Natanz, Jabr Ibn Hagan and Parchin[6], and one more in its center, target Fordow, near Qom.

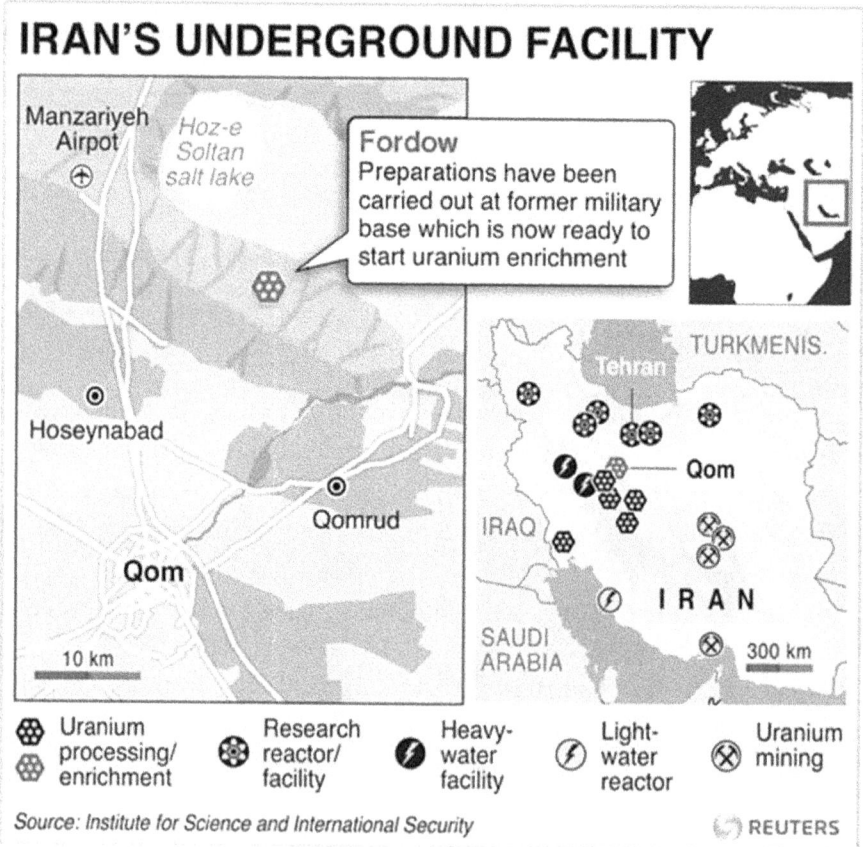

IRAN'S UNDERGROUND FACILITY

Source: Institute for Science and International Security — REUTERS

Figure 1 - Iran Nuclear Underground Facilities –
Courtesy of the Institute for Science and International Security.

A few seconds later, the mushroom cloud. Nobody could tell whether it was due to the Israeli missiles, or to the Iranian nuclear sites.

At 21:20, the Presidents of Russia and the United States walked into the United Nations conference room. They were flanked by all the members of the Permanent Security Council, and their aides. The first to speak was the Russian:

> "The Security Council strongly condemns the attack by Israel on its neighbor Iran, and deplores the loss of civilian lives that has resulted. This is not an act of self-defense, as Iran has not threatened Israel by any means. We are working on a resolution that shall prevent Israel from conducting any such operation in the future, and are urging its leaders to implement an immediate cease-fire. It will include sanctions to make her regret her senseless act of terror."

He then shook the hand of the American, and handed the pulpit over to him:

> "My fellow Americans, and citizens of the World, we are witnessing an historical moment. My predecessor would have certainly agreed with the Russian President, having let him take-over most of the Middle East, and turned his back on our allies in the region. But I do not. To the contrary, I reiterate my long held belief, that Israel not only has the right to self-defend herself – Iran acted first, and not for the first time -, but also, and more essentially, the right and duty to exist. In annihilating Iran's nuclear force, Israel and her allies have not only eliminated a threat to themselves, but the Russian threat to the world. You see [showing a chart of the Middle East], the red dots on this chart mark the countries where Russia has a strong presence, military or otherwise. It is pretty clear, and it is called the Russo-Islamic Alliance. The objective is no less clear. Russia has no economic interest in most of these barren lands,

with the exception of Iran, Iraq, their oil, and that of their neighbors. Russia's real interest lays in the access to the Arabian Sea, through the Strait of Bab el Mandeb on one side of the Arab Peninsula, and the Strait of Hormuz on the other. Through these Straits flow more than twenty percent of the world's oil products[7].

Why the Arabian Sea? In geopolitics, it is called the Gate to India. And India is the gate to China, as in Asia. And Asia is the final destination in Russia's Big Journey, the conquest of Eurasia. [Turning to President Putin] So, Vladimir – may I call you Vladimir? -, you just lost the key to the Big Journey. It is now time to change focus. Would you work with us on World Peace? [Turning back to the audience] I want to thank Israel for her patience through the years, for her tenacity, for her courage and determination. I want to thank all our friends and allies in the region, his Royal Highness King Salman, President al-Sisi, Sheikh Al Maktoum, President Masum, the Peshmerga, and all who understand that Peace is the only option. And I want to thank our men and women in uniform, here, in Israel and wherever they are to protect us, with their military might. God bless you, and God bless America."

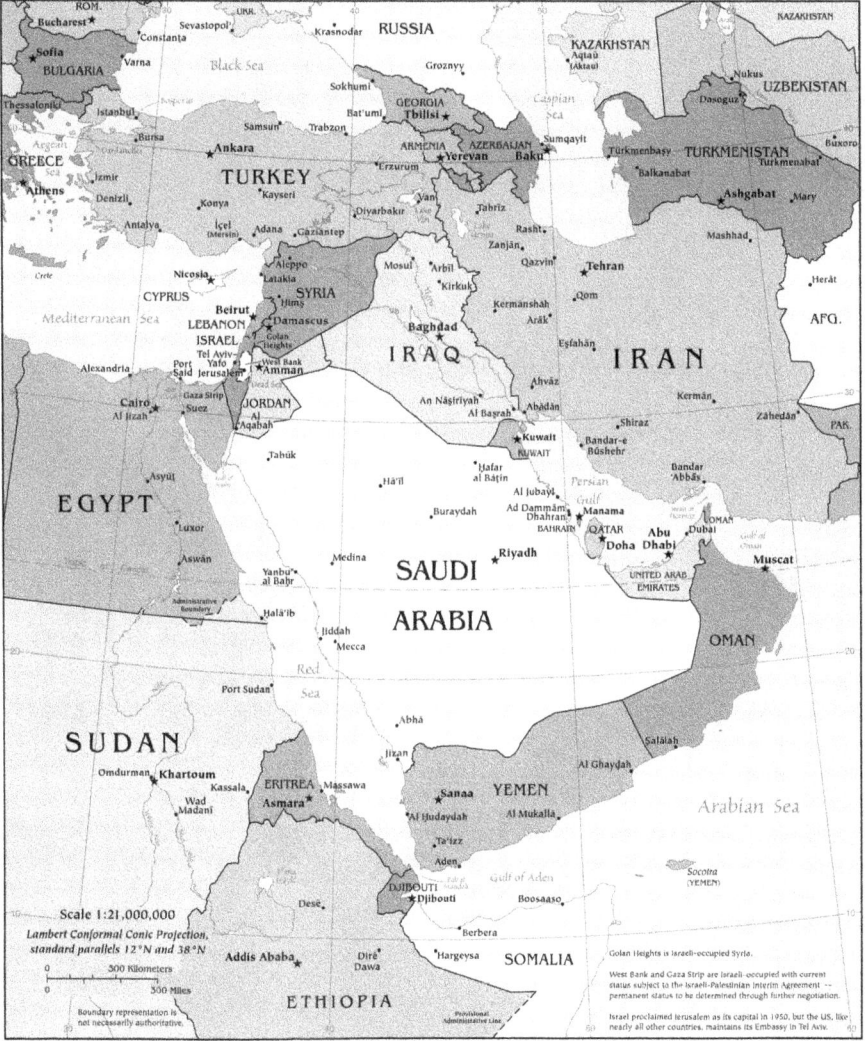

Figure 2 - The Middle East, and the Straits of Hormuz and
Bab el Mandeb to the Arabian Sea - Courtesy of the University
of Texas Libraries, The University of Texas at Austin.

2

Yuri's Trojan Horse

In late 1983, Yuri Andropov was confined in the Central Clinical Hospital of Kuntsevo in Western Moscow. Mikhail Gorbachev was his protégé[8].

"Mikhail Sergeyevich, how old are you?"

"I am fifty two, General Secretary."

"Well, I am sixty nine, and you are going to be the next General Secretary. I have so instructed the Central Committee. I do not have much longer to live, and this country needs young blood with fresh ideas. I have to bear my own load of good and bad. The old guard is corrupt, stale and awaiting its own death. Reagan may be a cowboy, he may be seventy two, but he will outlive them all. Trust me, once KGB, always KGB[9], I know. He needs a strong opponent, or Mother Russia will implode and all our sacrifices will have been in vain. I am the Evil, you are the nice guy. If this is going to happen, comrade, let's do it our way."

Gorbachev was remembering the omen from his mentor. On what would become his death bed, Andropov was still running the Politburo. What Andropov did not know was that the old guard would not surrender that easily. Upon his death in February 1984, instead of Gorbachev, the Central Committee appointed Konstantin Chernenko as General Secretary of the Communist Party of the Soviet Union, and chairman of the Presidium of the Supreme Soviet. Chernenko was not a nice guy, but he was fortunately quite ineffective. A pale imitator of Leonid Brezhnev, he mostly shared his penchant for vodka and personal piggy banks.

Andropov was right, however, as if he was still pulling the KGB strings even after his death. Chernenko, who had long been ailing, lasted ten months and died. Mikhail Sergeyevich Gorbachev was now General Secretary of the Communist Party of the Soviet Union. At the age of fifty four, he was defying the gravity of the phantom leaders before him. If there was to be a new dawn, this was his chance.

Forget Brezhnev, Khrushchev, and Stalin before them. The question was, how to get the Soviet Union into the 21st century? President Reagan saw three Soviet leaders die in less than three years. Hopefully, the fourth one would last long enough to strike a deal. This was 1985.

Gorby, as he became known, was lucky. His arch rival, Ronald Reagan, while a staunch anti-communist, shared the same "official" goal, Peace. Twenty odd years earlier, Eisenhower, on the advice of his own visceral anti-communist phobic Dulles Brothers, had rejected any détente proposal by Khrushchev. This time around, under the advice of State Secretaries Haig and Shultz, and Defense Secretaries Weinberger and Carlucci, time was ripe for a deal.

Official was a misnomer. The last time Peace was an international goal was in Yalta, in 1945, a mockery. Forty years later, the world was still in the same place – except for China, which had become a power of its own. Each side was spending gigantic sums of money to win an impossible war. For sure, there were Korea, Indonesia, Vietnam, the Middle East. But the overall conflict was America vs. the Soviet Union. Everybody knew this was a nuclear non-starter, despite the rhetoric and Khrushchev's shoe[10]. Time to act for the Gorby and Ronnie show. As high as the political and economic stakes were, the real underpinnings of the negotiations were personal and emotional. They both wanted to go down in history as the pair who had finally achieved "Peace." As in any chess tournament however, the next question was, who had the foresight for the nth move? The Russians were pretty good at chess.

President Reagan had won the first game in 1983. To paraphrase him: *"I am calling the USSR's bluff. You are an Evil Empire* [Andropov had gotten that right…]. *Our response is the Strategic Defense Initiative."*[11]

Reagan's "Star Wars" idea was simple. The Soviet Union had outspent itself in useless colonial wars but the United States still had deep pockets, even after the tough recession of the early eighties. If he was right, given the money involved, the Soviet Union would fold. He knew this, and he knew Andropov knew this too. You are not head of the KGB for fifteen years and a complete idiot. In August 1983, Andropov officially announced the end of all work on space-based weapons, preparing the stage for his protégé's deal with Reagan. In their shadow was Andropov's other protégé and future successor at the KGB, Vladimir Putin.

Looking out of the window, Gorby turned to Nikolai Ryskhov. He was rubbing his forehead as if a genie would come out of it. Nikolai was his economic counselor. The question before them was simple: now that the US was winning the Cold War, how could Mother Russia maintain its power over Europe – and then restore it to the World at large?

Longer term, the answer was the unpredictable chess tournament. In 1985, Gorbachev asked for a rematch, and it would be inspired by Greek tragedy, the Trojan Horse. It was the Russian's move.

"Niko, which country leads Europe?"

Ryskhov did not see it coming: *"West Germany, of course."*

"And West Germany is rich, right?"

"Yes…?"

"When did we build the Wall?"

"In 1961, I believe, General Secretary." When Ryskhov sensed a loaded question, he would stiffen with formal respect.

"How much does East Germany cost us, and what does it bring to Mother Russia?"

Ryskhov frowned. He was getting it. "Are you saying we should give the East back to the West?"

"Bravo Niko! Here is the plan. West Germany is the richest and most powerful country in Europe, and we are decaying because of war games that we have not been able to win for decades. East Germany burns an even bigger hole in our pocket, for no reason at all. We even had to build a Wall to keep our friends from leaving the party – no pun intended. Actually, if you ask me, I am not sure why we are fighting so hard to maintain our other Republics. Poland, Hungary, Czechoslovakia, Bulgaria – that's expensive yogurt. So, for starters, why not be "generous" with the West? I know Helmut Kohl well, real well[12]. He needs a coup to stay in power. Let him "force us" to give him East Germany."

"But, comrade, this is impossible. The East Germans are our people. We cannot turn back on two generations. President Reagan is a cowboy, it's a question of time before he runs out of money himself. And he is now a lame duck anyway. We are not going to play into his hand, are we? And if we lose East Germany, we could lose the other dominoes. Mother Russia will implode."

Gorbachev had Ryskhov trapped. "He may be quite smart, but he is still thinking inside the box," he thought to himself. "Niko, funny you would say that. It is exactly what Yuri Andropov told me a couple of years ago, and he clearly knew what he was talking about. The question is not if we will implode, but how. By "gifting" East Germany to Europe's strongest, we weaken the whole of Europe and with it its U.S. ally. We will then have to deal with only one problem, China, and the United States will look after themselves, as usual. We must lead the process, and act as if we did not see it coming. Otherwise, the old guard, the KGB, or worse, Stasi[13], will take us out."

So Gorbachev started building his Trojan Horse. The dominoes were worth sacrificing to save Mother Russia, and Perestroika and Glasnost were the smokescreens for Stasi[14].

President Reagan had to know about Anatoliy Golitsyn, the famous Soviet Major, senior analyst in the NATO section of the KGB Information Department, who had defected to the U.S. in December 1961. He had to know he was the one who led to the uncovering of the most famous Soviet double agents, the Cambridge Five[15], and that he wrote the 1984 book titled "New Lies For Old," about the Soviet long-term strategy of deception[16]. On June 12, 1987, President Reagan willfully took the bait. Standing tall in front of the West Berlin Brandenburg Gate,

"Mr. Gorbachev, Tear Down This Wall" he said.

Two months later, West Germany' Chancellor Helmut Kohl unilaterally decided to remove the joint U.S. – West German Pershing missile systems. On December 8, Gorbachev and Reagan signed the Intermediate-Range Nuclear Forces Treaty, or INF, later ratified by the U.S. Senate, 93 to 5. The Soviet Union was on a carefully orchestrated implosion schedule, much like an old plant is retired, and much like Yuri Andropov and Golitsyn had predicted. Both President Reagan and Secretary Gorbachev had their own public image to deal with, and the Peace Dividend was now at hand, to both men's posterity. Neither cared about Europe, really, and both knew East Germany was a poisoned gift. It would weigh on Germany for a generation or so, which would give ample time for the United States and Russia to carve out their own world. Britain also got it, it was Yalta all over again.

On October 18, 1989, Erich Honecker, the hardline leader of the German Democratic Republic since 1971, was forced to resign. He was replaced by Egon Krenz. Three weeks later, on November 9, 1989, Krenz opened all the gates of East Germany, including those leading to West Berlin. The Wall was down and Germany was officially reunified on August 31, 1990.

Secretary Andropov was still pulling the strings from his grave. You are not head of the KGB for fifteen years and a complete idiot. The breaking down of the Wall was a lure, Gorbachev's Trojan Horse, that President Reagan took at the first degree. The Russians had succeeded in planning the nth move. To the World, Russia was defeated, and the Cold War had ended.

First degree. No one suspected this could only be a draw. It would take some time, but the chess, tournament was not over, and Mother Russia would come back to win. Not to share the World, but to rule it, this time. The Wall was down, but the KGB was not[17].

Within two years, the Soviet Union imploded in tumultuous waves, including riots and rogue military coups. Every satellite state wanted independence, and got it. Andropov had failed to warn Gorby that he would be collateral damage. On December 27, 1991, Boris Yeltsin, newly elect President of the Russian Federation and leader of the Russian nationalist movement, moved into Gorbachev's office, two days after both had agreed to dissolve the Soviet Union.

Yeltsin was a brash nationalist reformer not very good at reforming. Instead of creating a market economy for the benefit of the people he was quite popular with, he enriched a minuscule new class of Russians, the oligarchs. With it came heavy corruption and deep economic and financial woes, which saw his popularity ultimately fade and his leadership contested.

In 1998, he appointed Putin head of the FSB, and Dugin, who had published "Foundations of Geopolitics" in 1997, became his Rasputin. One year later, Yeltsin, who under political pressure had also appointed Putin as Vice President, resigned with a surprisingly apologetic discourse[18]:

> "*Russia must enter the new millennium with new politicians, new faces, new intelligent, strong and energetic people. As for those of us who have been in power for many years, we must go. […]Why holding on to power for another six months, when the country has a strong person, fit to be president, with whom practically all Russians link their hopes for the*

future today? [...]In accordance with the constitution, as I go into retirement, I have signed a decree entrusting the duties of the president of Russia to Prime Minister Vladimir Vladimirovich Putin."

The reign of Vladimir Putin had begun. So did the preparations for the new chess game.

Upon Dugin's advice, he first had to replenish Russia's coffers, which he did, in particular through its oil and gas industry. He then restructured the military and police. For constitutional reasons, Dmitry Medvedev became Russia's President in May 2008 but, de facto, Putin remained in charge as Prime Minister

Putin had spent sixteen years in the KGB and two in the FSB. This was enough for him to know against whom he would want to play the next game. President Bush was too much of a hawk, but up and coming Senator Obama was a pacifist, possibly a friend for Russia. Coincidentally with the end of the Bush era, and in violation of the 1987 INF Treaty, Russia restarted its ballistic missile testing program in October 2008. She launched a SS-25 Sickle which hit its target in the Kamchatka peninsula in the Pacific, 6,000 kilometers away, and two others from a submarine in the Bering Sea[19]. Putin had chosen President Barack Obama as his next challenger, and Obama did not blink.

Mein Kampf was written in 1925. Eleven years later, in 1936, Hitler had established his Axis road map for a New Order, signing the Rome-Berlin pact with Mussolini, and the Anti-Comintern pact with Japan. Even Winston Churchill agreed, in support of the Hoare-Laval pact to partition Ethiopia. The U.S., for its part, was in non-intervention isolationist mode, with the Nye Committee[20] and the Neutrality Acts of 1935, 1936, 1937 and 1939.

In Dugin's case, 1997 plus eleven equaled 2008. It was Putin's turn to map his New Order, Eurasia. This is when the Obama Administration's Foreign Policy lapses became exposed, but Russia no longer seemed to be the enemy. Not only the new President did not blink about missiles in 2008, but four years later, he still was not blinking, witness a private conversation he had with President Medvedev, caught on a hot microphone at a conference in Seoul on March 26, 2012:

President Obama: *"On all these issues, but particularly missile defense, this can be solved, but it is important for him* [incoming Russian President Putin] *to give me space."*

President Medvedev: *Yeah, I understand your message about space. Space for you..."*

President Obama [with a friendly tap on Medvedev's hand]: *"This is my last election. After my election I have more flexibility."*

President Medvedev: *"I understand. I will transmit this information to Vladimir. I understand you."*[21]

3

The Red Web

A lot was happening in the late Fifties, early Sixties, which would define the years to come between the United States, Russia, and the rest of the world for that matter.

There was a short cut to describe this state of affairs: the Cold War. President Truman is credited for coining the term, with his address before a joint session of Congress in March 1947[22]. Then, he expressed what was to become the Truman Doctrine - the United States was to support Greece and Turkey, economically and militarily, against the Communist threat in the Middle East:

> "One of the primary objectives of the foreign policy of the United States is the creation of conditions in which we and other nations will be able to work out a way of life free from coercion. This was a fundamental issue in the war with Germany and Japan. Our victory was won over countries which sought to impose their will, and their way of life, upon other nations".

> "If Greece should fall under the control of an armed minority, the effect upon its neighbor, Turkey, would be immediate and serious. Confusion and disorder might well spread throughout the entire Middle East".

He had to. Aside from Germany and Japan, there was only one country, or block of countries, the U.S.S.R.[23], *"which sought to impose their will, and their way of life, upon other nations."* At the Potsdam Conference in July-August 1945, the Allies had agreed, among other things, to withdraw from Iran within six months. The British and Soviet forces had occupied it since 1941 in order to control the supply route to the U.S.S.R., known as the "Persian Corridor."[24] Stalin decided otherwise, and expanded the Soviet presence in the country, establishing two communist Republics, the Azerbaijan's People's Republic, and the Kurdish Republic of Mahabad. It took the new Shah's army, backed by the United States, to liquidate the Soviet groups in 1946. In the meantime, Stalin had negotiated a majority ownership in Iran's natural resources. On the strength of the Truman Doctrine, with assurances of U.S. economic support, the newly elected Iranian parliament reneged on the agreement. This cemented the U.S. - Iran relationship, effectively displacing British and Soviet control.

Stalin died in 1953, and Nikita Khrushchev succeeded him. Three years later, in a pivotal "Secret Speech[25]" titled *"On the Cult of Personality and its Consequences*[26]*,"* he denounced Stalin's purges and started advocating a 180 degree shift to de-Stalinization and "Peaceful Coexistence" with the West, known as the "Khrushchev Thaw".

Easier said than done. In the U.S., President "Ike" Eisenhower had taken over after Truman, with John Foster Dulles as Secretary of State and his brother Allen Director of CIA. The Dulles Brothers were phobic anti-communists. Truman disliked them, Eisenhower could not do without. In 1954, President Eisenhower had signed NSC 5412, the "National Security Council Directive on Covert Operations" under which the newly created and secret NSC 5412/2 "Special Group" would operate. It only had five members: the President, the National Security Advisor, the Undersecretaries of State and Defense, and the CIA Director.

Despite their reluctance, it looked as if Detente could work. In the aftermath of Khrushchev's leaked "Secret Speech," public outcry about the revelations of the Great Purge had decimated the ranks of the CPUSA – which is why we do not talk about it anymore[27], hence this walk down memory lane. In September 1959, Khrushchev had visited the United States, in a much mediatized and somewhat candid way. The American people bought it, if for no other reason that Marilyn Monroe and Dean Martin did[28].

The Dulles and Eisenhower did not. John Foster, then dead, had distorted the Truman Doctrine to the extreme, and his legacy was vivid. In his animus, there were two sides, with no room for interpretation. The Communists and the Free World. Allen Dulles was easier to understand. Without a communist enemy, he would have no "raison d'etre". This left President Eisenhower with a choice, Détente or no Détente. He chose the latter.

1960 was a wake-up call for Khrushchev. On May 1, as American spy plane missions had resumed over the Soviet Union, a U-2 was downed. Its pilot, Francis Gary Powers was captured, failing to commit suicide. He was under Allen Dulles' command and Eisenhower, not knowing of Powers' capture for five days, made up a story about a weather research aircraft that had been lost in a storm. Unfortunately, the captured plane's spy cameras were intact. Khrushchev blew up. Détente was no longer an option.

In June of that same year, Congo had gained independence from Belgium. Its first President was the puppet Joseph Kasavubu. His Prime Minister was the popular nationalistic Patrice Lumumba. Congo had been under the strict and bloody rule of the Belgium Kingdom since 1885[29], so it was not much of either the Soviet Union or the United States business.

Until the Belgians, fearing for their interests in this resource-rich country two-thirds the size of Western Europe[30], tried to maintain control. In a matter of weeks, the struggle had turned into a bloody civil war, and Lumumba, naively committed to neutrality, asked for help from both sides of the Atlantic. Khrushchev, no longer in a conciliatory mood with the West, reverted to the old Comintern policy of international expansion, and offered his support, much like he had in Ghana, the Gold Coast. This naturally upset Eisenhower's Special Group. To them, in John Dulles' tradition, there was no such thing as a neutral nationalist.

Not only Lumumba's request fell on deaf U.S. ears, but the Special Group decided to have him assassinated[31]. And so he savagely was, on January 17, 1961, by the Katangese rebels under CIA and Belgian command.

This was not the first time the Eisenhower Administration would be upset at an active nationalist. Before Lumumba, the CIA and State Dulles duo had removed Mohammad Mosaddegh in Iran in 1953[32], and Jacobo Arbenz in Guatemala in 1954. In 1956, they were unsuccessful at removing North Vietnam's Ho Chi Minh, and in 1958, they botched a similar attempt on Indonesia's Sukarno.

Next would be Fidel Castro, in Cuba. If there was a doubt about how communist the others on Dulles' list were, there was none in Castro's case. Together with his brother Raul and Che Guevara, they had created the notorious guerilla revolutionary movement "26th of July," back in the early 1950's. On New Year's Eve 1958, having lost support from the U.S., the Cuban dictator Fulgencio Batista fled the island with some two hundred of his closest associates, and Castro took over.

This was way too close to comfort. President Eisenhower, true to the Special Group, approved Allen's proposal to remove him. Young Senator Kennedy, then running against Vice President Richard Nixon in the 1960 Election, had to be appraised of the situation. An early detractor of Batista, he nevertheless endorsed the idea, but under one condition, no official U.S. boots on the ground. In April 1961, the Bay of Pigs Invasion, as it became known, failed miserably, and exposed U.S. involvement. President-elect Kennedy was more pragmatic than Eisenhower, he fired Allen Dulles. His days at the CIA were over, seemingly for good[33].

All and all, these turned out to be among the biggest blunders of the post WWII "Men In Charge and Their Intelligence." Iran ended up with the Ayatollahs, South America became a communist bastion, the Ho Chi Minh debacle led to the Vietnam War, and Islam would dominate Indonesia.

With Congo, and Ghana before it[34], Khrushchev had realized the importance of pan-Africanism in the pursuit of pan-communism. In 1960, he created the People's Friendship University, to proselytize future leaders from Africa and other Third World countries. After Lumumba's murder, he renamed it the Patrice Lumumba PFU. But this was not the first Soviet University to spin the red web around the world.

In 1919, Lenin had created the Communist International, also known as Comintern or the Third International, to fight,

> "*by all available means, including armed force, for the overthrow of the international bourgeoisie and for the creation of an international Soviet Republic as a transition stage to the complete abolition of the State[35]*".

Comintern was dissolved by Stalin in 1943. Despite the non-aggression Ribbentrop-Molotov pact he had signed with Germany in 1939, which itself strangely invalidated the 1937 Anti-Comintern pact Hitler had signed with Italy and Japan, Germany had invaded the Soviet Union in June 1941. By necessity, Stalin was now in the Allies' camp and could not have it both ways. So he closed down the communist gospel machine – for a while. In the meantime, however, the mantra had been spread through a score of international red webs, some kind of carrier pigeon network, which included two fairly well-kept secret schools. The first one was the Communist University of the Toilers of the East, known as KUTV, or the Stalin School, founded in 1921 to train Bolshevik cadres to infiltrate and promote communism in the colonial world. At the time, the main colonial empires were French, Dutch, Belgian, Spanish, Portuguese, and British. Kenya was under British rule.

The second one was the International Lenin School, founded in 1926, two years after Lenin's death, to achieve the same in Europe and the United States.

One of the notorious alumni of both schools was Nebraskan Harry Haywood, born Hall[36]. Starting in the late Twenties, he became a prominent figure of the Communist Party of the United States, known as CPUSA[37], and of various other U.S. Communist organizations, such as the Provisional Organizing Committee for a Communist Party (POC), which he founded in 1958. A notable POC member was Coleman Young, who became the first African American Mayor of Detroit in 1974. Haywood also worked with Malcolm X and was a prolific leader of the African American Civil Rights movement. He was a staunch communist[38].

Another alumnus of KUTV was Jomo Kenyatta, Kenya's Prime Minister in this strange year of 1961. He became President in 1964, one year after Independence. It was in 1932-1933, when he was in his late thirties, that he was schooled in the Communist University of the Toilers of the East, KUTV. He had moved to England in 1931 to attend the Woodbroke Quaker College in Birmingham – Kenya is home to the largest Quaker population in the world[39]. There he befriended British Communists who brought him to KUTV's attention. He then returned to the London School of Economics from 1935 to 1938, where he followed the teachings of world renowned anthropologist and socialist Bronislaw Malinowski[40], "The Comparative Study of Culture".

Attending the same seminar was Ralph Bunche, of distinguished fame as U.S. political scientist, civil rights activist, diplomat and future Nobel Peace Prize[41], and they became friends.

While in London, Kenyatta also became an active member of the pan-African, anti-colonial International African Service Bureau, founded by the international communist leader George Padmore[42]. Padmore had joined the CPUSA in 1927, and was active in the

American Negro Labor Congress. In 1929, he was tapped by the General Secretary, Chicago-based radical labor organizer William Z. Foster, to go to Moscow.

There, he briefly headed the Negro Bureau of Profintern, i.e. the Red Internationale of Labor Unions, whose agent in the United States was the same Foster. Small world indeed, Bunche had taught Padmore at Howard University, where he chaired the Department of Political Science from 1928 to 1950. And Padmore was Kwame Nkrumah's official advisor on African Affairs during Ghana's fight for independence[43].

During his career, Padmore worked closely with W.E.B. Du Bois, the first African American to earn a doctorate degree from Harvard and also a leader of the pan-African and Civil Rights movement, widely credited for his contribution to the Civil Rights Act of 1964.

For most of his life, Du Bois was officially ambivalent about Communism. However, he associated with enough leftists that the Justice Department indicted him in 1950, alleging he was a foreign agent as chairman of the Peace Information Center. Du Bois had created the Center to promote the work of the Soviet-backed World Peace Council, based in Helsinki and chaired by the communist French nuclear physicist and Soviet spy Frederic Joliot-Curie. The Center was advocating an international ban on nuclear weapons. In fact, it had been buying time, as the Soviet Union was badly lagging in nuclear warfare behind the United States. She had finally detonated her first test device in August 1949, four years after Hiroshima and Nagasaki, but was still ways behind. So the U.S. Soviet spy ring, led by Klaus Fuchs, David Greenglass, Harry Gold, and the famous Ethel and Julius Rosenberg, was to do its work. At the same time, Joliot-Curie was sharing similar secrets with the Soviets from the French side. It was only in 1961 that Du Bois joined the CPUSA, at age 93, and finally stated:

> "On this First day of October 1961, I am applying for admission to membership in the Communist Party of the

United States. I have been long and slow in coming to this
conclusion, but at last my mind is settled.[...] In the end,
Communism will triumph. I want to help to bring that
day." [44].

Among the other alumni of the Lenin School still ruling in the Sixties were Tito from Yugoslavia, Gomulka from Poland, Honecker from the German Democratic Republic (East Germany), Ho Chi Minh from Vietnam, Deng Xiao Ping from China, and General Secretaries from the French, Greek, Iraqi, Syrian and South African communist parties.

On August 13, 1961, a strange year indeed, the German Democratic Republic, member of the Union of Soviet Socialist Republics and known as East Germany, started building the Berlin Wall, effectively isolating West Berlin, controlled by NATO, from the rest of East Germany, controlled by the Warsaw Pact. With Checkpoint Charlie, it was a symbol of the borders that characterized the Iron Curtain[45] since the end of World War II.

A few days earlier, on August 4, a boy was born in Hawaii, to a Kenyan father. A story in earnest:

4

The Cold War

C old was a misnomer. World leaders were fighting with nuclear threats and spies. On the ground, this meant proxy wars, from Africa to Asia, from Congo to Korea to Vietnam. And a whole generation perished, on both sides, with no claim to victory except for death.

In 1946, the Intelligence and Secret Police of the Soviet Union had been retooled as the Ministry of State Security, or MGB. In response, President Truman signed into law the National Security Act of 1947, in essence creating the Central Intelligence Agency and the National Security Council, to succeed the Office of Strategic Services[46]. It was high time. By then, Russian spies had infiltrated the Administration, left and left[47]. Names like Jacob Golos, Elizabeth Bentley, Alger Hiss, Whittaker Chambers, Harry Dexter White, the Perol Group or the Silvermaster ring may not sound familiar, but a little research or a visit to the International Spy Museum in Washington will leave you speechless. In 1953, the MGB morphed into the Committee for State Security, known as KGB.

On the U.K. side was the unwavering British Secret Intelligence Service, or MI6, but it too had been infiltrated, with the infamous Soviet agents Harold "Kim" Philby, Donald Maclean and Guy Burgess of the "Cambridge Five" ending up in the British Embassy in Washington[48].

The Philby's deserve a special mention. It is fascinating to see how just a couple of secret service agents can shape history. Kim's full name was Harold Adrian Russell Philby, the son of Harry St. John Bridger "Jack" Philby[49]. While Kim ended up as your not-so-run-of-the-mill Russian double agent in the late Fifties, Jack had a much bigger claim to fame[50]. A British Intelligence Officer turned rogue, it was him, in 1925, who helped Ibn Saud retake the holy city of Mecca from Sharif Hussein bin Ali, whom the British were backing, and whose clan, the Hashemites, had ruled for seven centuries. In 1927, the British recognized Ibn Saud as the ruler of what is now Saudi Arabia. Philby, by then a free agent converted to Islam under the name of Sheikh Abdullah, and a British rule renegade, had become Ibn Saud's close adviser. As such, in the early Thirties, he played a leading role in snitching the Arabian oil fields from his former British bosses[51]. When oil was discovered in 1938, his new side job, commission wise, was the California-Arabian Standard Oil, a subsidiary of U.S. SoCal and Texaco which later became the Arabian-American Oil Company, or ARAMCO. WWII had not been declared yet, but all knew that a big piece of the puzzle had just come into play. Ibn Saud, officially neutral, was now owner of the Black Gold.

Of course, to pull that big one, Jack had to have some cooperative friends on the American side. Needed to look no further than Allen Dulles. He headed the State Department Near East Division, stationed in Constantinople, a.k.a. Istanbul, in Turkey. For two, there was Haj Amin al-Husseini, at the time Grand Mufti of Jerusalem, president of the Supreme Muslim Council, arch enemy of the British Mandate and advocate of a Judenrein Palestine[52], a policy Ibn Saud and Jack Philby publicly endorsed.

The Kim Philby story was not dull either[53]. In 1951, shortly after having been promoted from CIA Deputy Director for Plans, i.e. in charge of all foreign covert operations, to Deputy Director, period, Allen Dulles set out to infiltrate and foment guerilla operations in communist territories[54]. In a failure of epic proportion, with hundreds of agents killed or captured in Europe, and thousands in Asia, it turned out that the cause of failure was your "run-of-the-mill" double agent Kim Philby, officially the senior British intelligence officer assigned as liaison to Allen's CIA. In 1963, on the verge of being exposed by Anatoliy Golitsyn, among others[55], Kim Philby defected to Moscow.

On yet another side of the table was China. In 1921, the Communist Party of China, of Comintern substance, had been founded and Mao Zedong was one of its first two hundred members. In 1941, Chiang Kai-shek's Chinese Kuomintang was our "friend". In 1949, after defeating Chiang in the civil war that had been raging since 1927, Mao founded the People's Republic of China, with the backing of Stalin. She was now our foe.

The Cold War was in full swing and espionage was the thing. One way to fight the Soviet web was to play the same game and create a home-grown international army of anti-communist civil servants - spies, that is, mole for mole. The recruiters were mostly college officials, and the recruits were not only educated, but also Ivy League. In 1951, part of the former WWII Navy Construction Battalions Seabee[56] training base in Camp Peary, Virginia, was closed to the public and renamed "The Farm".

It was a Mole farm, and its products had an eager buyer, the Office of Policy Coordination (OPC). George Kennan, architect of the Soviet Containment Policy, had led to its creation in 1948, and Frank Wisner, Allen Dulles' long time OSS and operative friend[57], was its executive director. Wisner[58] had been recruited by Dean Acheson, then Under Secretary of State, soon to be Secretary of State himself. Kennan was Acheson's Director of Policy Planning Staff. Little by little, five of these Cold War power figures were involved. They were to later be called the Wise Men, six of them[59]. Averell Harriman, Robert Lovett, George Kennan, Dean Acheson, and John McCloy. Only Charles "Chip" Bohlen, the Soviet expert and the "dove" in the group, was missing from the Mole farm. He had been advocating a policy of accommodation with Stalin and was only the official top Russian translator.

The OPC was ruled by document NSC 10/2 of the National Security Council, dated June 18, 1948[60].

> "1. The National Security Council, taking cognizance of the vicious covert activities of the USSR, its satellite countries and Communist groups to discredit and defeat the aims and activities of the United States [...] has determined that, in the interest of world peace and U.S. national security, the overt foreign activities of the U.S. Government must be supplemented by covert operations. [...]
>
> 5. As used in this directive, "covert operations" are understood to be all activities (except as noted herein) which are conducted or sponsored by this Government against hostile foreign states or groups or in support of friendly foreign states or groups but which are so planned and executed that any U.S. Government responsibility for them is not evident to unauthorized persons and that if uncovered the U.S. Government can plausibly disclaim any responsibility for them. Specifically, such operations shall include any covert activities related to: propaganda, economic warfare; preventive direct action, including sabotage, anti-sabotage, demolition and evacuation measures; subversion against hostile states, including assistance to underground resistance movements, guerrillas and refugee liberation groups, and support of indigenous anti-communist elements in threatened countries of the free world. Such operations shall not include armed conflict by recognized military forces, espionage, counter-espionage, and cover and deception for military operations."

The directive could not be clearer. McCloy, the Dulles Brothers, the other Wise Men, were all essential to the Cold War. Regardless of the outcome, military strategy was not the only tool. The nerve was money but the brain was intelligence, as in espionage. Every major country had finally read Sun Tzu, Machiavelli and Clausewitz, and was perfecting their teachings. Through his spy mistress Mary Bancroft,

Allen Dulles had even introduced a new psychological dimension, in the person of the famed Swiss psychiatrist Carl Gustav Jung[61].

McCloy, for one, was later nicknamed "The Chairman", praised by many in the Establishment, yet his past was tainted by inconvenient memory lapses.

In 1947, after a stint at the Rockefellers' personal law firm of Milbank Tweed, he had been appointed President of the newly created World Bank. This was the man who had previously been the counsel of Rockefeller's Standard Oil of New Jersey and of her partner and major shareholder, I.G. Farben, the owner of I.G. Auschwitz.

The Bank, and the International Monetary Fund, had been created in 1944 as part of the Bretton Woods Agreement which a U.S. Treasury official, Harry Dexter White, had masterminded. White had been appointed assistant to Franklin Roosevelt's Secretary of the Treasury Henry Morgenthau, McCloy's "Jewish friend" and his brother-in-law Lew Douglas' arch enemy[62].

Herein laid one of the best example of the complex underground and Machiavellian mechanism, commonly known as Intelligence. Clearly, McCloy was anti-Soviet and, by definition yet in not so many words, pro-German. White, the man who put him in charge of the World Bank, then of the Bank for International Reconstruction, was later identified as a member of the Soviet NKVD[63] Silvermaster spy ring. It took until the testimony of other spies, Elizabeth Bentley and Whittaker Chambers[64], for the charges against White to be taken seriously. In August 1948, a couple of days after denying them before the House Un-American Committee, known as HUAC, White died of a heart attack apparently caused by an overdose of digitalis[65]. In the meantime, President Truman, still unconvinced, had appointed him head of the newly created International Monetary Fund.

Irony of ironies, not only John McCloy owed his promotion to the Jew Morgenthau, much decried by his anti-Semite brother-in-law, but also to the communist mole Harry Dexter White.

Coincidentally, in January 1948, the otherwise healthy director of the Thyssen Dutch bank, and former director of Averell Harriman's Union Banking Corporation, H.J. Kouwenhoven[66], also died of a heart attack. This is another story but in the Cold War era, even banking was a lethal business. Union Banking had been set up in 1922 to manage the interests of Fritz Thyssen, the German steel tycoon and early backer of Adolf Hitler. Through its Harriman 15 holding company, Harriman owned, among others, a majority interest in the Consolidated Silesian Steel Company, together with Thyssen, and Friedrich Flick, the other German steel magnate. It was located in Oswiecim, in Polish Silesia, renamed Auschwitz after the Nazi invasion. This is when Thyssen broke with the Nazis and ended up in Dachau. Flick, for himself, persisted and was indicted as a war criminal in the Nuremberg trials[67]. And while Union Banking and Harriman 15 were seized in 1942 by the Alien Property Custodian, under the Trading with the Enemy Act, Harriman remained one of FDR's closest advisor throughout. One of the Six Wise Men of the Cold War.

In 1949, McCloy, the former counsel of I.G. Farben, was back in Government, as U.S. High Commissioner for Allied Occupied Germany. The fox in the hen house, I.G. Farben had been one of the main defendants in the Nuremberg trials[68]. In his remarkable biography written by Kai Bird, "The Chairman", the author recounts McCloy's first meeting with Konrad Adenauer, who had just been elected Germany's first post-WWII Chancellor in September 1949. According to Bird, McCloy did not know much about him, and did not even know where he lived. When he found his house, Adenauer greeted him with these words,

"*I believe we are related*"[69].

They were indeed, and it is a stretch to think that McCloy did not know this. His best intelligence connections in the Administration were the Dulles Brothers. They were his business partners and knew the German political and industrial landscape inside out. So did he. McCloy could not have possibly ignored that Adenauer had been

Mayor of Cologne since 1917, the inventor of the autobahn, and a key anti-Nazi figure in the Rhineland. In addition, McCloy had married Ellen Zinsser in 1930, and Ellen's father Frederick was the first cousin of Adenauer's wife Auguste "Gussie", whom he had married in 1919. Since Ellen and her sister Peggy went to Germany to complete their education, it was unlikely they did not reunite. In those years, family ties were strong for those on both sides of the Atlantic.

Not only that, but the just married McCloy couple was sent to Paris in 1930, for McCloy to service his German clients. It would defy logic that he had not met with the reputable Mayor of Cologne, where Henry Ford had just opened a factory.

The fact was, McCloy, Douglas, Adenauer and with them John Zinsser, Ellen and Peggy's brother and partner of J.P. Morgan whom McCloy represented, were now in charge of Germany reconstruction. This looked like a family affair.

Klaus Barbie, the Nazi "Butcher of Lyon" was among McCloy's other inconvenient lapses. He had elected to keep him undercover as a U.S. agent of the Counter-Intelligence Corps, allowing him to later escape to Bolivia. Then, in 1950, he decided to appoint Reinhard Gehlen, another Nazi War criminal, as head of West Germany Secret Services. Gehlen was sought for war crimes by the Soviet Union, having led the German Foreign Armies East as their senior intelligence officer. To boot, in 1951, McCloy granted amnesty to Alfried Krupp, the steel and coal German magnate, Fritz Ter Meer, senior executive of I.G. Farben and his former client, and Friedrich Flick, each men having used thousands of slave laborers from S.S. concentration camps, killing most in the process. Not to mention he pardoned seventy nine of the eighty nine appeals from criminals indicted at the Nuremberg trials, and commuted the life sentence of five of the worst Nazi "Doctors", including the evil Dr. Herta Oberheuser. This led the outspoken Eleanor Roosevelt to write McCloy,

"Why are we freeing so many Nazis?"[70]

The answer on Gehlen was simple but politically incorrect[71]. He was one of Hitler's spymasters and had deployed some thirty five hundred agents in Eastern Europe and the Soviet Union. In 1945, he surrendered to the Americans. He had only one way to go, as he was carrying with him crates of intelligence on the Soviet High Command. This was enough for Captain John Bokor, Allen Dulles and "Wild Bill" Donovan, head of the OSS and known as the Father of American Intelligence, to circumvent the Yalta accords which required that Nazis from the Eastern Front be turned in to the Soviets[72]. He clearly was going to be of value to the United States in their upcoming fight with Stalin.

Whatever atrocities these criminals had committed, they were now supposedly needed in the field to combat Communism, whether it was in the coup brewing in Iran since Mohammad Mosaddegh had been elected Prime Minister, or in Korea where the one-year old war was pushing steel output worldwide. In October 1950, McCloy authorized Germany to increase its steel output from the previous ceiling of eleven million tons per year. For that, he needed the convicted Krupp, Flick, and Ter Meer. The means to the end, McCloy, the financier and lawyer of the previous humanity death squad, was now organizing the "Free World".

Nothing indicates that his fellow Wise Men Robert Lovett, then Secretary of Defense, and Dean Acheson, Secretary of State, agreed with his refreshed Nazi collaboration but, back then, it no longer really mattered. Hitler and his psychopath co-leaders had either committed suicide or been hung and it would take a while before the next Deus Ex Machina. For their part, John Foster and Allen Dulles certainly had no problem with McCloy's strategy. Gehlen, whom Allen had helped hire, was now reporting to him, as the means to the end of Stalinism. The trio McCloy, Dulles One and Dulles Two, was in charge.

Why then, in his exit speech on January 17, 1961, conservative Ike Eisenhower echoed what liberal Senator Nye had cautioned about, thirty years earlier, and what Senator Truman had been set to monitor, twenty years earlier – the threat and consequences posed by the "military-industrial complex?"

One had to read between the President's lines. This was the romanced version. In today's parlance, he was wiping his server clean for legacy purposes. President Eisenhower, the WWII hero, actually knew who was running the show. The trio, and the NSC 5412/2 Special Group, were the same who had advised, financed, and structured the military-industrial complex. The "Cloak and Dagger" policy that President Truman so despised was in full force. Eisenhower simply felt covert operations were more cost and people efficient than all-out overt wars.

John Foster Dulles had clearly laid out his anti-communist prophylaxis at his Senate confirmation hearing in January 1953:

> "*Therefore, a policy which only aims at containing Russia where it now is, is in itself an unsound policy; but it is a policy which is bound to fail, because a purely defensive policy never wins against an aggressive policy*"[73].

In Iran, in that same 1953 year, Mohammed Mosaddegh got a taste of prophylaxis. The year before, he had been appointed Prime Minister by the new Shah, Mohammad Reza Shah Pahlavi, after a 79 to 12 vote by the Parliament. Mohammad Reza had succeeded his father Reza, dethroned by the CIA and MI6 in 1941 for not allowing the British to supply the Soviets through the "Persian Corridor", i.e. the Trans-Iranian Railway. He was only thirty-years old, had been educated at the Swiss Institut Le Rosey for the rich and famous, and quickly beholden to U.S. interests and concepts, which included democracy. When Mosaddegh, the western educated and highly popular leader of the National Front, was appointed, this was prime time for the Iranians, used to the autocratic rule of Reza Sr. He was championing the growing resentment of continued pillage of Iranian industries by foreign interests, from caviar to tobacco to oil to railroads, ferry lines, post office, banking and so on[74]. So he nationalized the Anglo-Iranian Oil Company, known as British Petroleum

But he had the support of the outlawed communist party Tudeh, and it smacked of Soviet influence. Not only that, but he reneged on a $650 million contract with Overseas Consultants Inc., a construction and engineering conglomerate of American firms, sponsored by the Dulles Brothers[75], and commissioned by the new Shah to "advance" Iran's already impoverished economy. Mosaddegh viewed it as yet another way of looting his country. The British did not like the Oil takeover. The Americans, led by Allen and John Foster Dulles, happily confused anti-colonial nationalism, communism and economic interest. In 1953, with the approval of President Eisenhower, Mosaddegh was overthrown in a CIA and MI6-led coup.

This would not be the last of the Dulles and the Special Group prophylactic interventions, but the one that terminated Allen Dulles' "cloak and dagger" career was the attempted assassination of Cuba' Fidel Castro, in the 1961 Bay of Pigs debacle. On April 17, 1961, the CIA-led Cuban refugee troops, all fifteen hundred of them and poorly equipped, landed in Playa Giron. As expected, they were met by the overwhelming Castro forces. Contrary to Allen Dulles' expectation that he would cave in, and sticking to his word, newly-elect President Kennedy stuck to his word and refused to provide official air cover. By April 19, the foolproof invasion had failed.

For that one, President Kennedy fired the man who had directed the CIA for eighteen years. Two years later, in November 1963, JFK was assassinated in Dallas. In 1964, the Warren Commission was established to look into his murder and delivered its report to President Johnson in September. Lee Harvey Oswald was solely responsible. Among the nine members of the Commission were President Johnson, JFK's former Vice President, successor, and proponent of the Vietnam War, Congressman Gerald Ford[76], who would become President after Richard Nixon, Johnson's successor, and the old permanent fixtures of covert operations, John McCloy and the recently dumped Allen Dulles.

For his services, John McCloy was appointed chairman of Rockefeller's Chase Manhattan Bank in 1953, and of the Ford Foundation in 1958[77]. The Ford Foundation was one of the established conduit for the funding of covert operations, so much so that in that same year, while he was sitting between the chair of Deputy Director of the CIA and the coveted chair of Director, the operative-at-heart Allen Dulles himself had volunteered to be its chairman.

This was the way Foreign Policy was conducted. Presidents were only the public face, and Eisenhower was a telling example. Between the lines, the real thing happened under the curtain of Intelligence, secretly except to a few.

Fast forward to 1997. Putin was on the launch pad, unbeknownst to most, and Aleksandr Dugin's "Foundations of Geopolitics" was the new script.

Simply put, it debunked the claim that the Cold War ended in the late Eighties, with Glasnost, Perestroika and the fall of the Berlin Wall[78]. Anatoliy Golitsyn was vindicated, even though not in so many words. Dugin's resume was unambiguous[79]. Neo-fascist, former leader of the anti-Semitic Russian People's National-patriotic Orthodox Christian movement, or Pamyat, leading organizer of the National Bolshevik Party and Eurasia Party, close to the Kremlin and the Military. His ultimate objective followed – to restore Russia's control over Eurasia. The Middle East was just part of the plan. He called it the Russo-Islamic Alliance, *"the foundation of anti-Atlanticist strategy."* Here are excerpts, well translated by John Dunlap, Senior Fellow of the Hoover Institution, of what is an otherwise quite obtuse treatise[80]:

> *"In principle, Eurasia and our space, the heartland Russia, remain the staging area of a new anti-bourgeois, anti-American revolution. ... The new Eurasian empire will be constructed on the fundamental principle of the common enemy: the rejection of Atlanticism, strategic control of the USA, and the refusal to allow liberal values to dominate us.*

This common civilizational impulse will be the basis of a political and strategic union."

With regards to Ukraine, he did not mince words either:

"Ukraine as a state has no geopolitical meaning. It has no particular cultural import or universal significance, no geographic uniqueness, no ethnic exclusiveness" [...] Ukraine as an independent state with certain territorial ambitions, represents an enormous danger for all of Eurasia and, without resolving the Ukrainian problem, it is in general senseless to speak about continental politics".

And on China, he was even clearer:

"Tibet-Sinkiang-Mongolia-Manchuria taken together comprise a security belt of Russia. [...] Eurasia-Russia must seek at all costs to promote the territorial disintegration, splintering and the political and administrative partition of the [Chinese] state. [...] Without Sinkiang and Tibet, the potential geopolitical breakthrough of China into Kazakhstan and Siberia becomes impossible."

So, while for years we had fought the Cold War, and thought we had won it with the implosion of the U.S.S.R., here was a guy, backed by the Russian military and the new President, readying for a rematch. Even Turkey's Prime Minister Recep Erdogan liked the idea[81]. A NATO member. Repeat. A NATO member, willing to play in Russia's sand box. The Truman Doctrine was on its death bed.

Few understood the concept at the time, and still do not as of this writing. The Soviet Union had been involved in the Middle East forever. Few noticed when, in May 2001, President Bush and Secretary Powell added the word "Eurasian" to the Bureau of European Affairs." There was a reason for it. The new Russia was back in business, and it had a plan. Eurasia.

5

Luau For A Luo

On August 4, 1961, a boy was born in Honolulu, Hawaii, officially to a Kenyan father. They both had the same name, Barack Hussein Obama.

The boy's "father" was a Luo, eager to earn a higher education in America before returning to Kenya's politics. The Luos were the third largest ethnic group after the Kikuyus, and likely to partake in the lead of the country's upcoming Independence. Much like in the rest of Africa, there was a strong whiff of pan-African communism in the air.

When Kenya was let go from the United Kingdom in 1963, the prominent communist Luo leader Ogingo Odinga yielded to the forceful Kikuyu and former Mau Mau[82] leader Jomo Kenyatta. Thirty years earlier, Kenyatta had studied in Birmingham Woodbridge Quaker College, and had been an active member of the London-based pan-African, anti-colonial International African Service Bureau, founded by George Padmore. In Padmore's footsteps, he had been selected to go to Moscow to attend the Stalin School, known as KUTV, officially the Communist University of the Toilers of the East. It had been founded in 1921 to train Bolshevik cadres to infiltrate and promote communism in the colonial world but Stalin closed it during WWII, when he joined the Allies camp. In 1960, Khrushchev went back at it and founded his own People's Friendship University. There was no shortage of communist schooling in Africa – or in Asia and Latin America, for that matter.

Back to Kenya, Kenyatta quickly forgot the underpinnings of Marxism-Leninism and Quaker pacifism. What he did remember was the Hegelian part. He was the State, and the people were his subjects. His regime became one of the most brutal and totalitarian in all of Africa[83].

In his wings was a younger but powerful Luo leader, Thomas "Tom" Mboya. Born in 1930 and a center socialist partisan of Odinga, he had organized Kenya's Local Government Workers Union. The British Trade Unions Congress rewarded him with a scholarship to attend Rushkin College in renowned Oxford. Upon his return, recognizing how pan-Africanism would fit in the emerging yet momentous Civil Rights and African-American movements, he actively campaigned in the U.S. where he became quite popular. Together with the newly created U.S. based African American Students Foundation (AASF), in 1959, Mboya founded the Airlift Africa project. The original sponsors of the AASF were the American Committee on Africa, to include baseball star Jackie Robinson, performers Harry Belafonte and Sidney Poitier, Martin Luther King, Jr., Philip Randolph, a lesser known but prominent civil rights and Union leader, and Mrs. Ralph Bunche. Mrs. Bunche was the wife of the first African American to be awarded the Nobel Prize in 1950, for his peace mediation efforts in the Arab-Israeli conflict of the late Forties. Mr. Bunche himself was a close friend of Jomo Kenyatta for having studied together in London way back then. His wife was the "woman on the ground", raising scholarships from American Universities. Aside from the conservative Robinson, who was a supporter of Vice President Richard Nixon, everyone else involved was pretty liberal – which at the time meant left-leaning, and then some.

In its first airlift, on September 9, 1959, eighty one Kenyan students were sent to American Universities[84].

In 1960, the State Department was asked to sponsor the next airlift of another two hundred and thirty students, this time not only from Kenya but also from neighboring countries. They had collectively received an impressive $1 million or so worth of scholarships. The Department was run by Christian Herter, former Under Secretary for John Foster Dulles. He was part of the Establishment, having married into the empire Charles Pratt had built on the petroleum industry he pioneered with John D. Rockefeller. Promoting the education of foreign students in the U.S. to prevent the communist web from spreading was an integral part of Herter's job, who knew Africa was a prime target for the Soviet Union. The objective was to counter the Communist Schools. The implosion of the Old Continent colonies was an opportunity the U.S. could not afford to ignore, especially after the communist experience in Ghana's Independence[85].

Indeed, for efficiency sake, Herter had identified the need for a better coordination between the tens of departments, agencies and bureaus in charge of foreign aid of one form or another, and he had been appointed chairman of the Operations Coordinating Board, the OCB, established for this purpose:

> "The Board included the Under Secretary of State, the Deputy Secretary of Defense, Director of Intelligence, Director of the U.S. Information Agency, Director of the International Cooperation Agency and one or more representative of the President. By standing invitation of the Board, the Under Secretary of the Treasury and the Chairman of the Atomic Energy Commission regularly attended the meetings[86]".

Remarkably, there was no representative from the Education side. It was all about U.S. Intelligence.

The AASF was asking for was a mere $100,000 for the second airlift, while Herter's total budget was some $300 million. This seemed like a dirt cheap way to buy into Africa's wave of independence, and by the same token, into the civil rights movement spreading throughout the

United States. He had all the reasons to agree. His father-in-law was committed to the education of the "have not's", having founded the Pratt Institute in 1887, *"among the first* [college]*in the country to welcome students regardless of class, color and gender"*[87]. On the Foreign Policy side, Herter was not a novice either. In 1919, he had participated in the creation of the Council on Foreign Relations. In 1947, he had co-founded the Middle East Institute, another Washington think tank[88]. He also was a trustee of the World Peace Foundation, the U.S. oldest secular peace foundation, founded in 1910[89], to promote "peace and goodwill among all mankind", a mission dear to Herter's heart as a Master Mason.

Yet he refused the AASF request, for no recorded reasons.

Jackie Robinson then asked Richard Nixon to intervene. He did, again to no avail.

Why did Herter refuse is a matter of conjecture. In this Cold War, Herter could have been fearful of the liberal pan-African group behind the AASF, suspecting communist infiltration of some sort. After all, it included George Padmore, W.E.B. Du Bois[90], William Foster, Vincent Harding and Harry Haywood, whose activism was well documented. To boot, the leading contenders for Kenya's Independence, Odinga and Kenyatta, were communists.

But why be afraid of Vice President Nixon? He was a staunch anti-communist, known for his pursuit and conviction of State Department and communist spy Alger Hiss.

Maybe Herter simply distrusted Nixon's Quaker faith? The American Friends Service Committee, set up in 1917, had been quite communist friendly. Or maybe, like most in the Eisenhower Administration, he had had a bad experience with his predecessor, Under Secretary Herbert Hoover Jr., whose father and former President was also a Quaker? Maybe he distrusted the strong link between the Religious Society of Friends and Kenya, where it had the largest following worldwide? Or maybe Herter simply wanted a revenge for failing to replace Nixon as Eisenhower's Vice President in the 1956 election[91]?

The fact is, he denied the request up until young Senator and Presidential Hopeful John F. Kennedy got involved. Against the will of the State Department, and with the support of Nixon, his political and dogmatic rival, the Joseph P. Kennedy Foundation agreed to fund the $100,000 project. What made sense to them and did not to the State Department illustrated the bipolar thinking of the United States at the time. Herter folded. John F. Kennedy came to office as the 35th President of the United States, on January 20, 1961.

Regardless, contrary to most press accounts, the boy's "father" was not brought into the United States by Airlift Africa. Robert Stephens, the U.S. Cultural attaché in Kenya and member of a four-man selection committee which included Tom Mboya, had not been impressed by his potential[92]. He did not even mention Barack Sr. in his 2013 book, "Kenyan Student Airlifts to America, 1959-1961." Instead, by his own means, he reached Honolulu on August 9, 1959[93], one month before the first airlift. He was a close friend of Mboya and managed to get some pocket money from African friendly institutions, but it was under the auspices of Elizabeth Mooney Kirk, who ran the Laubach Literacy Institute[94] in Nairobi, that he got to fund his trip to the United States[95].

According to Sally H. Jacobs, the convincing narrator of Barack Sr.'s biography[96], Betty Mooney had some kind of platonic crush on him and one thing lead to another, first a secretarial job at the Institute, then the failed Airlift Africa application, and ultimately the trip to Hawaii. This was pre-independence Kenya, in the midst of the Mau Mau uprising. Barack Sr. was an ambitious man of skilled intellect and personal presence, in the best of Luo tradition. A U.S. degree would allow him to come back to Kenya in a high post, but one thing would remain. His Airlift Africa experience had been humiliating for a proud Luo, Muslim and budding communist to boot, and that would become an integral part of his legacy.

Obama Sr.'s story was interesting[97] and clearly inspired Obama Jr., even if he met him only once before his death in 1982. So much so that the book he wrote in 1995, "Dreams From My Father," launched his political career. But in that book was another story, that of "Uncle" Frank's, an essential part of "The Red Web[98]," an intimate slice of his teenage years and a prominent surrogate father figure. We need to talk about him now.

His full identity was never disclosed in the 1995 book and strangely, Frank actually disappeared in the 2005 audio version. But by all accounts, later confirmed by a Cambridge Public Library video of Barack Jr., he was Frank Marshall Davis, born in Arkansas City in December 1905, red as red in the then color spectrum[99]. Frank Marshall Davis, CPUSA card # 47544.

At age seventeen, he attended Friends University, the Quakers school in Wichita, Kansas. In the Twenties, he moved to Chicago where he first worked for African American newspapers and later headed the Associated Negro Press until 1948. In the meantime, he started community organizing and founded The Chicago Star, to *promote cooperation and unity between Russia and the United States*[100]. It was then and there that he befriended Vernon Jarrett[101], who will come to life later in the story, as well as Robert Rochon Taylor[102]. Both Taylor and Davis were part of the American Peace Mobilization group which would be listed on the Attorney's General List of Subversive Organizations as the sequel of a Soviet Comintern and CPUSA affiliate, the American League Against War and Fascism. Created in 1933, it was renamed the American League for Peace and Democracy, and included among its many members Helen Silvermaster, leader of the Soviet Silvermaster spy ring[103].

It was also then and there that he got acquainted with Harry Canter, who was part of a group that bought his Chicago Star newspaper in 1948, just before he left for Hawaii. Harry Canter had been secretary of the Boston Communist Party in the late Twenties and jailed for his support of Sacco and Vanzetti, the notorious anarchists who had been executed, albeit for debatable reasons. Upon his release, he went to work for Stalin in Moscow. This was the early Thirties. He turned back up in Chicago in 1946 and later moved to San Francisco but remained a member of the Communist Party of Illinois. His son David carried the communist torch in Chicago, working with, among others, Abe Feinglass, Vice President of the Soviet KGB front World Peace Council[104]. With fellow CPUSA member LeRoy Wolins, he owned Translation World Publishers, located at Suite 900, 22 West Madison Street, Chicago, Illinois. In the Sixties, the U.S. Government had it listed under the Foreign Agents Registration Act as an agent of the Soviet Union.

David Canter also partnered with a man by the name of Don Rose, to create a far-left newspaper called Hyde Park-Kenwood Places, and they would become the mentors of another essential character who will also come to life later, David Axelrod[105]. These were the early Seventies. Thirty years later, Axelrod had become the Democrats' kingmaker, advising famous politicians such as Rod Blagojevich, Hillary Clinton, Eliot Spitzer, Christopher Dodd, John Edwards, Rahm Emanuel, and Barack Obama. Among others.

The Star was a front publication for the CPUSA, and had been founded and headquartered in Chicago on September 1, 1919. So said the 1951 report of the Commission on Subversive Activities to the Legislature of the Territory of Hawaii, where "Uncle" Frank had moved in 1948. There he worked for the Honolulu Record[106], published by the International Longshore and Warehouse Union. The ILWU was so dominated by communists that it was expelled by the Congress of Industrial Organizations in 1950[107]. The CIO was the precursor of the AFL-CIO.

On a more personal level, Davis' passions included nude photography and pedophilia[108]. He was a member of Chicago's South Side Writers Group, who championed Social Realism in the arts, to focus on the everyday conditions of the working classes, and criticism of the social structures responsible for these conditions. In that sense, U.S. Social

Realism was a close cousin of the Soviet Socialist Realism movement, whose purpose was to further communism through the Social Arts. "Uncle" Frank was not just a Communist, he was a full-fledged activist.

There were no Jim Crow laws in Hawaii, so he may have moved there for convenience sake. His second wife was the white Chicagoan socialite Helen Canfield, eighteen years his junior, member of the Paul Robeson Club of the CPUSA in Chicago, carrying card number # 62109.

There was another simple reason. In 1948, the Kremlin had ordered the CPUSA to push for a U.S. withdrawal from Hawaii, as U.S. forces were an obstacle to Soviet expansion in Asia[109]. Japan was decimated, yet, in August 1945, "Little Boy" had been dropped on Hiroshima, and "Fat Man" on Nagasaki. The official purpose was to force Emperor Hirohito and his Generals into unconditional surrender, which was a done deal for all intents and purposes. The unofficial purpose was to stop the Soviet invasion of Japan, which had started with Manchukuo, hence Hawaii's strategic importance to both sides. Davis had the credits to be the man in charge[110], to the dismay of the local National Association for the Advancement of Colored People, a.k.a. the NAACP. To be sure, all one had to do was to read his blog[111] from the Honolulu Record.

Ten years later, on August 9, 1959, Barack Sr. also landed in Hawaii, allegedly at Betty Mooney's directive. The waters were blue, there were no Jim Crow laws, but this was a strange choice, especially since he had also been accepted to San Francisco State College[112], home to the Beat Generation and the San Francisco Renaissance. Hawaii had just joined the Union as the 50th State, but, in comparison, its University was still way under par relative to its continental peers, and certainly to San Francisco. It was to those universities that his peers who had made it to Airlift Africa were going. So, for a twenty-three year old African eager to learn about the United States and come back to enter the higher ranks of the upcoming new Kenyan political life, with a communist inclination to boot[113], liberal San Francisco sounded like a perfect fit. Even though Mooney had highlighted

Hawaii's cosmopolitan appeal, she must have known that there were no black people on the Island, so to speak. Obama Sr. would stand out as the only black African at the University[114].

Be it as it may, the "Center for Cultural and Technical Interchange between East and West at the University of Hawaii" was created in May 1960 by President Eisenhower, under the Mutual Security Act of 1960. The East-West Center, as it was known, had been in the works since the spring of 1959[115]. It was the United States belated answer to the Lenin and Stalin Schools, and the Patrice Lumumba People's Friendship University[116]. Obama Sr. was older than most undergraduates and spent most of his free time at the Center, where he could engage in more meaty debates on communism, in the footsteps of his idol Kwame Nkrumah[117], not only on campus but in town. And party harder. He had quite a reputation, as a flirt and a heavy drinker[118].

In 1962, in three years rather than the regular four, Obama Sr. had completed his BA in Economics. He had worked hard for it, constantly running out of money despite some small grants, and doing menial work to fund his lifestyle[119].

Constantly running out of money. How then did he fund the next step, his Harvard years, 1962, 1963, and 1964? The probing source is the Immigration and Naturalization Services' file for Barack Hussein Obama Sr.[120] One of the documents, dated June 8, 1964, states:

> "[...] *in view of correspondence in his file, Harvard was contacted telephonically. They weren't very impressed with him and asked for us to hold up action on his application until they decided what action they could take in order to get rid of him. They were apparently having difficulty with his financial arrangements and couldn't seem to figure out how many wives he had.*"

Leaving the polygamy question out, Obama Sr.'s only source of funds were three self-declared grants, $1,500 from Harvard, $1,000 from Laubach Literacy, and $1,000 from the Phelps-Stokes Foundation. In today's terms, this sounds like pocket change, but in 1964, Harvard's tuition was the lowest of the Ivy League, at $1,520. On average, housing was running at $1,100[121], so Obama Sr. had a little wiggle room to accomodate his social habits. Until Harvard fell through, in May:

> *"We have also been informed that neither the Department of Economics nor the Graduate School of Arts & Sciences has any further funds to support you in Cambridge. As you know this office has no money of its own for foreign students. We have, therefore, come to the conclusion that you should terminate your stay in the United States and return to Kenya to carry on your research and the writing of your thesis. In order to give you time to make arrangement for your departure we have asked the Immigration & Naturalization Service to give you until June 19 to make the necessary preparations.[…]"*[122]

Pretty brutal for a dad with an American-born son, but this is another story.

In the meantime, his half-brother, Onyanga[123], eleven years his junior, had been airlifted in 1963. Senior had found him a boarding school in Cambridge, and it was no cheap school either. Then called Browne & Nichols, a boy's school established in 1883, it later merged with the Buckingham girl's school. Today, the Buckingham Browne & Nichols School is considered one of the top fifty prep schools in the world, and the most expensive day school in the country. Fortunately, still according to Sally Jacobs, Senior had befriended a lady whose husband was the school's treasurer[124]. Whether this was a reason good enough to explain how Onyanga's tuition and board was funded is questionable. In 2007, BB&N was challenged to assess a potential achievement gap at the school based on race. The conclusion was

> *"It was difficult to argue with these numbers. BB&N did have an achievement gap* [to the detriment of the African-American and Latino students][125].

If there was a race-based problem in 2007, one can only imagine what the demographics were in 1963. But Mrs. Jacobs was a trusted source, according to the Pulitzer Center[126], so we will take her word for it.

Of note, however, the liberal Peter Osnos was her publisher at PublicAffairs. The same Peter Osnos who, sixteen years earlier, had published Obama Jr.'s "Dreams from My Father" after Simon & Schuster had pulled out of the deal[127]. Even though Mrs. Jacobs' book shed a different light on some details, such as Sr. not making it to Hawaii via Airlift Africa, the "biographies" conveniently complemented each other. But when all was said and done, Obama Sr. was still *"constantly running out of money."*

The parents of Barack's mother also had decided to move to Hawaii in 1960, one year after Barack's father. Seattle was great, but the business opportunity in a new State was supposedly calling. Barack's grandmother-to-be was the bread winner and would lose her well-paying job as vice president of a local bank, but her husband, a furniture salesman, would certainly make a killing. The Dunham family would leave Mercer Island, *"a rural [...] quiet, politically conservative, almost lily-white place"*[128], to go to the engaging and destined-to-grow Hawaii, two thousand six hundred eighty two miles away.

While at the University of Hawaii at Manoa, Barack's father was black as black, and the only African student. Barack's mother, Stanley Ann Dunham, was white as white. Even though there were no Jim Crow laws in Hawaii, black-on-white relationships, let alone marriages, were pretty much frowned upon at the time. This was 1960. Maxine Box, Ann Dunham's best friend in Mercer Island High School and a retired teacher in Bellevue, Washington, later recounted that she was stunned:

> *"I can't think of anything she said or did that would lead to such a radical thing. At that time, you practically crossed the street if you saw a black man and a white woman. Black and white didn't go together at that time. [...] We could see her, with her good grades and intelligence, going to college, but not marrying and having a baby right away"*[129].

Ann Dunham and Barack Sr. had apparently met in a Russian language class. Nothing wrong with that, it was emerging as a third language, after Spanish and French, for one reason. In 1957, the U.S.S.R. had launched its first spacecraft, Sputnik. The space race had begun, a sequel to the nuclear race. However, while this made sense for the young aspiring African communist, it sounded strange for an eighteen year-old girl, off the boat from Seattle.

But it actually made sense for a girl who had attended The Mercer Island High School and the East Shore Unitarian Church in Bellevue, known as the Little Red Church on the Hill[130]. A John Stenhouse was chairman of the board of the school, and president of the church. Born in China in 1908, he had emigrated to the U.S. in late 1940. In 1955, he admitted to the House Un-American Activities Committee, HUAC, that he was a CPUSA member from 1943 to 1947[131]. The hallway where two of Ann Dunham's avant-garde teachers professed, Jim Wichterman and Val Foubert, was dubbed "anarchy alley." And according to Wichterman, she would question anything, in particular

> *"What's so good about democracy? What's so good about capitalism? What's wrong with communism? What's good about communism?"*[132]

It seemed they both had Russian under their skin.

Barack Jr. was conceived that same year of 1960, and did not have the best of childhoods. His mother, then barely eighteen, left his "father" in August 1961, a few days after Barack was born, taking him with her while she would go back to study at the University of Washington in Seattle[133]. There she would take night classes in Anthropology 100, Political Science 201, History 478 and Philosophy 120[134]. It is as if she was following the footsteps of Ralph Bunche, thirty years later, but what she was doing during the day remains a mystery. So is the way she funded her three thousand miles trip from Hawaii to Seattle, her education and her living arrangements, to include Mary Toutonghi, her presumed baby sitter for her one-month old baby. For an eighteen-year-old, she had some motivation alright, as her high school teachers and friends had noticed. Somehow, she must also have had some financial support, but there is no evidence that it came from her family. Maybe it had something to do with the fact that Seattle was a hotbed for communism[135], the subject she and Barack Sr. were fond of and may have made them friends. Maybe it had something to do with "Uncle" Frank's connections. She returned to Hawaii in 1963 but it is unclear what degree she had in her Washington University pocket – her name is not even mentioned in the Alumni Association website.

She had not seen Barack Sr. since she had left for Seattle. In the meantime, he had gone to Harvard. Maybe because of the INS inquiry, or earlier from the stir her "marriage" had caused in both families, she found out he had another wife in Kenya, and a couple of children. While he was at Harvard, she had herself met Lolo Soetoro, a young Indonesian who was studying geography at the East-West Center. She divorced Barack Sr. in 1964 and married Soetoro the next year, just before he was called back to Jakarta at his government request. He was an army colonel. In 1958, Allen Dulles' CIA and the British MI6 had pulled the plug on their foiled Operation "Archipelago"[136] to remove Sukarno, too neutral in their view. Sukarno reacted by empowering the Communist Party of Indonesia, known as PKI. In 1965, fearing a communist overthrow, General Suharto and his army took over. Two years later, the Parliament appointed Suharto President, and Sukarno lived under house arrest until his death in 1970. This was the time of Indonesia's "New Order", when the PKI was eliminated in a bloody purge by the military and militant Islamists. At the time, it was the largest non-ruling communist party in the world, after Russia and China. After the purge, Indonesia had just become the largest Islamic country in the world.

Upon receiving her BA in anthropology or mathematics in 1967[137], Barack's mother moved to Indonesia with her six-year old son, to reunite with her new husband. Whether she disliked what she saw, or whether she found herself unwillingly involved in the communist purge, something must have ran counter to her beliefs and her second marriage turned sour. She sent Barack back to Honolulu in 1971. There, he attended the Punahou School, one of the finest private school on the Island, and in the Nation for that matter. And the first red flag in the story.

He was to be one of four black pupils there, out of thirty six hundred, and neither the mother nor her parents had enough money to pay for the expensive tuition[138]. Granted, the grandmother had just been promoted to the post of vice-president at the Bank of Hawaii. The grandfather, for himself, had become an insurance agent and counted the chairman of the school as his client. However, this was a fairly fairy tale for a ten-year-old who, coming from nowhere, was now in one of the top American boarding schools.

This is when the first real question popped up about Barack's real identity. Not only his "father" had scant money to pay for his own schooling, let alone that of his "half-uncle", but by whom were young Barack's Punahou years financed?

It is in that year that Barack's "father" came back from Kenya to visit him, for one month. This was to be the only and last time he would see him before he died in 1982, and he did not get a penny from him.

It is also around that time that Gramps, Grand'Pa in Hawaiian, introduced young Barack to his friend Frank Marshall Davis[139]. Frank, as Barack refers to him in "Dreams", had moved to Honolulu in 1948. Barack Sr. had moved there in 1959, and Gramps in 1960. The three men had many things in common. Frank had been educated by the Quakers – Barack Sr. came from Kenya, host to the largest Quaker population in the world. Frank was thirteen years older than Gramps, but they both came from Wichita, Kansas and all three loved Jazz. "Uncle" Frank was a communist anti-colonialist African American with a very active sex life. Barack Sr. was a communist anti-colonialist African with a very active sex life, and they both had a strong penchant for whiskey. History does not say whether

Gramps was liberal or conservative, but one of his favorite bar was in Honolulu's red line district[140]. One thing was for sure, Barack Sr. was one of the first African to be enrolled at the University of Hawaii, and aside from "Uncle" Frank, there were not a lot of black people in Hawaii at the time[141], let alone outspoken communists. Chances were great that Barack Sr., Frank Marshall David and Gramps knew each other back then, before Barack's father left for Harvard. And that "Uncle" Frank did not need to be introduced to young Barack.

The main thing was, they all had mixed race children, or grandchild in Gramps' case. Although they had divorced in 1970, Frank and Helen Davis would both live in Honolulu until their death in the late Eighties, and had five children, four girls and a boy. In the absence of Barack Sr., they had a free rein to educate Barack as one of their own. Whether Gramps agreed or not with their strong communist beliefs, he could not have ignored them and they did not seem to deter him. Nor did they deter Ann Dunham, obviously, who had returned to the Island in 1972 after separating from her second husband.

For the next three years, Barack's mother completed her studies, earning an MA in Anthropology, and returned to Jakarta. Strange, as communist sympathizers were not welcome there, and she no longer had a husband to speak for. Be it as it may, Barack preferred to stay with his grandparents – fourteen years old, and having fun. As Gramps told him,

> "*Hell, this is no school, this is Heaven*"[142].

Heaven it was, for sure, but who was paying for it? "Dreams" paints a dire picture:

> "*There was a long waiting list, and I was considered only because of Gramp's boss, who was an alumnus[143]. [...] For three years I lived with her and Maya in a small apartment a block away from Punahou, my mother's student grants supporting the three of us. [...] remark about the lack of food in the fridge or the less-than-perfect housekeeping [...][144].*"

While Ann Dunham Obama Soetoro *"appreciated the fine education [Barack] was receiving,"* no one else seemed to have been supporting the family who apparently lived beyond their unsubstantial means. If there had been another story, something as simple as a free ride from the school, this would have likely been part of the narrative. Punahou never released any records relating to young Barack, whether academic – and the curriculum was extensive – or financial. And there is no information on Ann Dunham's grants either. The boy was attending a school he could not afford by a mile.

Gramps had other friends than his boss who could have helped. Frank Marshall Davis was one. In "Dreams," he is portrayed as this almost senile eightyish poet, living *"in a dilapidated house in a run-down section of Waikiki."* But at the time, he really was in his mid-sixties, and a CPUSA leader strategically located in Hawaii. His network ran deep in Chicago and elsewhere.

Neil Abercrombie could also have been in the loop. He was a good friend of Senior and Ann, from their early days at the University of Hawaii at Manoa, and soon to become a leading Democratic Hawaii politician.

And there sure were other schools than Punahou that would have better fit the budget of the class conscious and modest Ann Dunham.

Who knows? This was 1975.

6

Red Herrings From Chicago

1975. This is what we knew about Barack Hussein Obama II, at this point in time.

He was born in Hawaii in 1961 to a free electron mother who, at the young age of eighteen, was intellectually intrigued by communism. Officially, his father was a young Kenyan who had landed there by some strange coincidence, one of the few black men on the Island, with a communist bent to boot. The black and white couple was certainly non-conventional. Barack's birth certificate itself was controversial.

As his mother separated from her husbands, one time and a second time, Barack was raised from age ten by his maternal grandparents. They had moved from Seattle to Hawaii, twenty seven hundred miles away, for some New Frontier calling. They were of little means, yet he attended the top private and quite expensive Punahou School, as one of four black pupils out of thirty six hundred. Source of funds and transcripts undocumented.

In his teen years, he was mentored by "Uncle" Frank and "Aunt" Helen. They too were black and white, but also red as red was to communism. They were Chicago's CPUSA outpost in the Pacific.

Then, in 1979, Barack attended the equally prestigious and expensive Occidental College in Los Angeles[145], known as "Little Moscow", allegedly as a transfer student with a Fulbright scholarship.

Pause for a second here. Mark Twain said it best, "Get your facts first, then distort them as you please." The main challenge when writing a non-fiction book is to figure out whether "information" is factual or not. Much like the funding of Barack Sr. and Onyanga's years in Cambridge is a stretch as conventionally reported, the Fulbright story came from some "trusted" source but did not make sense, since Fulbright Scholarships were, and still are not, awarded to undergraduate students[146]. If Barack Jr. had ever been a Fulbright Scholar, it would be front-line public knowledge, but he was conspicuously absent from the list of Fulbrighters Nobel Price laureates[147].

So, back to the question. Since he was not a Fulbright scholar, how were the two-year Occidental College expenses funded? And where were the Transcripts?

Next, in 1981, Barack transferred to Columbia University in New York, where he reportedly graduated in 1983 with a Bachelor of Arts in Political Science and International Relations. Source of funds and transcripts still undocumented.

His first job was for Business International Corporation, in New York. BI, as it was called, was an international consulting or publishing firm, and by some accounts, some kind of covert CIA training operation. This was not an exception among "consulting firms." Today, Booz Allen Hamilton, owned by the Carlyle Group[148], claims the title of "The World Most Profitable Spy Organization," and we certainly know of one of its ex-employee, Edward Snowden[149].

Barack's second job, in 1985, was with the New York branch of the U.S. Public Interest Research Groups, PIRG for short. From these formative four years he spent in New York, nothing much is said in "Dreams" which he published a short ten years later. Inconvenient memories maybe, since the book was 450-pages long, and since his work at both BI and NYPIRG was investigative reporting.

Let us start with NYPIRG. In the early Seventies, Donald Ross, a public interest lawyer, had created the PIRG movement with

Ralph Nader, of Green Party and serial Presidential candidate fame. PIRGs were mostly recruiting on college campuses. The purpose was summed up in Ross' 1971 book, *"Action for change. A Student's Manual for Public Interest Organizing"*. It was, and still is, to use grassroots organizing, direct advocacy, investigative reporting and litigation *"to stand up to powerful special interests"*[150]. There was little pay involved, so the question was, why did Barack leave BI, which he later described in his book as somewhat of a dream first job?

> *"I had my own office, my own secretary, money in the bank. Sometimes, coming out an interview with Japanese financiers or German bond traders, I would catch my reflection in the elevator doors – see myself in a suit and tie, a briefcase in my hand – and for a split second, I would imagine myself as a captain of industry [...]".*

The problem with this account is two-fold. First, according to some people who knew him then, such as Dan Armstrong, his BI closest associate at the time, or Ralph Diaz, BI's vice president, Barack never had a secretary, his office was the size of a small cubicle, and

> *"he was not in this high, talking-to-Swiss bankers kind of role. He was in the back rooms checking things on the phone"*[151].

Second, in his exit interview from BI, Louis J. Celi, then Vice-President, recalled him saying

> *"he had bigger fish to fry"*[152].

Barack was twenty-four at the time. What fish was he talking about? Given his upbringing, on the left side of the spectrum, did he have a problem associating with a possible CIA incubator? Bottom line, he left his pseudo dream job for the social activist and quasi volunteer NYPIRG. From Captain of Industry, he was now a very modest New York City College Organizer. Quite an epiphany at age twenty-four.

Later in 1985, in another Prince Charming story, he left NYPIRG and moved to Chicago. He had just been hired by Gerald Kellman, head of the Developing Communities Project[153], or DCP.

Kellman was looking for an African American to organize the South Side of Chicago, by then the largest black ghetto in the United States. A mighty endeavor, for sure. He *"had put an ad in a number of newspapers,"* and Barack sent his resume. Kellman *"did a phone interview"* and although he was *"fairly convinced he must be Japanese"*, he nevertheless went on to interview him in New York. There, he *"found out"* that Barack fit his bill, despite his young age and Kellman's own account of the job description:

> *"tough"*, *"we had not had good experiences with people who were as young as he was in organizing"*, *"there was a lot of failure"*, *"And the fact that someone had been successful in previous endeavors, including in their academic career, was not necessarily a plus in terms of organizing [...]"*.

For him to say that, Kellman must have been privy to Barack's academic records, whatever those were. But he could not have been impressed by his record as an organizer. The New York City College experience was only a few months old.

Regardless, Kellman had wanted to hear Barack's story. He must have been desperate for candidates, or cued to something by someone. So he did hear it, and hired him. (*Note: I usually do not highlight endnotes, which are only to supplement the text, but # 153 is worth reading. It is Kellman's interview on the subject, at the time of the 2008 Presidential race, by the award winning Frontline*). Of the "things" Kellman took home, one was that Barack was an "outsider". Penetrating view of the obvious. Kellman should have stopped there. Instead, he took the proverbial extra step off the short pier and added

> *"For the work we were doing, people were poor. People had faced racial discrimination. They are certainly outsiders"*.

Barack was going to identify with "these people" because he was bi-racial, and as such would bridge the gap with black and white poors? There was one difference though. None of "these people" had gone to Punahou, Occidental College, or Columbia College. They were poor for real, Barack only looked poor.

After working three years for Kellman's DCP, Barack decided to go to Harvard for a law degree. This was in late 1988. He is said to have graduated in 1991 with a JD "magna cum laude," but here too, source of funds and transcripts undocumented. According to Kellman's 2008 interview, he had borrowed the money and the Saving Grace came as a book advance from publisher Simon & Schuster.

> *"He gets this book contract, and the major thing is that it's a big advance. And he owes a ton of money for law school and law school debts. But he's so busy he can't get himself to write the book. He finally graduates, and he's almost at the deadline. And he goes off on the beach to write the book."*

Kellman did not say how Obama was able to borrow "a ton of money," nor from whom, but we will leave it to that for now.

In 1990, Barack had been elected the first African American president of the Harvard Law Review. To become a member of this prestigious journal, one had to be

> *"selected on the basis of his/her performance on an annual writing competition,"*

to be submitted at the end of the first year[154]. Aside from two "poems" he had written while at Occidental College, the only article that he was "known for" was a fairly scholarly paper titled

> *"Why organize? Problems and promise in the inner city"* [155],

published in 1988 by the University of Illinois at Springfield under the sponsorship of the Woods Foundation. So, while his 1989 performing submission to the Review was never made public to this day, he still got the job. True, according to the well-known and respected Percy Sutton, he also came in highly recommended by some Khalid al-Mansour friend of his, as we will see in a moment.

And through his work as an organizer at Columbia, Business International, NYPIRG, and then DCP on Chicago's South Side, to include the Gamaliel Foundation[156], he presumably knew about race relations. Presumably too, he could write a book about it, hence Simon & Schuster lofty $125,000 advance. Numbers vary but in today's dollars, the amount would easily be double.

Kellman does mention that newly-wed Barack went to the beach with his wife Michele, Bali to be specific, and that there was a deadline. What he omits to say is that Barack did not finish the book in time, and that, in 1993, Simon & Schuster cancelled the contract. His literary agent, Jane Dystel, found a more gullible Times Book, a division of Random House, to advance another $40,000 – the earlier mentioned Peter Osnos. Eventually, the book on race relations became the best-seller known as Obama's Memoirs, "Dreams from My Father", published in 1995. Suffice it to say, there is a high level of controversy as to who really penned the book[157]. And as to who convinced two top publishers to advance such big money to an unknown author with no platform.

So, aside from this Saving Grace book advance, who had been funding this allegedly extremely bright student whose records were totally undocumented? And why? And why was the question still out there?

There were three potential trails, all rooted in Frank Marshall Davis's Alma Mater, the South Side of Chicago, and all with crossovers. The first revolved around the socialist/socialite Vernon Jarrett[158], "Uncle" Frank's friend and partner in the Associated Negro Press. The second was in the lineage of the communist Harry Canter, who bought "Uncle" Frank's Chicago Star in 1948. The third trail, not necessarily in that order, was that of the U.S.-born pan-African radical Islamist

Khalid Abdullah Tariq al-Mansour, who had asked Percy Sutton to recommend his protégé to Harvard.

Al-Mansour first. A few years before Barack came to Chicago, al-Mansour, a San Francisco lawyer born Donald Warden[159], and mentor to Black Panther founders Huey Newton and Bobby Seale in the mid-Sixties, had been interviewed by none other than Vernon Jarrett. The article was published in the Chicago Tribune in November 1979 under the title *"Effects of Arab Aid to US blacks"*, and syndicated to the St. Petersburg Evening Independent as *"Will Arabs Back Ties to Blacks with Cash?*[160]*"* Al-Mansour, a prolific author[161], speaker, and hatemonger of many sorts – Jews, Christians, and Whites alike -, let Jarrett know that that he had made a proposal to Rene Ortiz, then General Secretary of OPEC, to provide $20 million per year for ten years to ten thousand American minority students. No such announcement was ever acknowledged by OPEC and al-Mansour disappeared from the news.

Until much later, in 2008, when his long-time friend and associate Percy Sutton asserted on national TV that, in 1988, al-Mansour had a protégé for whom he was raising money, Barack Obama, and had asked him for a letter of recommendation to Harvard as well as to the Harvard Law Review. Sutton was a figure in New York City politics, once considered a viable Mayoral candidate running against icons of the likes of Bella Abzug, Mario Cuomo and Ed Koch, and did write the 1988 recommendation. At the time of the 2008 interview, he was even more emphatic about Obama's Presidential bid, calling him a genius[162].

Overnight, the mainstream liberal media challenged his reference to al-Mansour, portraying him as senile. He was eighty eight years-old and died a year later[163]. In this election year of 2008, it sounded like the liberal media was going into damage control, all in to protect the background of its newly found Hope and Change Champion and President Hopeful, Barack Obama. As far as he was concerned, he had no idea who al-Mansour was, and al-Mansour asserted he only noticed him for his 2004 DNC speech. The idea of a virulent black Islamic pan-African supremacist being close to Obama, let alone one of his early mentors, had to be just ludicrous.

The exact nature of the relationship between al-Mansour and Jarrett was unclear, but they were both real pan-whatever activists. One thing was clear, though. Al-Mansour's aim had been to infiltrate America from its base, and Jarrett knew from Subversive Warfare 101 that the school system was the weakest link and the most effective way to accomplish this.

What was al-Mansour' claim to fame which allowed him to be so proactive, back then if not now, trying to influence the American educational system? Money, and big money at that. He was Special Advisor to His Royal Highness Prince Al-Waleed Bin Talal of Saudi Arabia, no less, and his partner in the law firm of Al-Waleed, Al-Talal and Al-Mansour. He also served on the Board of the Saudi African Bank and the United Bank of Africa[164]. Maybe, by a stretch, Vernon Jarrett did not know this in 1979, but it was no secret. In 2012, al-Mansour was to speak at the University of Technology in Jamaica. The news release, dated September 27, read as follows, despite Team Obama's denials four years earlier:

> *"Al-Mansour who made the news in 2008 when it was revealed that he had been a patron of Barack Obama and had recommended him for admission to Harvard Law School in 1998, is co-founder of the international law firm of Al-Waleed, Al-Talal and Al-Mansour and Special Advisor to Saudi Arabian Prince, His Royal Highness Prince Al-Waleed Bin Talal Bin Abdulazziz."*[165]

Sutton did not have a senile moment, after all.

These days, the Prince was quite mediatized as a "friend of America", given his substantial stakes in many U.S. flagship companies. But back in 1979, and even 1988, the world was quite different. In the early Seventies, there had been the Yom Kippur War and an Oil Embargo to countries supportive of Israel. Yasser Arafat's PLO was in full force. The tensions with the Arabic Peninsula were tangible and it was quite conceivable that the leaders of the Muslim World would want to infiltrate the American psyche. Years later, in October 2001, a month after the September 11 attack, the Prince was quick to offer a $10 million check to the Twin Towers Fund, and even quicker to add that

> *"The United States should re-examine its policies in the Middle East and adopt a more balanced stand toward the Palestinian cause. [...] our Palestinian brethren continue to be slaughtered at the hands of Israelis [...]*[166].

Naturally, Rudy Giuliani, then Mayor of New York, refused the "donation," but it illustrated the lingering presence of Islamic interference in U.S. public affairs.

Which begged the next question. When did al-Mansour start backing Young Barack? More importantly, how did he know him, and when did he know him? 1988 for Harvard? 1979, the year of the Jarrett interview and of Occidental College? Before that, Punahou? The fact is he did, at some point, and al-Mansour was not just your regular passer-by. So this counts as trail number one.

Trail number two. Vernon Jarrett was a powerful voice in the Chicago liberal intelligentsia and, as such, was in the inner circle of Thomas Ayers, the socialite and wealthy chairman of Commonwealth Edison, the largest electric utility in Illinois. Tom was the father of the Marxist-Leninist and/or Maoist and/or anarchist William "Bill" Ayers. This was the troika of trail number two.

Bill Ayers' claim to fame, together with his life partner Bernardine Dohrn, founders of the Weather Underground Organization in 1969, was to have been on the FBI's "Ten Most Wanted" list for bombing government buildings and a number of other "revolutionary" acts, including a "Declaration of War" against the United States in May 1970. The WUO fell apart in the late Seventies. In December 1980, Ayers and Dohrn turned themselves in and with years passing, were now romanticized as simple local Chicago's Hyde Park activists, figments of the Sixties' Counterculture.

They were not.

In July 1969, in the thick of the Vietnam War, they had travelled to Cuba to meet with representatives of the North Vietnamese and Cuban governments. While some may have considered the anti-war protests as just that, Ayers and Dohrn did not. They were among the hard-core revolutionaries whose real motive was to help the Viet Cong[167] inside South Vietnam to fight along the North People's Army of Vietnam, in order to topple the South Republic of Vietnam. The activist duo and their friends did not mind and could not care less about the "domino theory," the Asian version of the Truman Doctrine that President Eisenhower had enunciated in 1954[168], which Senator J.F. Kennedy had reiterated in 1956 in a speech to the American Friends of Vietnam[169]:

> "Burma, Thailand, India, Japan, the Philippines and obviously Laos and Cambodia are among those whose security would be threatened if the Red Tide of Communism overflowed into Vietnam".

Bill Ayers and Dohrn were not figments, they were real Marxist-Leninists, in the footsteps of Che Guevara and Malcom X, and explosive-laden activists to boot. In their manifesto titled "Prairie Fire: The Politics of Revolutionary Anti-Imperialism", published in 1974, they wrote

> "We are a guerilla organization. We are communist women and men, underground in the United States for more than four years."

The Weather Underground and the Black Panthers had different platforms, but were quite close in their revolutionary approach. Once their Revolution failed, Bill turned into a teacher, and Bernardine into a lawyer, then a teacher.

Malcolm X' Muslim name was El-Hajj Malik El-Shabazz, so Malik become a popular first name in the counter culture of the late Sixties. In 1967, Black Panther Bobby Seale had named his son Malik. In 1980, the couple Ayers-Dohrn named their second son Malik. In 1998, the Obamas named their first daughter Malia.

In yet another example of how tight-knitted the Chicago elite was, in 1984, Bernadine was hired by the prestigious Chicago law firm of Sidley & Austin, for their New York office. Howard Trienens, a fellow trustee and former classmate of Thomas Ayers at Northwestern University, was running the firm. It did not bother him much that she had not been admitted to the New York or Illinois bars, despite having passed both exams. It did not bother him either that the reason she was turned down was because she refused to file applications to demonstrate good moral character, under the Character and Fitness rule of bar admission. Thomas Ayers, her father-in-law, was his friend, and one of his biggest clients.

Her past did not deter the prestigious Northwestern University School of Law either, maybe because both Thomas Ayers and Howard Trienens were on the board of Trustees. It hired Dohrn as adjunct professor of law in 1991. An anarchist wanted by the FBI turned law professor. Anything could happen in Chicago.

As for Bill Ayers, he went on to teach at the College of Education at the University of Illinois in Chicago[170].

In 1988, Thomas Ayers founded the Alliance for Better Chicago Schools[171], a.k.a. the ABCs Coalition. Newcomer organizer Barack Obama joined as Kellman's DCP representative[172], and the contact person running the meetings was anarchist-turned-a-new-leaf education teacher Bill Ayers[173]. Contrary to Obama's assertions, twenty years later, that he barely knew Bill[174], this is when their relationship officially started, and it did not stop there. Ayers went on to found the Chicago Annenberg Challenge (CAC) in 1995, after winning a $49Mn grant from Walter Annenberg's "Challenge to the Nation". Annenberg was already a large donor to Northwestern University, so Annenberg and Tom Ayers were close. They also shared the same counsel, Sidley & Austin, the same prestigious firm that had hired Bernardine Dohrn, Bill Ayers' wife. Annenberg's counsel was Newton Nimow, Ayer's was Howard Trienens.

CAC's first Board appointed Obama President for a four-year mandate. Bill Ayers had assembled the Board so for all intents and purposes, he had appointed Obama. So much for the two not knowing each other[175]. When CAC phased out in 2001, it morphed into a new institution called the Chicago Public Education Fund, where Obama continued to serve on the "Leadership Council," together with Thomas Ayers and his other son John.

Obama had also joined the Woods Funds of Chicago as director from 1993 to 2002, and vice chair in 1997, and Ayers became director in 1999[176]. The same Woods Foundation that had sponsored the article Young Barack had written in 1988, titled *"Why organize? Problems and promise in the inner city"*. While this seemed to be just another foundation, it was not. Its chairman at the time was George Kelm[177], President and CEO of the largest Illinois Coal Company, Sahara Coal. Naturally, Sahara was a large supplier[178] of Thomas Ayers' Commonwealth Edison.

Together, Ayers and Obama granted money to minorities and schools in the Chicago area, which was their job. Strangely, however, among the recipients were the well-known left-wing activist group and now barred Association of Community Organizations for Reform Now, a.k.a. ACORN, to the tune of some $70,000 per year from 2001 to 2005[179], and the much lesser known Arab American Action Network, or AAAN, which received $40,000 in 2001 and $35,000 in 2002, a fifth of all their reported contributions. AAAN board member, Ali Hasan Abunimah, was the Palestinian Radical Islamist and founder of ElectronicIntifada.net, which needs no further qualifier than its website home page.

AAAN's co-founder was Rashid Khalidi, professor of Modern Arab Studies and director of the Middle East Institute at Columbia University. Close to, and allegedly affiliated[180] with Arafat's Palestinian Liberation Organization (PLO) when it was designated a terrorist group in the Seventies, it is fair to say that he was and still is a vocal anti-Israel and pan-Arab voice. Interestingly however, his Wikipedia page does not mention AAAN in his long list of affiliations[181]. It does say, though, that his wife Mona Khalidi is the Assistant Dean of Student Affairs and the Assistant Director of Graduate Studies of the School of International and Public Affairs at Columbia University. And her own Wikipedia page also says that in the late Seventies and early Eighties, she was working at Wafa, the official news agency of the PLO, and that she is President of AAAN[182].

So, at least two networks were emerging that could have backed Young Barack, way back. One was the liberal-radical political activists and socialites of Chicago's Hyde Park. The other was the pan-Arab Muslim connection. The two had several potential crossovers, and poor Percy Sutton kind of fell into it.

The third network was visibly communist. At the inception of the Cold War, no less, Frank Davis' Chicago Star's goal was to

> "*promote a policy of cooperation and unity between Russia and the United States.*"

Harry Canter, Secretary of the Boston CPUSA, had bought it with a "group of friends", in time for Davis to move to Hawaii. One of his son David's associates in the Illinois State Bureau was Abe Feinglass, a fierce opponent of the Vietnam War, much like a young vet, John Kerry. And David Canter owned Translation World Publishers with Le Roy Wolins, registered as a Soviet Union agent[183].

At about the same time, 1966, David Canter partnered with a Don Rose to publish the Chicago Hyde Park-Kenwood Voices[184]. Don Rose had been a communist radical since the Forties when he had joined former Vice President Henry Wallace's Progressive Party, but he was not just "a" Don Rose. His claim to fame was to have been the Chicago press secretary for Dr. Martin Luther King Jr. A few years later, the pair became mentors to a young Hyde Park Herald journalist they had spotted, David Axelrod[185].

While Don Rose had been Jane Byrne's campaign manager, successfully seeing her through as the first woman Mayor of Chicago, both he and David Canter were also instrumental in getting their longtime friend Harold Washington to beat her in 1983, and to become the first African American Mayor of Chicago. The man who ran his 1987 reelection campaign was none other than David Axelrod. He had good mentors indeed.

Three trails. One Frank Marshall Davis.

From 1981, when Young Barack went to Columbia College in New York, to 1985, when he landed a job in Chicago, apparently, and from nowhere, there were many people ready to help him. All had the money, the connections, and all were organizers, of one sort or the other. So, why didn't Barack go to Chicago in the first place? Why all the zig and zag? Why was the deciding factor a fortuitous job posting by an unknown Gerald Kellman, picked up by another unknown, the young Obama with a Japanese sounding name?[186] Why were his New York years but a fleeting moment in his 450-pages "memoirs"? And why were the transcripts and funding of all of his school years never disclosed, to this date?

The expression "Red Herring" comes from a smoked kipper – the herring. From Merriam-Webster,"

> [from the practice of drawing a red herring across a trail to confuse hunting dogs]: something that distracts attention from the real issue."

The Red comes from the color of the herring's slow smoking process. In this case, it befitted the color of Obama's sphere.

The trail to Chicago was loaded with Red Herrings. As a ten-year old, Barack comes back from Jakarta with no money but goes to Punahou in Hawaii, then to Occidental College in Los Angeles, then to Columbia College, then lands in Chicago still with no money after all these very expensive years, and no records disclosed at age twenty-four. There, he gets a whopper organizer job, out of the blue, which puts him on the political map of the Chicago inner circle before he is even thirty. And he ends up at Harvard Law School, becomes President of the Law Review, and lands a mega book advance without having written anything worth noting, or even noticing, with no records, whether financial or academic, known to anyone except, apparently, to Khalid al-Mansour and George Kellman. This is 1991, Obama is now thirty, and the rising star in the Chicago School of Herrings, home to his first known mentor, Frank Marshall Davis, "Uncle" Frank, full circle.

In that same year of 1991, and out of the blue again, a lady by the name of Valerie Jarrett hires Barack's fiancée, Michelle LaVaughn Robinson, to work in Chicago Mayor Dailey's office where she herself is Deputy Chief of Staff. As the story goes, before Michele accepts the offer, she asks Barack to meet Valerie, and vice versa.

Valerie Jarrett was one smelly Herring.

She was Vernon Jarrett's daughter-in-law, the same Vernon Jarrett who was "Uncle" Frank's best friend, the same "Uncle" Frank who was Michelle's fiancé's mentor, the same Vernon Jarrett who had befriended, somehow, Khalid al-Mansour who also was Michelle's fiancé's mentor and one of his likely financial backers. What were the odds that Vernon and Valerie Jarrett knew of Obama the day he set foot in Chicago in 1985, and maybe before, either through "Uncle" Frank or Khalid al-Mansour, or both?

Valerie had officially started her political career in 1987 as Deputy Corporation Counsel for Finance and Department in Mayor Harold Washington's administration – the same Harold Washington who Don

Rose, David Canter, and Vernon Jarrett had helped elect, and who David Axelrod had run the 1987 reelection campaign for. The same Harold Washington who was Obama's idol and who shook his hand at the ribbon cutting ceremony for the Development Community Project's office on once-thriving Michigan Avenue in Roseland[187].

Her full name was Valerie Bowman Jarrett, the daughter of James Bowman and Barbara Taylor Bowman, whose father, Robert Rochon Taylor, was the early housing activist chairman of the Chicago Housing Authority from 1942 to 1950[188]. For many years, Mrs. Bowman ran the Chicago Erikson Institute she had co-founded in 1966 with the help of philanthropist Irving Harris, and with who else but Thomas Ayers on her Board[189]. The Institute was named after Erik Erikson, the "father" of child psychology who had coined the term "identity crisis."

Bill Ayers, Tom's son, was not only a friend of Vernon Jarrett but also of the Bowman family. On page 82 of his book, *"A Kind and Just Parent"*, he wrote:

> *"Just South I see the Robert Taylor Homes named for the first head of the Chicago Housing Authority, whose daughter, a neighbor and friend is president of the Erikson Institute."*

Indeed, he, the Marxist, and Mike Klonsky, his communist friend and partner[190], were themselves pioneering educators, clones of Erik Erikson But Klonsky was not the only communist. The FBI had extensive files[191] on James Bowman and his friend Alfred Stern, Robert Rochon Taylor, and, more obviously, Vernon Jarrett and Bill Ayers.

So, while the story has it that before Michelle accepted Valerie's job offer, she asked that she meet her fiancé, Barack, and that all three had dinner, and that Michelle then accepted, let us recap the timeline:

1979: Vernon Jarrett interviews al-Mansour, Percy Sutton's friend. The connections are the Black Panthers on al-Mansour's side,

Malcolm X on Sutton's side, and Franck Davis on Jarrett's side. All three end up rooting for Barack, one way or the other, and at various points in time.

1985: Twenty-four year old Barack lands in Chicago, "Uncle" Frank's Alma Matter and Jarrett's turf. He works for Kellman's DCP, and instantly becomes a highly visible organizer in Greater Roseland in the Far South East Side, home to the poorest and most violent slums in the city. Jesse Jackson was the then leader of the Civil Rights movement not only in Chicago, but also of international renown. Barack attends several of his meetings of the People United to Save Humanity, or PUSH[192]. Mayor Washington comes to the opening of the DCP office in Roseland.

At the time, twenty-nine year old Valerie Jarrett is Vernon's daughter-in-law, just divorced. Valerie is the daughter of Barbara Taylor Bowman, and a close friend of the Ayers. Valerie and Barack, who supposedly do not know each other until the famous 1991 dinner, are roughly the same age and have one passion in common: organizing and inner city activism, to include housing and education. They also share the same political wavelength and both operate in Hyde Park and the South Side of Chicago. She works for Mayor Washington who is Obama's idol.

1988: Barack officially connects with Vernon Jarrett's inner circle, the Ayers, and joins the ABCs Coalition. The Cast, at this point, includes Vernon Jarrett, Barbara Taylor Bowman, Tom Ayers, Bill Ayers, Bernardine Dohrn, David Axelrod, Khalid al-Mansour, Percy Sutton, Don Rose, David Canter, David Axelrod, Harold Washington and, in the background, "Uncle" Frank.

Yet, for some reason that defies logic, Valerie Jarrett is not part of the Cast, and did not know Barack Obama until their dinner in 1991?

Michelle LaVaughn Robinson. She had graduated with a JD from Harvard in 1988, the year Barack went for his own "degree". That same year, she was hired by Sidley & Austin, as one of a handful

African Americans. This was the firm that had hired Bernardine Dohrn in 1984 because of the Ayers /Annenberg connection. Whether Michelle and Bernardine knew each other is irrelevant at this point, except it would make the official timeline even stranger, for lack of a better word.[193]

"Naturally", in 1989, Obama also worked at the Sidley & Austin firm as an associate. "Naturally," because it made more sense given his own Ayers' connection. And "naturally," Michele was his mentor. But why did Sidley & Austin hire Michelle? Wasn't she an unknown? Or was she, really?

Her father was a precinct captain, who had been working for the Democrat machine of Mayor Richard J. Daley, chairman of the all-powerful Cook County Democratic Central Office, the father of Valerie Jarrett's Richard M. Dailey. At the Whitney Young High School, Michelle met Santita Jackson[194], Jesse Jackson's oldest daughter.

Jesse Jackson had been prominently known since the Sixties, when he worked, among other civil rights leaders, with Dr. Martin Luther King. He became one of the leading Democratic figures in Illinois, so much so that George McGovern, Presidential Democratic nominee in 1972, rejected Mayor R.J. Daley's elected convention delegation, to replace it with that, unelected, of Jackson. For his role in international affairs, he rose to the forefront of Chicago politics and, as Presidential candidate in 1984, he received more than three million votes in the primaries. In 1988, his tally was close to seven million votes, only to be narrowly beaten by Michael Dukakis. Needless to say, Jesse Jackson was a powerhouse in the Eighties.

So, Santita and Michelle were best friends since the late Seventies, and had a three-hour commute to the Whitney Young High School. They would car pool, and became so close that, later, Santita was Michelle's maid of honor at her wedding, and godmother of her oldest daughter, Malia[195]. Michelle was de facto Jesse Jackson's "adopted" daughter, and as such, certainly not an unknown[196]. Rather, she had to be part of the Cast. In addition to her own merits as a recent JD graduate, this seemed good enough reasons for Sidley & Austin to hire her.

Michelle's Cinderella version is that she met Barack in 1989, while at the law firm. This does not make much sense either. Not only they were involved with the same political groups, but certainly, twenty-two year old Santita and twenty-one year old Michelle, who were quite attractive themselves, must have noticed the twenty-four year old charismatic, eloquent, good looking, highly visible organizer of the South Side and avid participant of Jackson's PUSH meetings[197], way before he joined Sidley & Austin in 1989.

The reality is that a bare seven years later, at the young age of thirty-five, the Man from nowhere, Barack Obama, now married to Cinderella Michelle, was powerful enough to clinch the Illinois Senate from his former mentor and well-entrenched communist, Alice Palmer. This did not happen out of the blue either.

David Axelrod's name has appeared here and there in this book. It is time to get to know him a bit better because, contrary to the many characters who are marginal to the story, he is a linchpin, much like Ayers, Jarrett, "Uncle" Frank and the pan-Arab connection.

Little is known about Axelrod's father who separated on and off from his mother, and committed suicide when David was twenty-two. Before they got married in 1948, his mother Myril worked for a well-known left leaning magazine called PM. In her footsteps, David took up political science at the University of Chicago. In 1975, he wrote for the Hyde Park Herald, which is where the real story began. There, he was spotted by Don Rose and David Canter. Axelrod ended up at the Chicago Tribune, as political writer from 1977 to 1985, working with Vernon Jarrett[198], and earning praise for being the youngest of his peers. At the time, the Tribune was the leading newspaper in Illinois. Axelrod then went on his own as Axelrod & Associates, a political consultancy firm.

For the time being, we will stop the clock somewhere in the mid-Nineties. By then, in 1984, Axelrod had gotten Illinois Congressman Paul Simon elected to the United State Senate. In 1987, Axelrod had gotten Harold Washington, for whom Valerie Jarrett worked as lead counsel, reelected as Mayor of Chicago. When he died a few months later, Axelrod became the strategist for his successor, Mayor Richard M. Daley, for whom Valerie Jarrett was Deputy Chief of Staff. Richard M. Daley was the son of Richard J. Daley, the omnipotent head of the Illinois Democrat machine, and Mayor of Chicago for twenty one consecutive years. In 1992, Axelrod got Cook County Recorder of Deeds Carol Moseley Braun elected as the first African American woman to the United States Senate. He had not been born into the inner circle of Chicago, but by then, in the early Nineties, Axelrod had scored them all. He was Illinois' top kingmaker.

Which takes us to 1996. In that year, Obama went from organizer status to full-fledged leader. As such, he embraced two of Saul Alinsky's basic principles, self-interest and lust for power. He used them against Alice Palmer, the incumbent Senator of Illinois 13th District for whom he worked.

Alice was no Alice. She was a die- hard communist, member of the World Peace Council, in the footsteps of W.E.B. Du Bois and Abe Feinglass, and writer for the People's Weekly World. The World Peace Council had been founded in Prague in 1949 and was controlled by the International Department of the Communist Party of the Soviet Union, in other words, the KGB. As a professional, she had taught at Chicago's Malcolm X College. Her 13th District included Hyde Park, the middle-to-upper class South Shore and distraught Englewood. Not only she was a communist, but she also was a real Chicagoan. In 1995, she had decided to run for the United States Congress and had chosen Obama as her successor – which she announced at a fundraiser at Bill Ayers and Bernardine Dohrn's house, of all places and as a matter of course[199]. Ayers had just appointed him chairman of the Chicago Annenberg Challenge, and "Dreams" was about to be released. Little did she know of Obama's flickering loyalty, and the story does not say why he had become her carpetbagger chief of staff.

Good or bad, she was well on her way to lose the Congressional race to Jesse Jackson Jr., and decided she would run to keep her Illinois Senate seat, after all. Not so said her protégé Obama. Even though he was a rookie, barely thirty-five years old, he went as far as verifying the signatures on the nominating petitions for each of the other four Democratic primary candidates[200], Alice Palmer, Ulmer Lynch Jr., Gha-is Askia and Marc Ewell . Two-thirds of Palmer's fifteen hundred and eighty signatures were found invalid, and she withdrew from the race. So did the other three, and he ended up running unopposed in the Democratic Primaries. Not bad for a rookie. The carpetbagger exactly knew what he was doing, and why.

In addition to Carol Anne Harwell, his first campaign manager and veteran from Project Vote[201], Axelrod, Ayers and Jarrett must have been coaching him, together with their pal Rahm Emanuel. He also had the support of local politicians such as Toni Preckwinkle, Barabara Holt, Ivory Mitchell, Abner Mikva, socialites Bettylu Saltzman and Christie Heffner, and a couple of years under his belt in the civil-rights activist top law firm of Davis[202], Miner, Barnhill & Galland[203]. Combined with the Annenberg Challenge, the fuzzy memoirs book, and a non-competing slate of opponents, the unknown rookie from Honolulu was handed down the power, as in organizer turning leader, and became the 13th District Illinois Senator, effective January 1997. Jesse Jackson Jr. now was the U.S. Congressman representing Illinois 2nd District, and Rod Blagojevich the U.S. Congressman representing Illinois 5th District. The Chairman of the Democratic National Convention was Christopher Dodd and we will talk about all of them later. Blagojevich and Dodd were also Axelrod's clients. Together with his other successes, his reputation as kingmaker clearly established, Axelrod's next stop would be Washington. And Alice Palmer went on to teach Urban Planning and Public Affairs at the University of Chicago.

This was kind of strange. Jesse Jackson Jr., although barely thirty-years old, was a natural political rock star, given his father's leadership and his own charisma. Blagojevich was considered part of the Machine, having married Patricia Mell in 1990. Patty Mell was the daughter of Richard Mell, the influential Alderman of Chicago's 33rd Ward, on the Northwest Side. But Obama replacing Alice Palmer, out of nowhere? It is one thing to run a conventional platform. It is something else to run as the successor of a flamboyant communist and alleged Soviet agent of influence, in Chicago of all places.

What did Alice Palmer, much like Gerald Kellman before her, know about the Man Obama from Honolulu that we did not know? More importantly, what did Axelrod, Emanuel, Jarrett, Ayers and al-Mansour know about him?

Officially, he had a top curriculum. Punahou, Occidental College, Columbia, Harvard. But there were no transcripts and documented source of funds. Then there was BI, NYPIRG, and the DCP. The list of achievements there is not documented either, except for Obama connecting with Bill Ayers and the ABCs coalition, if that is to be considered an achievement. Certainly, becoming the Chairman of the $49 million Chicago Annenberg Challenge was remarkable, even if it was staying in Bill Ayers' family, not much of a politically conforming vetting by a former terrorist. There was also the Khalid al-Mansour-posing-as-Percy Sutton recommendation to Harvard. Where that came from, we still do not know, but being the first African American President of the Harvard Law Review would certainly help. Even if the submission to the Review Annual Competition was, well, still somewhere to be found.

If all of this should have ensured a shoe-in for the Primaries, why then go the extra borderline mile to kick all the other candidates out?

Even the book "he" had written should have been enough. Barack's father was a humble Kenyan goat herder, his mother was a hard working mind devoted to the poor, and Frank was just an old poet living in a decrepit house, an inspirational figure to a boy with absentee parents. The book was a tepid seller but to quote Aristotle, "*ha men pollois dokei taut age einai ohamen*", i.e. "*what seems right to many, we say is true*". Therefore, the book was "true". Nobody was supposed to know about the real Frank, or the whole cast of characters. Nobody was supposed to know about two key words, communism and pan-Arabism. And nobody could really check the story first hand. Obama Sr. had died in 1982, "Uncle" Frank Marshall Davis in 1986, Lolo Soetoro in 1987, "Gramps" Stanley Dunham in 1992, and Ann Dunham in November 1995. Only "Toot" Madelyn Dunham was alive and well, but would not talk to anyone. And while Elizabeth Mooney Kirk passed later in 2004, she had been mute on the subject.

The internet was of no help either. It was one year old, so was Netscape Navigator, and neither Google nor Wikipedia were born yet[204].

One thing about Red Herrings. After a while, the hounds get the idea. Simon & Schuster had been looking for a book on racial tensions in the inner cities, but it was not happening in 1993, Barack was somewhere with Michelle in Bali. Then someone had a brilliant idea, and the book became some kind of biographical political manifesto, just in time for the elections. Because he had no writing record to even mention, one story has it that Obama sketched the canvass for his friend William Ayers[205]. Seventeen years his elder, professional writer, self-described educator, apprentice identity crisis specialist, and in charge of Annenberg's $49 million, all Bill had to do was to ghost pen a romantically sanitized account of a dire reality. Why not? Certainly, Jack Cashill, known for his amazing literary detective work on Obama's writing skills – or lack thereof – was convincingly adamant[206, 207].

With the help of the many internet resources at our disposal today, we now can follow the maze, almost in that order: Saul Alinsky, Frank Marshall Davis, Ann Stanley Dunham, Barack Hussein Obama Sr., Harry Canter, Robert Rochon Taylor, Thomas Ayers, Barbara Taylor

Bowman, Vernon Jarrett, David Canter, Don Rose, LeRoy Wolins, Abe Feinglass, John Kerry, David Axelrod, Rahm Emmanuel, Khalid al-Mansour, Jesse, Jesse Jr. and Santita Jackson, Bill Ayers, Bernardine Dohrn, Rashid Khalidi, Ali Hasan Abunimah, Gerard Kellman, Valerie Jarrett, Alice Palmer, Percy Sutton.

This was Obama's Cast, in the movie that started in 1959 in Honolulu, Hawaii.

"Reverend" Jeremiah Wright, from the United Church of Christ, and his friend "Minister" Louis Farrakhan, the then leader of Chicago-based Nation of Islam, made cameo appearances but were way too inconvenient. They were later dumped, like Bill Ayers.

We were in 1996, what happened in Chicago stayed in Chicago. Al-Mansour and many other stories had been swept under the rug. And Putin, Medvedev, and Dugin were not even on the stage, yet. The story was barely beginning.

7

Mid-East Mess - v1

Add Zbigniew Brzezinski to the cast. In 1997, the National Security Advisor to the Carter Administration and co-founder of the Trilateral Commission had published a classic, "The Grand Chessboard", in which he described how the United States had become the leading World Superpower, and what she should do to remain so. No doubt this was a counter to Aleksandr Dugin's "Foundations of Geopolitics," published the same year. Dugin, for his part, laid the ground for the destruction of the Atlantic Alliance, and the Russian conquest of Eurasia. Some twenty years earlier, Brzezinski had warned President Carter of the Soviet ambition in the Persian Gulf:

> *"If the Soviets succeed in Afghanistan, [...] the age-long dream of Moscow to have direct access to the Indian Ocean will have been fulfilled."*[208]

Brzezinski had built his reputation as a staunch anti-Soviet, for personal reasons. Born into Polish nobility, his family was decimated during WWII, first by Hitler then by Stalin. Considered by many a grand strategist, his record was nevertheless controversial. Much like the Dulles Brothers, and the likes of John McCloy and the Wise Men[209], the end justified the means. Any means, to destroy the Soviets.

And like the Weather Underground and the Vietnam Veterans Against War before him, but for diametrically opposite reasons, he had no problem overtly backing China in her support of the Khmer Rouge leader and war criminal Pol Pot[210].

He also had no problem enabling the Islamic Mujahedeen to fight the Soviet invasion of Afghanistan, which had officially started in December 1979 under Brezhnev's rule. This earned him the nickname of "Father of al-Qaeda." Nor did he have a problem green lighting Pakistan's nuclear ambitions, to further assist the Taliban for the same reason, and counter the Soviet-Indian Treaty of Peace, Friendship and Cooperation of 1971[211].

This is why Brzezinski is part of the Cast. An expert on the Middle East pivot, Dean of the Institute on Communist Affairs at Columbia from 1960 to 1989, perfectly aware of Russia's Persian Gulf strategy, he later became foreign policy advisor to Barack Obama during his presidential bid. One could have inferred President Obama would take his praised advice into consideration[212]. He partly did – except for the Russian part.

So, what was happening in the Middle East in 1979, when the Soviets decided to play hard ball?

These days, Afghanistan may sound like a mountainous barren country, with poppy fields and land mines everywhere. While unfortunately true, this was not always the case, as the area goes back to the dawn of civilization. In the 18th century, it even had its own Empire, named after Ahmad Shah Durrani[213]. The Durrani Empire extended to northwestern India, northeastern Iran and eastern Turkmenistan. Capital Kabul, winter capital Peshawar.

For centuries, Afghanistan had been a coveted pivot on the Silk Road to China. Finally caught between the ambitions of the Greater British Empire and that of Czarist Russia, it was only after the Third Anglo-Afghan War, in August 1919, that the United Kingdom recognized its independence and its borders – which had been drawn by the British

Indian diplomat Sir Mortimer Durand in 1893. In the Empire usual "divide and rule" manner, he split the indigenous Pashtun people in two[214], which explains much of the legacy fighting in the area. Aptly called the Durand Line, it was still debated as of this writing, much like the other British gerrymandering of the Middle East in 1916, the Sykes-Picot Agreement[215].

During the Cold War, the United States replaced Britain in its quest for influence in the region, and in 1947, Pakistan had literally come on the map, to the East. The Indian side of the Durand Line had just become Pakistan's problem but Afghanistan was doing fine, on the other side of the border. In 1919, King Amanullah Khan had declared it a sovereign, secular, independent constitutional monarchy. One coup after another, it was Zahir Shah's turn to take the throne in 1933, for the next forty years. He made one mistake. In 1953, he appointed his cousin and brother-in-law, Prince Mohammed Daoud Khan, Prime Minister.

King Zahir had been close to the Axis in WWII, and Daoud Khan was leaning Soviet. Also, Daoud did not recognize the Durand line and wanted to reunify all Pashtuns, creating tensions with Pakistan. King Zahir did not like that and Daoud had to step down in 1963. This was the King's second mistake. In 1973, Daoud came back and took over from his cousin the King. Interestingly, to reflect his secular ideology, he did not become Shah, or King, but took the title of President of the new Republic of Afghanistan.

All in all, Afghanistan was opportunistically non-aligned, a popular position for many peripheral countries. The U.S.S.R. was Daoud's Big Brother, but he had other friends too. In 1974, he asked India for military training, and Iran for economic development. Then he turned to the Gulf countries, China, even to the United States. And in 1977, Daoud Khan asked Brezhnev to lay off his support of the Afghan communist party. This turned out to be his government and personal death sentence.

Although Détente was in the air during the Nixon years, he had resigned in 1974 over Watergate. The following year, with the

Helsinki Accords, President Ford had recognized Soviet hegemony over Europe, in exchange for some human rights promises. When President Carter was elected in 1976, he pushed Brezhnev's human rights button a little too hard. Emboldened by the end of the Vietnam War, the hawkish Brezhnev saw an easy opponent in the dovish Carter. Now seemed a good time to break the Cold War stalemate. In April 1978, banking on a split within the communist People's Democratic Party of Afghanistan (PDPA), Moscow backed a coup by the Marxist faction, the Khalq[216]. Daoud Khan was killed with most of his family in the Arg, the presidential palace in Kabul. The Democratic Republic of Afghanistan was now under Soviet supervision. The Khalqis were not done. They had a revolutionary ax to grind and started purging the other PDPA faction, the Parcham, and every non-communist in sight.

A few thousand miles away, something else was happening in the Middle East. In September, the United States sponsored the Camp David Peace Accords between Israel and Egypt. The Soviet Union did not like that either, as it created a powerful anti-Soviet military block to include Operation Bright Star, a biennial joint training exercise between the American and Egyptian military[217].

And by mid-1979, the Afghan "Lion of Panjshir", Ahmad Shah Massoud, barely twenty-six years-old, was organizing the Islamic resistance against the communist intruders.

There is a difference between the terms "Islamic" and "Islamist". Whereas Islamic describes a religious belief, Islamism adds a political and radical dimension to it, in particular the strict adoption of Sharia law. The Islamist branch was being organized by Gulbuddin Hekmatyar. He was the bad guy. Massoud was the good guy. They would work together for the cause, but not hand in glove.

In the meantime, Iran was in the midst of its own revolution. The Shah, who had been restored to his throne in 1953 with the overthrow of Prime Minister Mosaddegh[218], had overstayed his welcome, a combination of the extensive use of his secret and savage police aptly named SAVAK, and the rise of fundamental Islamism led by the Ayatollahs. He flew into exile in January 1979, in the hope that calm be restored, but never returned.

President Carter had praised him as late as December 1977 and initially offered him asylum. A couple of months later, he wobbled, leaving the Shah a wandering Monarch until he agreed to let him in for medical treatment in late 1979. Carter feared the Ayatollahs' retaliation but the Men in Charge, the "Triumpherate" as it was known, prevailed[219]. They were David Rockefeller of the Chase Bank, his Milbank Tweed personal counsel and one of the Wise Men John McCloy, and McCloy's love-hate protégé Henry Kissinger. Their official argument was "humanitarian", skipping the bloody part of the Shah's story. In reality, the Shah was their U.S. asset and client state crown jewel.

In April, Prime Minister Shapour Bakhtiar, the feeble remnant of the Shah's government and his former political opponent, was also overthrown. The new man in charge was the Spiritual Ayatollah Ruhollah Khomeini. Spiritual, but not joking. He had long opposed the Shah's policies, and was deported to Turkey in 1964. From there, he went in exile to the Iraqi Holy Shia city of Najaf, continuing his campaign against the Shah. In 1978, however, Saddam Hussein let him know it was time to leave. Saddam was Sunni, and the Sunnis in Iraq were a minority. He did not want to have the Shia leader knocking on the doors of his own Shia population at a time when Iran was in turmoil, and when the Soviets were gearing up to something. The Ayatollah chose to go to France, land of asylum for many leaders of obscure alliances, where he stayed until February 1979. He returned to Iran in great pomp, a short month after the Shah left.

Although all religions purport to forgive, one way or the other and under different conditions, most really do not. Khomeini was in the camp of "do not forgive under any circumstances". In the U.S. hosting of the Shah, he saw the opportunity for an Islamist show of force against the Western world, and allowed for what was to be called the hostage crisis.

In November 1979, a group of revolutionary students – among them Mahmoud Ahmadinejad who would later become Iran's President – stormed the U.S. Embassy in Tehran and took fifty two Americans hostages. In Farsi, the official Iranian, Afghan and Tajik language, this was called the "Conquest of the American Spy Den" and would last for four hundred and forty four days. Under different circumstances, it may not have happened. Under President Carter, Zbiegniew Brzezinski, John McCloy, Kissinger, and Rockefeller, it did. Same McCloy, another President, another team, another blunder[220].

Egypt, Israel, Iran, Pakistan, and the Afghan Khalqis killing everyone in their own backyard, the situation was becoming a little too iffy for the Soviets. In December, Brezhnev deployed his 40th Army in Afghanistan, ambushing the Khalqi leader Hafizullah Amin in the process, and installed Babrak Karmal as new General Secretary of the PDPA Central Committee. He did not want the Ayatollahs, who were bold enough to thumb their nose at the U.S. after they had allowed them to rise to power, to expand their sphere of Shiite influence to Afghanistan, or even think about their fifteen hundred miles of common border with the Soviet Union. As for Pakistan, it had its own large and oppressed Shiite minority ready to rise, and was a menace in itself. De facto, Brezhnev was keeping the same eye on Iran than Stalin did in 1945. This was his window of opportunity after twenty five years of close U.S.-Iran relations. To its West, Iran was the key to Iraq, Kuwait and Saudi Arabian Oil. And it was not only the gate to the Caspian Sea to its North but also the gate to the Strait of Hormuz and the Arabian Sea to its South. The Arabian Sea was the gateway to India, and he was not about to let Iran lock it[221].

One thing for sure, neither Brzezinski nor Carter could secure the hostages' release. They were fully aware of Brezhnev's Afghan threat, and any forceful intervention in Iran could embolden the Soviets to get involved. Things could get even worse given Moscow's long-lasting relationship with Iraq next door. Their hands were tied, all they could try was an election-time, face-saving covert rescue operation code named Eagle Claw, in April 1980. Destined to fail, it did, with helicopters unable to cope with desert sandstorms, in the desert. This was a major blow to both men and their Administration, led by nice-to-everybody Secretary of State Cyrus Vance, who resigned in the process.

In parallel, the 1978 Camp David Accords fired back, literally, on President Sadat, a friend of the United States and the first Arab leader to promote peace with Israel. Egypt was suspended from the Arab League in 1979, and President Sadat was assassinated in 1981[222].

The turmoil was also getting iffy for the other hegemonistic hopeful, Saddam Hussein, something he had anticipated when he kicked Khomeini out of Iraq. Without getting in the history of the ruling Ba'ath Party, fascinating as it is, suffice it to say that Saddam was the de facto leader of Iraq since 1976, before forcefully assuming power from General Ahmed Hassan al-Bakr in July 1979. It was a propitious time to try and make a run at his pan-Arab goal, his friend Brezhnev surely would not mind.

He also had to deal with its own Kurdish separatist issue. If he let the Northern Iraqi Kurds unite with the Western Iranian Kurds, the North Eastern Syrian Kurds and the Eastern Turkish Kurds, they would soon create a forty-million people strong Kurdistan State. This was not acceptable either.

Figure 3 - Kurdish Areas in Iran, Iraq, Syria, and Turkey. Courtesy of the University of Texas Libraries, The University of Texas at Austin.

So Iraq invaded Iran in September 1980, and President Reagan was elected in November 1980. He was no Jimmy Carter.

Iran now had three threats to face – Afghanistan under Soviet control to the East, Iraq to the West, and Reagan in the White House. The day before his inauguration on January 20, 1981, Iran and the United States signed the Algiers Accords that ended the hostage crisis. A few minutes after President Reagan was sworn into office, the hostages were released into U.S. custody.

Fast forward to the late Eighties.

The Iraq-Iran War officially ended on August 20, 1988. By then, Iran had inverted the roles, and was making forays in Iraq. During this deadly period, it became apparent that Iraq had used chemical weapons against civilians, with a heavy toll on its own Kurdish and Shiite populations[223]. In mid-1988, Saddam had warned Iran of a full-scale chemical weapons attack. On August 2, it bombed the Iranian border town of Oshnavieh with poison gas, killing and wounding two thousand civilians out of a population of less than thirty thousand. Earlier, on March 16, during the al-Anfal campaign, it had dropped bombs containing mixes of sulfur mustard, nerve agents tabun, sarin and VX, and blood agent hydrogen cyanide on the Iraqi Kurdish village of Halabja. Five hours of bombing from Iraqi Russian-made MiG and French-made Mirage aircrafts, killing an estimated five thousand Kurds, mostly civilians, injuring thousands more.

It also became apparent that the suppliers of these chemical weapons, to include their highly engineered precursors, were located in Western industrialized nations. As for conventional weapons, Iraq had been supplied mainly by the Soviet Union and France, with China supplying both sides. The United States was providing logistical and intelligence support. Saudi Arabia, Kuwait and the United Arab Emirates were Saddam's main bankers. Much like in WWII, when they had lost sight of the Soviet Union's real local ambitions, they were all united against the aggressor, the Ayatollahs in this case. Not to mention the real economic threat – Iran's potential control of the Persian Gulf and the Strait of Hormuz, the world's main choke point for the world's main oil producing region.

Which may explain why the West, the East and the Gulf did not react to Iraq's chemical violations, as if they condoned them. This was the deciding factor for Iran to accept the cease-fire, despite its territorial gains. Even the "accidental" downing of Iran Air Flight 655 by the USS Vincennes on July 3, 1988, killing all two hundred and ninety passengers including sixty six children on board, did not resonate. The Ayatollahs started to realize they were an endangered species. They had to fold, and they did.

The Iraq-Iran war was a draw, if it was not for its absurd death toll, not only military but also civilian, and so it ended, in 1988. So did the Soviet-Afghan war, with the Soviets pulling out in February 1989.

If only it was so simple.

In Afghanistan, the Resistance to the Soviets had been the "Peshawar Seven" and the "Tehran Eight". The "Peshawar Seven" were so called because of the alliance of seven Sunni factions, Pashtun[224] for most: the Khalis, Hezbi Islami, Jamiat-i-Islami, the Islamic Union for the Liberation of Afghanistan, a.k.a. Ittehad-I Islami, the National Islamic Front for Afghanistan, the Afghanistan National Liberation Front and the Revolutionary Islamic Movement. Peshawar was the main town in Northwestern Pakistan at the Afghan border, once the winter home of the Durrani Empire.

The Shi'a "Tehran Eight" were comprised of the Afghan Hezbollah, the Nasr Party a.k.a. the Islamic Victory Organization of Afghanistan, the Corps of Islamic Revolution Guardians of Afghanistan, the Islamic Movement of Afghanistan, the Committee of Islamic Agreement, the Islamic Revolution Movement, the Union of Islamic Fighters, and the Raad party.

A political landscape as difficult to map as the country's land mined fields.

In the meantime, in 1984, Osama bin Laden, Abdullah Yusuf Azzam, and Ayman al-Zawahiri had founded Maktab al-Khidamat in the same town of Peshawar. MAK, known as the Afghan Services Bureau, was established to channel funds and recruit mujahedeen for the war against the Soviets. In 1986, MAK started recruiting worldwide, including from the U.S. It established a presence in thirty three American cities, to include Boston, St. Louis, Kansas City, Seattle, Sacramento, Los Angeles, San Diego, and Chicago, where it was later known as the Global Relief Foundation in Bridgeview[225]. Its hub was located at the Al-Kifah Refugee Center at the Farouq Mosque in Brooklyn, New York. In 1988, bin Laden founded his own organization, al-Qaeda, to expand the Islamic Jihad beyond Afghanistan.

In November 1989, Azzam and his three sons were killed by unknowns, and bin Laden's al-Qaeda took MAK over.

That same year, the Soviets had withdrawn from Afghanistan, thanks to Gorbachev's Perestroika, and left the People's Democratic Party of Afghanistan, the PDPA, on its own. It collapsed in 1992, with the implosion of the Soviet Union, and was immediately replaced with the Islamic State of Afghanistan, or ISA, under the leadership of Sunni cleric Burhanuddin Rabbani.

A long-time leader of Jamiat-i-Islami, one of the Peshawar Seven, he was considered the respected spiritual leader of the Northern Alliance. His military commander was Ahmad Shah Massoud, "The Lion of Panjshir."

Naturally, another civil war ensued, still ongoing as of this writing. Not only this was mostly a tribal conflict, with a confusing number of ethnic, political and religious groups involved, and an even more confusing list of international backers, but the land itself was now physically devastated. Nothing much was left of its forests, two percent maybe, and agricultural land almost immediately became dedicated to poppy fields, the source of the international narcotics trade. The unexploded land mines, with estimates ranging from one hundred thousand to millions, were now part and parcel of the landscape, with Afghanistan in the pack of the most land-mined countries in the world[226].

Despite this literally devastated state of affairs, many were fighting for control of this now barren mountainous region. It was still one of the main land locks to Eurasia, with Iran to the West, the Persian Gulf to the South, Pakistan to the South East, China to the East, and Russia's former republics to the North.

There was another reason, the narcotics trade was extremely lucrative. With oil, this was the main source of jihadist revenue, with opium accounting for some 90% of the world's production.

If there is one thing Brzezinski could be commended for, it is the choice of his book title, *"The Grand Chess Board"*. It was a chess board alright, but to this author it looked more like a Grand Board of Go[227]. The Pashtun-Tajik-Uzbek-Hazara Northern Alliance, led by Rabbani and Massoud, was a threat to Pakistan's regional aspirations. This new Islamic movement could potentially appeal to its moderate Sunni population, so instead, Pakistan backed the drug lord and dissident Islamist Gulbuddin Hekmatyar, Massoud's arch rival and leader of Hezb-I Islami. Hekmatyar went on to bomb half of Kabul, earning him the nickname of "Butcher of Kabul" in the process. Saudi Arabia naturally backed the Wahhabi Ittihad-i-Islami faction of the former Peshawar Seven. And Iran stood behind its own Nasr Party of the former Tehran Eight.

Nobody knew where the chips would fall. A bloody war it was, far from civil.

Then, in 1994, Mullah Omar officially founded the Taliban, the Islamist version of the Islamic State of Afghanistan, in Kandahar. The Taliban's credo was strict Sharia law, and then some. In September 1996, with the help of Pakistan's intelligence service ISI, of Prime Minister Benazir Bhutto, of General Pervez Musharraf, and of the "opposition" leader Nawaz Sharif, it took over Kabul and declared its rule as the Islamic Emirate of Afghanistan – to be internationally recognized only by Pakistan, Saudi Arabia and the United Arab Emirates. That same year, Osama bin Laden was expelled from Sudan and joined Omar, his friend and mentor, in Eastern Afghanistan. The Islamics, led by Rabbani and Massoud, were now at war against the Islamists, led by the Taliban and al-Qaeda. Hekmatyar had overstayed his Pakistani welcome. He fled to Tehran where he stayed in exile for a while.

Benazir Bhutto was in her second term as Pakistan Prime Minister, in the footsteps of her father Zulfikar Ali Bhutto. Nicknamed the Matron of the Taliban, she allowed for the opening of the Taliban embassy in Islamabad. A couple of months later, in November 1996, she was excused by Pakistan President Farooq Leghari, on corruption charges. This did not change much. She was replaced by Nawaz Sharif, who followed the same pro-Taliban policy, with the same assistance of the powerful ISI, Pakistan's Inter-Services Intelligence agency. When General Musharraf deposed Sharif in 1999, unlike when General Zia-ul-Haq had deposed Prime Minister Zulfikar Ali Bhutto in 1977, this time Saudi Arabia and the United States pleaded in favor of Sharif so that he would not be hung, like Ali Bhutto had been. In a pragmatic gesture of goodwill, Sharif was allowed to go into exile in Saudi Arabia, and Musharraf got to support the Taliban and al-Qaeda for a couple of more years – that is, until late 2001.

Where was Iraq during all of this? Saddam Hussein, in a typical psychotic fashion, whether he thought he had won the Iran war, or believed his atrocities would go unnoticed, kept going on. He had a pan-Arab job to do, and a lot of debt. Next would be Kuwait. The Emir Jaber Al-Ahmad Al-Jaber Al-Sabah had lent him the tidy sum of fourteen billion dollars in his eight-year war against Iran but Saddam, true to his word, refused to pay him back. The Emir was not happy and started drilling into Iraq's oil fields. So, on August 2, 1990, Saddam's army invaded little Kuwait, with an eye on its next door neighbor and other major creditor, Saudi Arabia, to whom it owed twenty six billion dollars – some say thirty. Saddam's army was not exactly small. It was the fourth largest in the world, with some one million standing soldiers, about the same in reservists, five thousand tanks, three thousand artillery pieces, seven hundred combat aircraft and helicopters, and a strong air defense. One million soldiers for thirty million people.

Within one day, Kuwait was done with. The Emir was somewhere in the Saudi desert, his half-brother killed and then, to make sure, run over by a tank, and half of the 2.5 million population in exile. As a pre-emptive measure, and acting on its own, the United States immediately sent troops to Saudi Arabia, under the code name Operation Desert Shield. This was August 7, 1990. It took seven months for the International community to get its act together, even with the support of the Soviet Union and China. They had finally turned on Saddam, the threat to the Gulf oil fields was universal. After the United Nations Security Council had passed twelve resolutions to no avail, the United States finally led a coalition force, code named Operation Desert Storm, which included Saudi Arabia and Egypt among its leaders. It launched on January 17, 1991, and whatever was left of Iraqi troops was sent home by the end of February.

This is when the United States and President George H.W. Bush decided to play a dangerous game, and let Saddam off the hook, literally. Officially, it was Mission Accomplished. Unofficially, convenience ruled. Iraq, albeit weakened, was nevertheless the heavy-armored pawn which would act as a buffer against Iran. This game of chicken continued all through the Clinton years, under the watch of Secretaries of State Warren Christopher and Madeline Albright.

William "Bill" Clinton, the next President, would now operate under bluer skies, cleared by the implosion of the Soviet Union in 1992, presumably free of Cold War compromises. His foreign policy plate was full – the Yugoslavian civil war, the tribal genocides in Somalia and Rwanda, and continued unrest in the Middle East.

He started on a hopeful note. In November 1993, he achieved the unthinkable, a peace accord between Israel's Prime Minister Yitzhak Rabin and P.L.O. Chairman Yasser Arafat. The Oslo Accords, as they were called, allowed for a limited Palestinian self-rule in the territories of Gaza and the West Bank. To boot, in 1994, he brokered a truce between Israel and Jordan, which became the second Arab state after Egypt to normalize its relations with Israel. Awesome, but Iran, Iraq, and al-Qaeda were still kicking, and President Clinton's second term Middle East policy was less than clear.

Since 1993, the veteran State Department point lady was Robin Raphel, Assistant Secretary of State for South Asia, usually described as warm to totalitarian regimes, cool to human rights, and deeply anti-communist. She openly promoted the Taliban takeover of Afghanistan and even asked Massoud, the "Lion of Panshjir," and the popular hero of Afghan resistance since the Seventies, to surrender the Northern Alliance fight – which he flatly refused. By the same token, she endorsed Pakistan and its support of the Taliban. She was a career diplomat, married for a couple of years to the late Arnold Raphel, U.S. Ambassador to Pakistan in the Zia era, and therefore very much in the Pakistan know. Yet, she did not seem to worry about al-Qaeda, despite the 1993 bombing of the World Trade Center. And she could not care less about India either, which was too close to the Soviet Union for her taste. In November 1997[228], most likely because of her iconoclastic views, she was appointed to the much less visible post of Ambassador to Tunisia.

In 1998, President Clinton again started paying attention to the Middle East mess, a much needed diversion in the midst of his sex-related impeachment proceedings. In August, in a first of its kind, al-Qaeda made the news. Until then, its Jihad had been confined to the Near War, in the Middle East. It was now engaging in the Far War, hence the large scale bombings of the U.S. embassies in Dar es Salaam, Tanzania and Nairobi, Kenya, which left some two hundred people dead and many injured. The idea was to scare the U.S. as in Mogadishu, in 1993.

It worked. In his weakened position, President Clinton could do little to retaliate against this new asymmetric threat. Operation Infinite

Reach targeted some missiles at al-Qaeda bases in Afghanistan and a factory in Sudan, suspected to manufacture chemical weapons. The search was on for bin Laden but it failed, to the satisfaction of his growing supporters. So the President, even more in need of a diversion, dusted off an old foe. Bin Laden was an emerging threat, maybe, but Saddam Hussein was still his non-compliant genocidal self, and, as such, was a ready platform worth exploiting, especially for a President battling some bad press at home.

In 1986, U.N. Sanction 582 had unanimously *"deplored"* the use of chemical weapons in the Iran-Iraq War. In 1988, Sanction 612 *"expected both sides to refrain from the future use of chemical weapons"*. In 1991, Sanction 687 provided for the formal ceasefire between Iraq and Kuwait, with a series of conditions: destruction of all of Iraq's chemical and biological weapons, all ballistic missiles with a range greater than 150km, no nuclear weapons development, and a schedule of inspections. Despite all of these, and then some, Saddam was still relentless in the murder of his Kurdish population to the North, and of his Shi'a population to the South. This prompted Bill Clinton to give a warm-up speech to the Joint Chiefs of Staff in February 1998[229], before the al-Qaeda bombings:

> *"Iraq admitted, among other things, an offensive biological warfare capability, notably five thousand gallons of botulinum, which causes botulism; two thousand gallons of anthrax; twenty five biological-filled Scud warheads; and one hundred and fifty seven aerial bombs. And I might say UNSCOM inspectors believe that Iraq has actually greatly understated its production... [...] And someday, some way, I guarantee you he'll use the arsenal..."*

In October, Clinton got his diversion and the Iraq Liberation Act became law, calling for the removal of the Hussein regime, with 360 votes for and 38 votes against in the House, and unanimity in the Senate. Remarkable given that Congress now had an absolute Republican majority[230], and great timing right when the House voted to impeach the President[231]. A few weeks later, in mid-December 1998, Operation Desert Fox launched a four-day bombing campaign, and a shot across Iraq's bow.

In 1999, the focus was back on al-Qaeda, with bin Laden now on the FBI Most Wanted list. The U.N. Security Council passed Resolution 1267, demanding that the Taliban extradite him and close all terrorists bases. Yet, Massoud was no longer receiving any international support, except from India, and, nominally, from Russia. When President George W. Bush took over in 2001, he discarded whatever was left of the Raphel doctrine and in August, with National Security Adviser Condoleezza Rice, he agreed on a plan to covertly support Massoud.

It was ten years too late. On September 9, 2001, Massoud, the forty eight years old "Lion of Panjshir," was assassinated by al-Qaeda suicide bombers posing as journalists.

Two days later, on September 11, 2001, "some" Middle Eastern terrorists struck the United States at its core. More than three thousand civilians were murdered in New York and Pennsylvania, short of the terrorists' goal of fifty thousand, and more than six thousand were injured. The Pentagon was hit. The terrorists, at first, were "some" terrorists. In a matter of days, if not hours, they were identified as nineteen members of al-Qaeda, under Osama bin Laden's orders, the same group that the United States, read Zbigniew Brzezinski, the United Kingdom and Saudi Arabia had financed to fight the war against Russia in Afghanistan some fifteen years earlier. As "Zbig" reportedly said in retrospect, "*we all make mistakes.*" Seventeen of the nineteen were Saudi nationals.

The response had to be immediate. President Bush declared the Global War on Terror, and there were three potential targets to go after. Saudi Arabia was an obvious no-go, for strategic and oily reasons. Some even reasoned that Presidents Bush, father and son, had close connections with the bin Laden family, even though Osama had had his Saudi citizenship revoked in the early 1990s[232].

Pakistan for itself was a bit too big to handle and did have a nuclear force. The third choice was Afghanistan. Even though al-Qaeda was based in Pakistan, it was operating mostly from there, working hand in hand with the Taliban. So Afghanistan it was. "We", meaning the United States and the United Kingdom at first, launched Operation Enduring Freedom on October 7, 2001, with the help on the ground of the Northern Alliance, Massoud's army. Within two months, most of the Taliban had fled to Pakistan, but al-Qaeda was still kicking.

Saudi Arabia, for itself, was caught between a rock and a hard place. The Royal Family had not forgotten "we" had saved her during the Iraqi invasion of Kuwait, but the Saudi Wahhabi clergy had long been in the best of terms with Pakistan's Musharraf, and with Nawaz Sharif, Benazir Bhutto and General Zia before him. However, the Royal Family knew it had only one Big Brother watching over its oil fortunes, and this was the United States. So it officially supported Operation Enduring Freedom, while looking the other way when its clergy was dispensing funds to Pakistan, the Taliban, al-Qaeda, and the Islamist Madrasas.

Pakistan was in an even hotter seat. Under Brzezinski and Raphel's auspices, it had become a nuclear power, with Sharif officially launching two successful tests in 1998. In the tradition of Pakistan's Islamism versus India's Hinduism, this was to counter India's own nuclear arsenal. Despite a bilateral Non-Attack Agreement signed in 1991, each country now had their finger on the trigger. India was the only South Asian country who had recognized the Soviet-backed People's Democratic Party of Afghanistan. Once the Soviets left, and the Taliban and al-Qaeda took over, India changed her mind. On orders of Mullah Omar, not only the Taliban had destroyed the 6th century Bamiyan Buddha monuments in March 2001, but the September 11 attack, only six months later, left no doubt as to their ultimate intentions. Since the Taliban and al-Qaeda were backed by Pakistan, the Saudi Arabian clergy and the United Arab Emirates, and given its own fairly large 170 million Muslim population, India saw this as a high-risk Islamist threat, with an unstable Pakistani nuclear arsenal. It joined forces with the United States and fully participated in Operation Enduring Freedom.

This was one reason why Musharraf temporarily turned coat on the Taliban and al-Qaeda. It was about to be squeezed between India and the Afghan theater. But the real reason were the words of U.S. Deputy Secretary of State Richard Armitage, in his meeting with Pakistan's Inter Services Intelligence Chief General Ahmed Mahmud on September 12, 2001, as reported in a declassified cable:

> "Pakistan faces a stark choice: it must either stand with the United States in its fight against terrorism or stand against us. There is no maneuvering room"

To which Mahmud replied:

> "[The President can] count on Pakistan's unqualified support, Islamabad would do whatever was required of it by the U.S.[233]".

What was the Coalition of the Willing to do next[234]? Much like Pearl Harbor sixty years earlier, 911, as it became known, was a dark and rare existential moment, certainly for the United States. In his 2002 State of the Union address, President Bush had defined the Axis of Evil as Iraq, Iran and North Korea. The next domino to go was Iraq, and the President had been clear:

> "While there are many dangers in the world, the threat from Iraq stands alone -- because it gathers the most serious dangers of our age in one place. Iraq's weapons of mass destruction are controlled by a murderous tyrant who has already used chemical weapons to kill thousands of people. This same tyrant has tried to dominate the Middle East, has invaded and brutally occupied a small neighbor, has struck other nations without warning, and holds an unrelenting hostility toward the United States.[235]".

Brushing off Clinton's Iraq Liberation Act and Operation Desert Fox, and the many economic and U.N. sanctions before and after, Saddam Hussein had shown the world that he had the most lethal force in the region and that he was not afraid of using it, starting with his own people. He did not fear international retribution for the extensive use of chemical weapons, and had defied the ban on nuclear development. His fight was "noble", to become the one and only secular Ruler of the Arab Nation, better than Nasser, better than Ataturk.

Iraq also had six borders with terrorists' havens – Iran, Jordan, Syria, Saudi Arabia, Kuwait and Turkey. And, lurking behind Iran, were Afghanistan and Pakistan. Saddam's biggest mistake was to claim, loud and clear, that he was the bully in the middle of the jihadi sand box.

Noticeably, several countries on the Global War on Terror hit list – Iraq, Iran, Syria, Lebanon, Libya, Somalia, Sudan, Yemen - had two things in common. Russia was backing them, one way or the other, and they were training most of the region's terrorists.

To be sure, there was substantial opposition to this next step, a military intervention in Iraq. Even though they all had participated in Operation Enduring Freedom, the other permanent members of the United Nations Security Council, Russia, China, and France, kept pleading there was not enough evidence of weapons of mass destruction. Germany echoed, as in P5 + 1. This was not surprising. WMDs required precursor chemicals[236], manufactured and stored with advanced technology which only major industrial countries in the world possessed - Russia, China, France, Germany among them. They did not want to make front-page news holding those canisters with their name on it. The United Kingdom was hesitating. And while the United States also manufactured these precursors, and the WMD that went with them, it had no choice. After 911, it had to hit back, and Iraq was the target of choice.

Regardless of objections, in 2002, four long years after Operation Desert Fox, with Russia and China watching, President Bush invoked the 1998 Iraq Liberation Act. On October 11, by an overwhelming majority, 77 yea against 23 nay in the Senate, and 296 to 133 in the House, Congress voted the Iraq Resolution, to authorize President Bush's use of force. Operation Iraqi Freedom was launched on March 20, 2003, at 5:34 am local Baghdad time, and ended on May 1. The multinational coalition was led by the U.S., the U.K., Australia, Spain, and Poland, with the notable help of the Kurdish Peshmerga in Northern Iraq, and the noticeable absence of Turkey and the P3 +1 – France, Russia, China and Germany.

The Global War on Terror did not stop there. To the contrary, this was the start of the Iraq Civil War, pitting Iraqi insurgents faithful to Saddam Hussein against coalition troops and a mismanaged post-invasion provisional government. On December 13, Saddam was captured. For their successful initiative, U.S. public opinion gave a sixty nine percent kudos approval rating to President Bush and Vice President Cheney. Saddam would later be sentenced to death for crimes against humanity by the Iraqi Special Tribunal, and hung on December 30, 2006.

This did not change much. In this land of eternal conflict between Sunni and Shi'a, the Iraqi political vacuum had been engulfed by terrorists groups of all kind, mainly al-Qaeda in Iraq (AQI) and Kata'ib Hezbollah. In February 2006, AQI bombed the sacred Shiite al-Askari mosque in Samarra. Ibrahim al-Jaafari, the Shiite Prime Minister of the first post-Saddam government at the time, refused a curfew, and hundreds of Sunni Iraqis were killed in reprisal. Two month later, the Shi'a Nouri al-Maliki, effectively a close ally of Syria, Iran, and Hezbollah[237], replaced Jaafari. He had been vetted by the CIA and, of all people, by Iran's Quds Force. The best of worse, he was deemed capable to bring some semblance of calm between at least the Sunni minority, the Shiite majority, the Iraqi Kurds, and the coalition troops. All in all, it was not just a Civil War, but a bloody war between civilian factions, Islamic religious denominations, terrorist groups, and coalition troops.

Iran was involved too, not just in Iraq, and not just in the war. At home, it was busy developing its own nuclear weapons, with the help of North Korea, Mother Russia, and China.

After the 1979 revolution, Ayatollah Khomeini had declared the Iranian nuclear weapons program illegal under Islamic law. Ten years later, his successor Ayatollah Ali Khameini had affirmed the fatwa. One could have taken their words for granted. After all, they were the Supreme Leaders. So the world did, not knowing that Khameini was a graduate of the KGB-inspired Patrice Lumumba People's Friendship University of Russia[238], and a protégé of the Soviet spymaster Evgeny Primakov[239].

Fast forward another ten years. Contrary to what the Ayatollahs had fatwa-ed, Iran did have a nuclear enrichment program, and it really looked more weapons grade than your grandfather's electric plant. In August 2002, Dr.Alirezza Jafarzadeh, an Iranian-American spokesman and congressional liaison for the dissident National Council of resistance of Iran (NCRI)[240], publicly revealed the existence of a uranium enrichment facility in Natanz, and a heavy water facility in Arak. In early 2003, the International Atomic Energy Agency (IAEA) started investigating, and sanctions kept getting worse. Iran, for itself, claimed all along it was within its rights, as defined by the Nuclear Non Proliferation Treaty it had signed in 1968[241].

Not only was Iran back in bed with Russia, to Brzezinski's chagrin and to Primakov's delight, but it was also harboring various terrorists groups – Hezbollah officially, the Taliban covertly, and the Muslim Brotherhood, Hamas, Palestinian Islamic Jihad, and al-Qaeda in Iraq, very covertly[242]. Shiites and Sunnis were killing each other in Iraq, but above all, they were brothers in terror to destroy the United States and Israel.

8

Obama Rising

In the international politics of the late Nineties, little should have possibly surprised Barack Obama, whether it be Dugin, Primakov, Brzezinski, and Russia' renewed quest for Eurasia. As his Columbia professor Michael Baron seemed to recall a while back, the gist of his senior thesis at was

> *"an analysis of the evolution of the arms reduction negotiations between the Soviet Union and the United States."*[243]

He got an A said Baron, pretty heavy stuff for a twenty-two-year-old. And did he not major in Political Science? Frank Marshall Davis had taken care of his Communist teachings, al-Mansour and Rashid Khalidi of pan-Arabism and Arab Socialism, Brzezinski and Dugin of the World's Chessboard, and Alinsky, Kellman, Ayers and Axelrod, of the How-to-Organize. The question was, what could he do with all this baggage, now that he was one of fifty nine Illinois Senators, and a rookie at that?

His heart was to the radical left, much like the father he barely knew. His religion was likely Muslim although he was deemed a Christian since 1988[244], when he was organizing churches in the South Side of Chicago. He allegedly had been baptized by Reverend Jeremiah Wright of the Trinity United Church of Christ, a controversial figure and a great admirer of Louis Farrakhan, the other controversial figure and leader of the Nation of Islam.

Add the al-Mansour and Khalidi connections to the fact that his father, paternal grandfather, and step-father were Muslims, the picture was definitively blurry.

The net of it, he was a rookie carpetbagger who had been elected on technicalities and lack of real opponents. As such, he did not have much of a platform, let alone to officially express sympathy for anything communist, pan-African, or Islamic.

But he did not need a platform. He was a charismatic young man, with a charismatic young wife, powerful newly-found friends, and a nice looking resume. His life story was a romantic account in an a-propos book about race-relations-turned-memoirs which had taken this prodigy, the first African American President of the Harvard Law Review recommended by a virulent Islamic hatemonger, more than five years to write, with no way to fact check the story[245].

Was he a wolf in sheep's clothes? He had a book alright, but we had to watch the story play out.

State Senator Barack Obama chose the easy way out, a back-game of sort[246]. At first, he simply rode the coattails of President Bill Clinton and Vice-President Al Gore, newly reelected in 1996, saying nothing much except for Health Care and Campaign Finance Reform. He also lectured on constitutional law, part-time, at the University of Chicago Law School[247]. This low profile strategy got him reelected in 1998 and 2002 as the charming Illinois Senator representing the 13th District of Chicago.

The downside was that he was not well known. A back-game can lead to a bigger win, but it has longer odds.

Indeed, in 2000, Obama suffered a bit of a setback. Despite some alleged objections from his wife, he had decided to run against veteran Bobby Lee Rush for the 1st District in Illinois in the United States House of Representatives. With the help of David Canter, again, Rush, a co-founder of the Black Panther Party and close to the CPUSA, had been elected to the House of Congress in 1992, winning eighty three percent of the votes in the general election. Eight years later, Rush was still quite popular and Obama, while in his fourth year as Illinois Senator, was still unknown, despite all of his Hyde Park political and media relations, and top notch resume. Report cards of the time showed that he entered the primaries with a ten percent name recognition, and got thirty percent of the vote, half of Rush's. In the general elections he was nowhere to be found, with Rush garnering eighty eight percent of the vote. Obama had thought Rush was just a deep-seated far-left radical who could do no better than "Act Local". Emboldened by his success in dethroning the other far-left radical, Alice Palmer, he was hoping to become the one who could "Think Global". He failed, but still had *a bigger fish to fry*[248].

In 2002, the back-game started to work. The Democrats regained control of the Illinois Senate, and the first Democrat Governor in twenty six years, Rod Blagojevich, was elected. Obama was one of his staunch supporters, together with their common friend and fundraiser, the now indicted felon Antoin "Tony" Rezko[249]. David Axelrod, a familiar face, was also in the Blagojevich loop, although he later denied having helped his former client in his gubernatorial bid.

"Scratch my back, I'll scratch yours", Blagojevich liked to say about Chicago politics[250]. Who lobbied for Obama in his 2004 U.S. Senate race? Rod, naturally. This is when he was quite popular and even thought off as Presidential hopeful. Of course, the wind turned when, in 2011, "Hot Rod" was sentenced to fourteen years in a Denver Federal prison. Corruption, including soliciting bribes to sell the Illinois Senate seat Obama had vacated in 2008 to run for President. Tony Rezko only got ten and a half, but this is another story.

In July 2002, State Senator Obama had launched his 2004 campaign for the U.S. Senate. The one-term Republican incumbent Peter Gosselin Fitzgerald had decided not to run, in disagreement with the

Illinois GOP on many issues, leaving his seat vacant. Both Republican and Democratic primaries were twenty-one months away. Who was helping Obama in his campaign? David Axelrod, naturally. By early 2004, he had been endorsed by the five largest newspapers in Illinois, to include the Chicago Tribune (hello Vernon Jarrett and David Axelrod), the Chicago Sun-Times (hello Vernon Jarrett again[251]), by three of the state's largest unions, including the Illinois Federation of Teachers (hello Bill and Tom Ayers, and Mrs. Bowman Jarrett), and by four of the nine Democratic Illinois congressmen, to include Jesse Jackson Jr. (hello Santita and Sr.).

Sheila Simon was also backing him up. She was the daughter of the late U.S. Senator Paul Simon, who had been elected in 1984 with, who else, David Axelrod and Rahm Emmanuel as his campaign managers. This is when Axelrod had made a name for himself, at age twenty-nine, and it was paying back. It would take a little longer for Emmanuel, but he was on the short list.

When it came to the March Primaries, Obama won by a landslide, fifty-three percent against twenty-four for his closest rival, Dan Hynes. Not only that, he had garnered 655,923 votes, whereas the whole Republican field had a total of 661,804. This did not go unnoticed by the Democratic Party and he was asked to deliver the keynote address at the Democratic National Convention on July 27, in support of Presidential Nominee John Kerry and his Vice Presidential Nominee, John Edwards, another of Axelrod's clients.

There were no lack of superlatives to describe Obama's speech. Passionate, electrifying, phenomenal, home run, so close to home, better than Clinton's, better than Kerry's. And Obama was adamant, he wrote it himself, in a lonely hotel room in Springfield, inspired by a sermon of his then Pastor, Jeremiah Wright, "The Audacity to Hope."

Maybe, but the affirmation was suspicious. Nobody was asking, really. Maybe he wanted to put to rest questions about who wrote "Dreams from My Father." So, no mention of the DNC editorial team. No mention of David Axelrod either, even though he was his campaign media manager. And no mention of Jon Favreau, who was Kerry's speechwriter and would become Obama's "mind reader[252]." This time, it was all about Obama, by Obama. At least, this is how the story went.

The speech did not contain any reference to Marxism, Communism, "Uncle" Frank, Organizing, Islam, and all that sort of things. The only race related tidbit was about

> *"An Arab American family being rounded up without benefit of an attorney or due process."*

If anything, it was centrist, as Pat Buchanan, the conservative politician, put it. But he was quick to add,

> *"He is hiding what he truly believes. What does he believe about this war?[253]"*

This was in reference to what Obama had said about the second Iraq War, which he had opposed since inception, contrary to John Kerry who had voted for it:

> *"There are patriots who opposed the war in Iraq and there are patriots who supported the war in Iraq".*

It was an all-American speech, based on hope, truth, and change, ending with

> *"And out of this long political darkness a brighter day will come"[254].*

Hope and truth were Motherhood and Apple Pie, but Change was a bit short on specifics. Even David Axelrod, who presumably had nothing to do with the speech writing, was a bit vague to say the least.

The motto of his AKPD Message and Media Agency, prominently displayed on his website[255], was:

> "*Change is something you have to fight for. Change is never easy. We are going to have to work for every vote. The change we need is worth the struggle; it's worth the fight.*"

It almost sounded as if Axelrod did not care about "what" to change, and what to change "it" into, as long as he got the job.

One thing was clear, however. Neither Alice Palmer nor Bobby Rush could have crossed over the racial divide the way Obama did. For the first time in U.S. history, an African-American politician, of origin unknown to boot, was seemingly in pole position to win the hearts and minds of the overall American public. And then some, around the globe.

From the March Primaries to the November elections, there was a long road. First, Obama had to face his Republican opponent, the young and charismatic multimillionaire ex-Goldman Sachs partner, Jack Ryan. Somehow, the Chicago Tribune had gotten wind of Ryan's nasty divorce proceedings, filed and sealed in Los Angeles five years earlier to protect the couple's emotionally challenged son. Whether this was the digging of David Axelrod or Vernon Jarrett, or whether it was a mere coincidence and good investigative journalism, suffice it to say that the Tribune and ABC's Chicago affiliate WLS-Ch.7 sought to have the documents released by the court. In spite of both parents' opposition[256], the court reversed its decision on June 22, 2004. That same day, the Tribune published an article titled "*Ryan file a bombshell.*" It bore fruit. A week later, for all intents and purposes, Ryan withdrew from the race and Obama was running unopposed.

This heavy-handed episode was reminiscent of how Barack had evinced all of his opponents in the 1996 Illinois Senate race[257]. This time around, Obama was trying to officially distance himself from the dark side of politics, in the spirit of his DNC love speech, but the damage was done, and the narrative was transparent. The means to the end, Ryan was replaced by Alan Keyes, who had no chance as a conservative Republican carpetbagger from Maryland.

Pause for a moment. Axelrod, the kingmaker? *"Show me who your friends are and I'll tell who you are."*

John Edwards, seven years later, was indicted on six felony charges of violating multiple federal campaign contribution laws to cover up an extra marital affair which he admitted to, although he was not convicted. He had been a client of David Axelrod.

That same year, 2011, Rod Blagojevich was indicted and later convicted to fourteen years in Federal Prison. Among those served with a subpoena in his trial were David Axelrod, Valerie Jarrett, Rahm Emanuel and Tony Rezko[258]. "Hot Rod" had been a client of David Axelrod.

He had also advised Eliot Spitzer in his 2006 Gubernatorial New York win. In March 2008, Spitzer resigned as "Client 9" of the prostitute ring known as the "Emperors Club VIP."

And Obama's 2004 discourse was on Truthfulness and Political Darkness? Maybe Axelrod had nothing to do with his convention speech, but he still deserved every penny for transforming the Man From Nowhere into a Globalist champion who knew good from bad.

At the end of the day, when the November 2004 general elections came, Obama had outspent his Republican rival Alan Keyes six-to-one, $14.2 million versus $2.5 million, an unexpected prowess for an Illinois Senator who had sponsored and passed a Campaign Funding Reform bill. He won by a landslide, seventy-three percent against twenty-seven.

Of note, as clever and successful as Obama's advisors were in foraging his opponents' files, nobody on the Republican side or conservative media had been able to tap into Obama's hodge podge past. No one even flinched when, in his DNC address, he asserted that

> "[My parents] *would give me an African name, Barack, or "blessed," believing that in a tolerant America your name is no barrier to success.*"[259]

Great figure of speech, what's in a name, really, except for a glaring omission? Barack was not just "*an African name*", it was his father's name.

Sally Jacobs, the longtime Boston Globe journalist and author of Senior's vivid biography we mentioned earlier, added an interesting etymologic twist to the name, according to the Obama family back in the village of Kanyadhiang in Kenya,

"*Obama is derived from the word bam, which means crooked or indirect.*"[260]

Hogwash. In mid-2004, Barack Hussein Obama II was simply a young, charismatic, well-educated multi-racial man, with a very likeable family to boot, a great story to tell, and a nice given name. Where he came from, who he was associated with, and who had paid for his resume, was still enshrouded in his memoirs, now a best-seller with an ominous title, "*Dreams.*"

On November 2, 2004, he was elected United States Senator from Illinois. Looking at the field of Presidential Hopefuls, there was no doubt. The Man from Nowhere had become a serious contender, if not "The Great Contender", for the next level. The Presidency.

9

On To the White House

November 2004. Barack Obama was now one of the two U.S. Senators from Illinois, both Democrats. The other was Richard "Dick" Durbin, soon to become Senate Minority Whip. The Presidential Election had been a toss-up, despite substantial Republican gains in the Senate[261]. Iraq, Afghanistan, our foreign policy was the topic, our troop deployment was the heartbreak, our Defense spending was the proverbial straw.

Pundits saw it two ways. The War on Terror was not going as fast as expected, despite the largely positive early results in both Afghanistan and Iraq. Forty thousand body bags had been planned for Iraq, for fear of chemical attacks, and, fortunately, the casualties were minimal, on the coalition side. However, while the coalition had been somewhat effective at regime change, it felt way short of nation-building. This was a major theme of the Presidential campaign, opposing the incumbent Bush-Cheney ticket, whose approval rating had dropped to fifty four percent, to the hopeful John Kerry-John Edwards ticket on the Democrat side.

Another theme was the vanishing of Weapons of Mass Destruction. The whole thing was depicted as a hoax to invade Iraq to simply gain control of its oil. This was a side issue. Most important was the on-the-ground intelligence gathering mission, long abandoned by Clinton and now implemented by Bush, but this escaped public opinion. How Iraq's well documented and self-acknowledged WMD disappeared remained a mystery for that very reason, the lack of intelligence. Suffice it to say, neighboring Syria ended up having the greatest stockpile in the region. Many observers, in particular John A. Shaw, Deputy Undersecretary of Defense for International Technology Security at the time, believed Saddam had sent them there at the last minute, and squarely put the blame on Russia's special forces Spetsnaz[262].

Unfortunately for his credibility, Shaw was later fired on corruption charges for trying to profiteer from the War, but that did not necessarily make him wrong on his WMD account. If Saddam Hussein's talk of WMD was a bluff, quite a stretch if all of his victims could speak, it did not work except to empower the critics of the War. And if it was not a bluff, somebody somehow got them to disappear. This was a very complex task, from a logistical and technological standpoint, as in very hazardous hazmat. Whomever did it had to be pretty sophisticated, and the Spetsnaz version made sense. But the there-is-no-WMD-in-Iraq narrative was powerful, enough to even ignore Bill Clinton's own 1998 arguments, and enough to validate the we-told-you-so position of Russia, China, Germany, and France – there were no WMD in Iraq, and the War had no raison d'etre. So said the pundits.

In 2000, President Bush had been elected in a hotly contested race against former Vice President Al Gore, despite the strength of a Republican Congress. In the 2002 elections, the Republicans managed to pick up a few seats, a rare mid-term occurrence when the President is of the same party, and gained control of the Senate with Vice-President Cheney as the tie-breaker. During that time, the economy had been greatly impacted by a fifty percent drop in the stock market, due to the Internet Bubble Burst, compounded by September 11, 2001. Opposing the Iraq war was good demagoguery, regardless of the "shock and awe" campaign of 2003.

In 2004, there were several Democrat Presidential Hopefuls. Howard Dean, an early leader in the Primaries, and a vocal opponent of the War, had lost it, figuratively and literally, in the Iowa caucuses[263].

Another candidate was John Kerry, one of the Senators who had voted for the use of force against Iraq in 2002. He had voted on one hand, but with a long list of preconditions on the other, including exhausting all peaceful avenues first, whatever that meant, and the need for a worldwide coalition. It was therefore no surprise that he decided to go with the other hand and campaigned that it was a bad thing, after all. Despite all the Kerry praise Obama had expressed in his famous DNC speech, he was promptly countered by a forceful anti-Kerry campaign called the Swift Boat Veterans for Truth. It reminded the public of his role during the anti-War protests of the Seventies, when he was associated with the communist Abe Feinglass' People's Coalition for Peace Protest[264]. The incumbent Bush-Cheney ticket won by a narrow margin, carrying thirty one States, and 286 electoral votes out of the required 270. It received shy of fifty one percent of the popular vote and Republicans regained full control of the Senate with fifty five seats.

The new Senator Obama was lucky. The 109th Congress met for 242 days, the shortest since World War II, and was aptly nicknamed after Truman's 80th Congress, the "Do Nothing Congress".

In 2006, the Middle East wars were growing more unpopular. Afghanistan was a stalemate even after NATO took over after U.S. troops. In Iraq, instead of peace and nation-building, the fall of the Hussein regime had the collateral consequence of a scenario that had been foreseen but not been wished for, a full-fledged civil war, with widespread jihadist participation. Abu Musab al-Zarqawi, the leader of al-Qaeda in Iraq (AQI)[265], had been killed in June, but it did not stop AQI a bit, to the contrary. His fellow jihadists, Abu Omar al-Baghdadi and Abu Ayyub al-Masri, took over and in October, renamed it ISI, for the Islamic State in Iraq. We will get back to this later.

Something else had been brewing in the background, of tectonic potential, which the public at large knew nothing about. The Shanghai Cooperation Organization. Founded in 1996, in Shanghai of course, its original name was the Shanghai Five, for the group comprised of China, Russia, Kazakhstan[266], Kyrgyzstan and Tajikistan, who had signed the *Treaty on Deepening Military Trust in Border Regions*. These three "stan" countries were the former Soviet Republics between China and now Russia. This treaty was followed by the *Treaty on Reduction of Military Forces in Border Regions,* signed in Moscow in 1997, the year our old foe Dugin's Foundation of Geopolitics was published. At the time, Yevgeny Primakov was Yeltsin's Minister of Foreign Affairs, and a strong proponent of multipolarism, a triangular alliance between Russia, China and India, to counter what he called U.S. unilateralism.

The public did not know either about the *Treaty of Good-Neighborliness and Friendly Cooperation* signed by Russia and the Peoples' Republic of China in July 2001. But the think tanks, the intelligence committees, and at least a few in Congress knew about it[267]. In short, including the "Observer States" – Afghanistan, Pakistan, India, Iran, Mongolia – and the "Dialogue Partners" – Belarus, Sri Lanka, Turkey -, the SCO, as it was known, would ultimately account for a quarter of the human race. In a sense, it was "another" United Nations, which excluded the United States and Western Europe, i.e. the Atlantic Alliance, and most of the Middle East and Africa. Powerful, yet under the public radar and despite the differing views of the two key players, China and Russia, the unspoken motto was "the enemy of my enemy is my friend". The spoken motto was "enough with U.S. hegemony". Their alliance was an additional force that opposed the Iraq War, music to Primakov's ears[268].

On the domestic side, Republicans were marred by a few too many scandals, including a botched attempt at Social Security Reform. By a landslide upset, with the undeniable energy of Howard Dean, then DNC chair, the Democrats regained control of both chambers, which they had lost in the "Gingrich Revolution" of 1994. Nancy Pelosi was now the first woman Speaker of the House, Harry Reid the Senate Majority Leader, and Dick Durbin his Majority Whip.

One word on the Gingrich Revolution. It was noteworthy. The Democrats had been in control of the House for all but four years since 1932[269]. Newt Gingrich, the veteran Republican Congressman of Georgia's 6th District, and Richard Armey, the Republican Congressman from Texas' 26th District, had co-authored the conservative "Contract with America", which had become the Party platform in the 1994 mid-term elections. The major themes were the shrinking of the Government's size, the lowering of taxes and the promotion of entrepreneurship, to include tort and welfare reform – much in the vein of President Reagan's policy and Supply Side Economics. It was in clear opposition to President Clinton's agenda, in particular his proposed health care reform plan, engineered by a task force chaired by the First Lady, Hilary Clinton. Dramatized by a year-long television campaign dubbed "Harry and Louise" after the actors' names, the plan was so unpopular and so complex that it led to the Republican sweep, with Gingrich becoming Speaker of the House.

Needless to say, 2006 was a major regression to the mean, no pun intended. A couple of years later, under Obama's tenure, an even larger health care reform than the Clinton proposal was passed by a Congress led by Pelosi and Reid, but this too is another story.

Senator Obama had started to work in 2004 as a Democrat with a Republican Congress and a Republican President. Then, he sat on a couple of minor committees, like the Subcommittee on Clean Air and Nuclear Safety, and the Subcommittee on Private Sector and Consumer Solutions to Global Warming and Wildlife Protection. Somewhat demeaning for someone of his alleged stature and education, whose college "thesis" had been on Soviet Nuclear Disarmament.

2006, however, would be his springboard, with 2008 as the goal line. Then he sat on more committees. Health, Education, Labor and Pensions, Homeland Security and Governmental Affairs, Foreign Relations, in particular as chairman of the Subcommittee on European Affairs. This was yet another back-game. All he had to do was to wait for an opportunity, listen to his long-time associate Rahm Emanuel, the Congressman from Illinois' 5th district, to the Majority Whip Dick Durbin, the other Senator from Illinois, and to David Axelrod, the kingmaker. Not to mention Valerie Jarrett, the ultimate confidant advisor. This was the new Illinois Machine, rebuilt in Washington.

The opportunity came from left field. 2008 was the worse Stock Market crash since 1929. Its corollary, the destruction of Household Net Worth, what you own minus what you owe, was hitting Main Street, big time. In 2004, it was $51.9 Trillion. It peaked in the third quarter of 2007 at $64.3 Trillion. By the end of 2008, it was back at $51.5 Trillion with no end in sight to the downfall. Worse, the Debt-to-Household Net Worth was now a whopping 27.6% versus its 2004 level of 21.2%, already high by historical standards. In plain English, we had leveraged ourselves into oblivion, and oblivion was knocking on the door.

Balance Sheet of Households and NonProfit Organizations

$ Trillion, nominal, not seasonally adjusted.

			Peak NW		
		2004	Q3, 2007	Q4, 2008	Q4, 2010
Assets		62.9	78.4	65.7	70.7
	of which:				
	Real Estate	20.2	23.7	20.5	18.2
	Fixed Income				
	Short Term	5.7	7.1	7.6	7.9
	Long Term	3.1	3.7	3.9	4.3
	Stocks	22.5	29.4	20.2	27.6
Liabilities		11	14.1	14.2	13.9
	of which:				
	Mortgages	7.8	10.4	10.4	10.1
	Consumer Credit	2.2	2.5	2.6	2.4
Net Worth		51.9	64.3	51.5	56.8
Debt as % of Net Worth		21.2%	21.9%	27.6%	24.5%

Figure 4 - U.S. Household Net Worth – 2004 - 2010. – Source: "Anatomy of the Meltdown – 1998-2008" page 74, Franck Prissert, 2011.

In the process, it felt like the engine of American capitalism, its banking system, was failing much like Karl Marx had predicted. The list of casualties included Bear Sterns, Countrywide Financial, IndyMac, Fannie Mae, Freddie Mac, Lehman Brothers, American International Group, General Motors, Chrysler, Merrill Lynch, Washington Mutual, Wachovia… To many younger readers, these names will not mean much. To most of us, they were "America". The United States needed a savior.

Fortunately, there were three, Treasury Secretary Henry "Hank" Paulson, Federal Reserve Chairman Ben Bernanke, and the Commander in Chief, President Bush. To be clear, this is this author's opinion, and not necessarily a fact. On September 20, two weeks after Fannie and Freddie had been placed into conservatorship by the Federal Housing Finance Authority, one week after the infamous week-end of September 13 which led Bank of America to "agree" to buy failing Merrill Lynch for $50 billion after allowing Lehman Brothers to file for bankruptcy, and just four days after the Fed had written a taxpayer check of $85 billion in exchange of an 80% stake in then worthless AIG[270], one of the largest insurance company in the world, Paulson and Bernanke asked for a $700 billion Bazooka, formally known as TARP, or the Troubled Asset Relief Program.

Originally a slim 3-page memo, the Democrat-led Congress morphed it into a 551-page legislation. On October 3, President Bush signed it into law as the Emergency Economic Stabilization Act. Needless to say, these were uncharted waters, and TARP was historical by any measure. At the time, the Federal Reserve Balance sheet was $800 billion. TARP, in essence, doubled it[271].

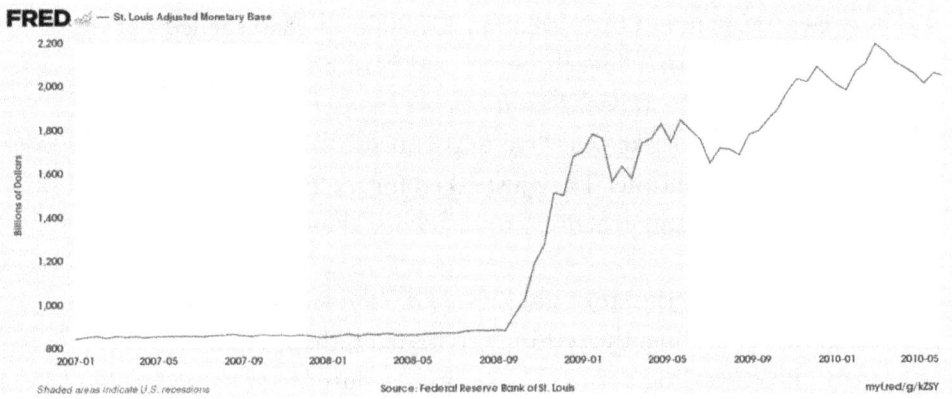

Figure 5 - U.S. Adjusted Monetary Base – 2007 – 2010.
Source: Federal Reserve of St. Louis, FRED®.

While the ensuing years proved the Bazooka theory right, it was forcefully debated at the time. Both sides were concerned about price expectations. Opponents feared easy money inflation. Proponents feared wealth destruction deflation. The analogies with the Great Depression abounded. Senator Barack Obama and Senator Chris Dodd had been top recipients of Fannie and Freddie's campaign donations. Yet, no one was pointing the finger at them, and certainly not their close friends and vocal Congressman Barney Frank and Senator Chuck Schumer, among others.

The only one who was on record for having anticipated this scenario was Ben Bernanke. On November 21, 2002, he had spelled out the bazooka theory in a speech before the National Economists Club, entitled *"Deflation: Making Sure It Doesn't Happen Here"*[272]. But neither Paulson nor Bernanke said "we told you so", a politically incorrect thing to do at the time. They just asked for the Bazooka, and no one dared, moaning and groaning, to challenge them.

Right or wrong, the story got legs, and President Bush's popularity continued to decline. Everything was his fault, the subprime mortgage crisis, the exploding deficits[273], the war "failure", you named it. Not that it really mattered, he was not up for reelection, having completed two consecutive terms. But anything that looked Republican was tainted, in particular Vice President Dick Cheney. He was not the usual decoy. Taking the lead on many issues, working hand in glove with the President, he had no place to hide. While the Iraq and Afghan wars had been early campaign issues, and while the 2007 troop surge in Iraq had been quite successful in fending off ISI[274], by the time the 2008 election came, it was all about your pocket book. And it did not look good.

In addition, the Republican platform was to the right of things, fiscally conservative yet pro-War, not a good combination in an economy which was on track to register two quarters of 6% GDP declines. There were some pretty good hopefuls, former Massachusetts Governor Mitt Romney, former Arkansas Governor Mike Huckabee, former New

York City Mayor Rudy Giuliani, and Senator John McCain. Noticeably absent, a first since 1928 and for all of the above reasons, the incumbent Vice President was not running. John McCain won the nomination in March 2008. In a bold move, he chose Sarah Palin, a woman "for God's sake", Governor of far away Alaska to boot, as his running mate. As she used to say, she could see Russia from her living room windows. She was much derided then, but in hindsight, she had foresight.

In the Democrats' camp, the race was not over until June. Rookie Obama had to face the former Iron Fist Lady, Hilary Clinton, and this was a tough one. Not only she had her own stature, but she also was from the David Axelrod School, and a personal friend of his[275]. Axelrod, however, had chosen Obama. She was "Experience", and therefore associated with the past and the current. He was "Hope and Change", which was the theme of his second campaign book, "The Audacity of Hope", published on schedule for 2008[276]. Charisma, bi-racial, Change, 2004 convention speech, he won the nomination, and chose Joseph "Joe" Robinette Biden as his "experienced" running mate. Why is an open question – Biden had been the U.S. Senator from Delaware since 1973 and Chairman of the Committee on Foreign Relations for a couple of years. But Vice President?

It worked. November 4, 2008. "Hope, Change, and Experience" won by a landslide. 365 electoral votes versus 173, and 53% of the popular vote. In Congress, Democrats rode the coattails big time, 257 versus 178 in the House, and 58 to 41 in the Senate. They had an open field, and people demanded Change. We were about to find out what this meant.

Obama and his team had understood the lay of the land, demographics, something Republicans had missed big time. Math is an exact science, and there were fourteen years between 1994, the year of the Gingrich Revolution, and 2008. In a little more than half a generation, the poorer had grown poorer, the migrant population had grown larger, and the pyramid-shaped demographic curve was now a rectangle, with Baby Boomers and GenXers being insidiously replaced by Millenials, themselves grandchildren of the Cultural Revolutionaries of the late 1960's. Things were different, people were different. Axelrod banked on it with "Bread and Circuses". No more troops in harm's way, be it in Afghanistan or Iraq, and health care for everyone. The McCain-Palin ticket, as ideologically attractive it may have been to the demographically declining conservatives, did not have the "Hope and Change" or "Yes We Can" catch-all slogans which appealed to the rising liberal audience.

The Man, Barack Hussein Obama was in, the 44th President of the United States. At age forty seven, he was one of the youngest U.S. President, and in good company – Teddy Roosevelt, John F. Kennedy, Bill Clinton, and Ulysses S. Grant. Frank Laubach, "the Apostle of the Illiterates," would have been amazed[277]. Joe Biden was second in command. Third in line was Nancy Pelosi, Speaker of the House.

Then there was Axelrod's genius command of words. To the grand majority of Americans, "Change" meant just that, a little here, a little there. "Hope" meant the usual, the American Dream. And "Experience", when it came to Joe Biden's foreign policy experience, most Americans did not even know what foreign policy meant, let alone their geography. But Experience sounded good as wars are never popular, and Change sounded even better in the worst stock market debacle since the Great Depression.

To President Obama, "Change" meant what he had in mind while at BI in New York,

"a bigger fish to fry."[278]

What had been lost in Axelrod's carefully crafted message was the word "left". The newly-elect President was not looking for change "a little here, a little there", he was going for radical change. This soon became clear in his domestic agenda. However, we would have to wait a few years to see what it meant for foreign policy. How far would he go in his relationship with Putin & co? From what we knew of him, the socialist model, or worse, was certainly within the realm of reality. From what we knew of historical misalliances, there was no such a thing as a stretch of imagination. Everything was possible.

Some may say it was a series of good luck and well-placed political bets. Some may even say Obama was not qualified for the job, in particular with regard to what this book is about, geopolitics. So we had a choice – qualified, unqualified, or worse. Before we came to any real conclusion, we had to wait for the tea leaves.

10

Change, Hope, Experience - And Apple Pie

Since its peak in October 2007, the stock market was having an acute case of the jitters. By March 3, 2009, the Standard & Poors 500 Index had crashed 58%, from an intraday high of 1576 to an intraday low of 666. In thirteen months, in a pivotal Election year.

More specifically, by June 3, 2008, when Candidate Obama was nominated, it had gone down by some 14%. When it reached the November 21 intraday intermediate low of 741, eleven days after President Obama was elected in a landslide, with the strongest Democrat Congress in two decades[279], the market had wrecked a further 47%.

In the meantime, on September 20, as leading U.S. companies were falling like flies, Treasury Secretary Henry "Hank" Paulson and Federal Reserve Board Chairman Ben Bernanke had asked for a $700 billion "Bazooka" to buy "toxic" securities, i.e. bonds that were poorly collateralized, to say the least. It took two long weeks for Congress to put it to President Bush's signature. The S&P was at 1255 and this was supposed to stop the carnage. It did not. The markets kept plowing down, to reach the final intraday low of 666 on the S&P, on March 6, 2009, a drop of 58% from the 2007 high. Interesting if you are a numerologist, 666, 3/6/9, but dauntingly scary to the rest of us. I was there.

Figure 6 - Standard & Poors 500 Index - Copyright (c)
2018 Interactive Brokers LLC - All rights reserved.

Net net, most of the damage occurred from June to November 2008. This made the decade ending that year the worst since the data had been recorded, handily beating the one ending in 1929.

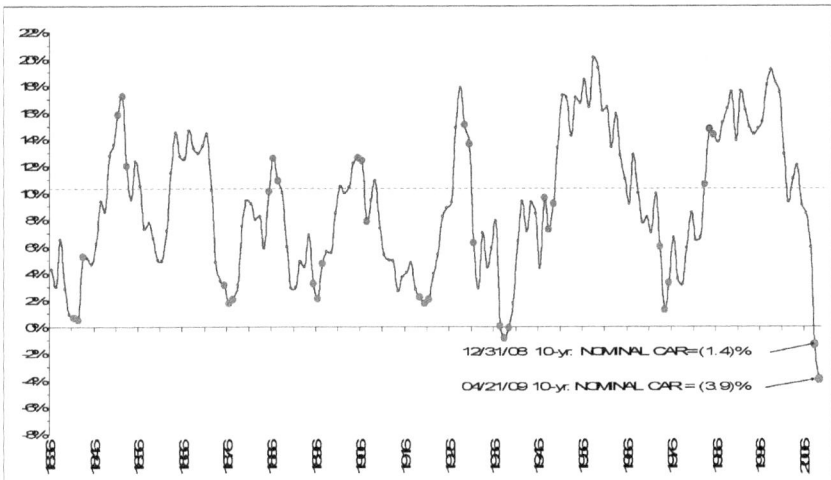

Figure 7 - U.S. 10-year Nominal Compound Stock Market Returns - 1827-2008.
Source: "Anatomy of the Meltdown – 1998 – 2008," page 3, Franck Prissert, 2011.

"Most of the damage occurred from June to November 2008." Really? We had just decided to double the size of the Federal Reserve Balance Sheet, an historic measure unheard off on any continent, presumably large enough to sanitize the whole banking system, and this did not stem the tide?

There were many reasons to account for the financial crisis, but the short answer was leverage. Not only were Households in above average debt, but so was the Treasury. This was true not only in the U.S., but also abroad. The one thing about leverage, it hinges on confidence. As long as the lender trusts the borrower, it works and increases the return on equity – for more on that, let me know. The cycle turns when the lender loses confidence, and this is mostly subjective. Could it be that, in the Man and his cohort, the market's Invisible Hand[280] saw the end of Supply Side Economics, and the return to Keynes? More spending, more deficits and more taxes, as in the looming American Recovery and Reinvestment Act, a.k.a. ARRA[281]. Could it be that it anticipated a hell of a decline in a leveraged economy, a scary thought in itself[282]? Or could it be that the two combined was the worst possible outcome?

A new fellow to the world at large, Timothy Geithner, had been rumored as the new lead candidate to head the Treasury department, should Obama prevail. They were both the same age, forty seven. Importantly, Geithner had an impressive resume. To the Establishment, he was a protégé of Treasury Secretaries Bob Rubin and Larry Summers, had worked for Henry Kissinger, the IMF, and was a member of the Council of Foreign Relations. Less obvious, but in yet another confirmation of his stature, he was a member of the highly exclusive international "Group of 30" leading financiers and academics[283]. Obama's curious resume paled in comparison.

More importantly, since 2003, Geithner had been the president of the Federal Reserve of New York, the largest of the twelve regional district banks that were mandated, back in 1913, to constitute the Federal Reserve System. As such, he oversaw most, if not all, of New

York financial institutions. Very few did not belong to the system, and the New York District was by far the largest in the Nation, with $2.5 trillion in assets, more than 50% of the total.

As the saying goes, a financial crisis, like many things that happen in life out of the blue, is usually the result of a process, not just an event. Tim Geithner, the next Treasury chief to repair the country's finances, the one with the fiat money[284] printing presses, was the same who had been supervising the inner workings of the ex nihilo money multipliers[285], the banks, so that the system would not need any repairs in the first place. Fact is, the whole thing had cratered under his watch. Despite his resume, he obviously was not the weapon of choice to restore confidence. Regardless, on November 24, 2008, at the apex of the worst financial crisis the U.S. and the world had experienced since the Great Depression, President Obama announced his upcoming Treasury nominee. Tim Geithner.

It seemed like Obama's Change platform, Geithner's failed experience, and the company of Congress radicals like Nancy Pelosi and Harry Reid, may have been the proverbial straw that broke the camel's back.

Paulson had to leave. Fortunately, Bernanke stayed. He was the only pilot left in the plane, he had a Bazooka, and both Obama and Geithner knew he was the only one who knew to use it.

When Obama took office in January 2009, who was his team? Rahm Emanuel, Chief of Staff. David Axelrod, Senior Advisor. And Valerie Jarrett, the other Senior Advisor and Assistant to the President for Intergovernmental Relations and Public Liaison. Add Arne Duncan, Secretary of Education, former CEO of Chicago Public Schools, and Ray Lahood, Secretary of Transportation, former Congressman representing the 18th district of Illinois, it looked like a meme of the Chicago machine.

And poor former First Lady Hilary Clinton was given the Kiss of Death, as Secretary of State. If anything was to blow up on the international scene, which was likely, she would be the fuse.

Then, to name a few, there were Susan Rice, Samantha Power, Eric Holder, Robert Gibbs, and Van Jones – one of the thirty plus President "Czars" who required no Senate confirmation.

Van Jones was appointed in March 2009 as Special Advisor for Green Jobs, Enterprise and Innovation, which was an offshoot of one of the Committees the President had served on while in the Senate. Together with Ken Salazar, strangely appointed Secretary of the Interior[286], and Steven Chu, the new Secretary of Energy and former director of the Lawrence Berkeley National Laboratory[287], they went on a Green splurge which cost taxpayers north of several billion dollars, with nothing to show but dubious endeavors. Solyndra, the solar panel company that filed for bankruptcy in 2011 and left taxpayers on the hook for $585 million, was a drop in the bucket. It had been the first project to be financed under Section 1705 of ARRA[288], a provision set to expire on September 30, 2011, which would fund:

> "Renewable Energy systems that create electricity, electric power transmission systems, and leading-edge biofuel projects that reduce Green House Gases".

Section 1705 was an extension of President Bush's 2005 and 2007 Energy Acts, but no such projects had been approved under his tenure. Solyndra, under Obama's watch, was the first. Another more successful one, Alamosa, in Colorado, cost $91 million, to create seventy five construction jobs, ten permanent operations jobs, and produce around 60,000 MegaWatt hours per year[289]. At the prevailing rate of $0.10 per grid-parity KWh, the plant would pay back in fifteen years – maintenance excluded. In the meantime, this was a gargantuan job cost. The Agua Caliente solar farm in Arizona was much larger, at $1.8 billion with $627 million in ARRA loan guarantees. It would eventually produce 620,000 MWh of electricity, with a payback of some thirty years. And it would create a whopping four hundred construction jobs, and ten permanent jobs.

By September 30, 2011, my notes say that $37 billion had been lent by the duo Chu-Salazar, creating 63,947 jobs at a cost of $605,000 per job[290]. The Department of Energy Loan Program office was even harsher. It tallied $16 billion in loans that supported more than ten thousand jobs. That would be $1,600,000 per job[291]. And if you took out the Vogtle Project, "America's first new nuclear reactors in thirty years," which would provide 3500 construction jobs and 800 permanent jobs, the loan per job of the other twenty four projects would rise to some $2,500,000[292].

In the case of Crescent Dunes Solar Energy Project, located in Nevada, state of the new Senate Leader Harry Reid, the $737 million in DOE loan guarantee -and-then-some-private money that was to be spent would create 600 construction jobs and 45 permanent jobs[293]. It would produce 480,000 MWh per year [294], which the local utility Nevada Power had agreed to buy at 13.5 cent per KWh for 25 years, commencing in 2014. Since customers were currently paying around 10 cent per KWh, either the taxpayer or the consumer would have to foot the 35% marginal increase of 3.5c/KWh. Apparently, nobody noticed, nor cared.

Nobody seemed to care either about the risks of the technology involved, United Technology's Rocketdyne. Solar Reserve, the developer of the site, was adamant on its "About Us" website, in September 2011:

> "Actually, the technology has been proven [...] at the Solar One and Solar Two power plants in Southern California."

It omitted to say that it was last used in 1982 at Solar One, which had been decommissioned in 1988. And that Solar Two had briefly operated from 1996 to 1999, both with a name plate capacity of a mere 10 MegaWatts.

Crescent Dunes was to be commissioned in early 2014. And so it was, in late 2015.

Interestingly, the main private investor in Solyndra, George Kaiser[295], a billionaire fund raising bundler for Obama, was also an investor in Crescent Dunes[296], albeit a smaller one this time[297].

Worth noting, none of these projects would displace the use of oil, which was the original concept. They were geared to electricity production, which barely consumed 2% of all our Petroleum resources. As one would have expected, Transportation accounted for 70%, and we were many many years away from a universal electric car. The real motto was job creation — at what cost? — and "harmful" CO_2 emissions, another figment of imagination and another story.

Primary energy consumption by source and sector, 2013
quadrillion Btu

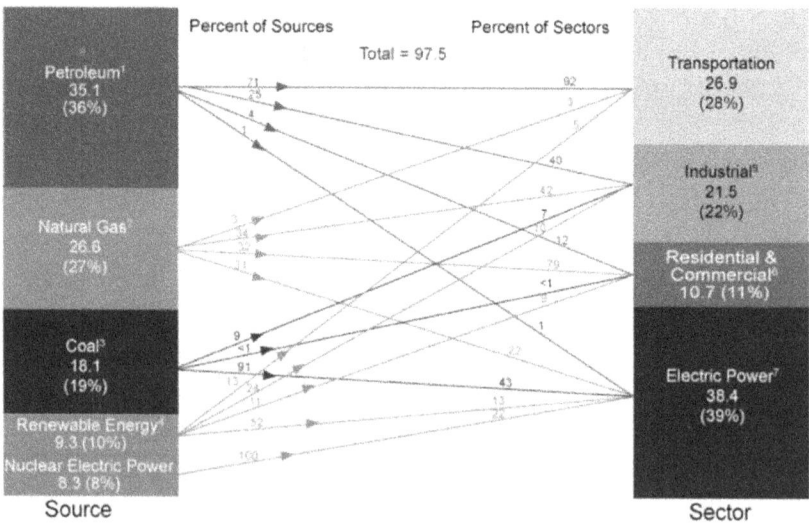

Figure 8 - U.S. Energy Consumption by Source and Use – 2013. Source: U.S. EIA, Monthly Energy Review.

Van Jones, in a rare occurrence for a "Czar", resigned on September 6, 2009, a short six-months after his appointment. As a Czar, he had not been subject to Senate confirmation but his background was quite non-conforming. The basic story, then, was that he had cofounded

"Green for All" in 2007, with the backing of former Inconvenient Truth Vice-President and Nobel Prize Al Gore. He was also on the Board of the Apollo Alliance, founded in 2003 by a coalition of major environmental groups and labor unions, with a plan to revitalize the American economy with a 10-year $300 billion plan to foster clean energy. In 2006, it morphed into the Blue Green Alliance, with Phil Angelides, the California State Treasurer and failed Democratic gubernatorial candidate as its chair, and well-known environmental activist and actor Robert Redford as fellow Board member.

This was a sequel to the Renewable Energy Policy Project created in 1995, during President Clinton's first term, by the Department of Energy, the National Renewable Energy Laboratory, and the Environmental Protection Agency. Under the tutelage of then Vice President Al Gore, the project had called for the creation of one million jobs by spending $200 billion to create 200 GigaWatts of Renewable Energy. The REPP.org website is no longer online, but to put things into prospective, in 2005, electricity production capacity in the U.S. was 1,000 GW, of which a mere 100 GW was from Renewable sources, with 60 GW coming from Hydropower alone. Ex Hydropower which had limited expansion capacity, maybe 20GW, this meant increasing Renewable Energy production, ex Hydro, by 350%, from 40 GW to 180 GW[298].

Noble cause indeed, if it was not for the fact that this would cost the taxpayer $200,000 per job created, an already gross and yet wildly optimistic estimate at the time, and that 90% of Renewable Energy, producing electricity otherwise known as stationary power, would not be a substitute for transportation anytime soon. Regardless, ARRA worked along the same premise, and was a great platform for Van Jones, Special Advisor for Green Jobs, Enterprise, and Innovation.

There had to be some other reasons for his prompt resignation.

A closer look at his resume showed that in 1991, Van Jones had co-founded STORM, *"Standing Together to Organize a Revolutionary*

Movement". The group's manifesto, published in 1994, "*Reclaiming Revolution*", left little doubt as to the group's aim:

> "*411: Political Education Committee: In 1998, STORM created 411[…] a formal committee in charge of providing structured training for both the Core and the General Membership. 411 was also responsible for orienting new members. 411 was important in collectivizing STORM's commitment to Marxist politics. […] later sessions covered more "contemporary" issues, including Marxism feminism, transgender liberation, and the Palestinian liberation struggle.*"[299]

STORM was dissolved in 2002.

Jones had also become known for organizing a 1999 march for the retrial of Mumia Abu-Jamal, former Black Panther and killer of Philadelphia policeman Daniel Faulkner in 1981[300], and for sponsoring rallies of 9/11 deniers[301]. His list of affiliations included International A.N.S.W.E.R., for "Act Now to Stop War and End Racism"[302], founded just three days after the 9/11 attacks.

Behind this well-intended acronym was Ramsey Clark, former Attorney General under President Johnson, and 1992 founder of the International Action Center. A civil rights lawyer by trade, Clark was a well-known anti-Vietnam War and pro-Communist North Vietnam activist. He was also known for his defense work in the trials of several war criminals, including Slobodan Milosevic and Saddam Hussein, whom he had both described as "*commanders who were courageous enough to fight powerful countries*". Birds of a feather, the Russian apparatchik spymaster Primakov was on the same page. Clark's ANSWER anti-Imperialist and anti-Semitic philosophy needed no further comment than a quick look at its website, www.answercoalition.org.

His association with the Marxist-Leninist group Workers World Party was also well-documented[303]. In 1981, in company of Abe Feinglass, he supported the defense of the communist trio who attempted to bomb the National Shipbuilding Company in San Diego, California, otherwise known as NASSCO3[304].

He then founded the International Peace for Cuba Appeal in 1994. On February 27, 2004, speaking after a press conference at the National Press Club to rally support for Haiti's Marxist dictator and drug-trafficker Jean-Bertrand Aristide, he endorsed no other than John Kerry in his Presidential bid – the same John Kerry who had asked for U.S. military intervention to support Aristide, and who, in 1985, during the Iran-Contra affair, had called Daniel Ortega of Nicaragua

"a misunderstood democrat rather than a Marxist autocrat."

This is a free country, and Ramsey Clark was one of Van Jones's mentor. By the end of 2009, Jones was the only Czar who had left the Administration. A year later, Clark was hosting a meeting in New York City in support of then Iranian President Mahmoud Ahmadinejad[305], another of Primakov's buddies.

In February 2013, John Kerry, Clark's and Feinglass' friend, became Obama's second Secretary of State. His other well-known friend was Bashar al-Assad[306] who Russia had been backing all the way.

Susan Rice was another secret weapon. Her resume was impeccable, and she brought something else to the party. Her husband, Ian Officer Cameron, was the executive producer of "This Week," an investigative Washington team at ABC News and a convenient amplifier of the President's pulpit[307]. However, Rice's record was not in sync with her impeccable resume, in particular when it came to her alleged upset at genocides.

She had graduated from Stanford University in 1986, went on to Oxford College in England, and joined President Clinton's National Security Council staff from 1993 to 1997. From 1995 to 1997, she was his Assistant Secretary for African Affairs, while Robin Raphel was Assistant Secretary for South and Central Asian Affairs[308].

Raphel would support any type of dictator, as long as they were anti-communist. Like the repulsive Mobutu Sese Seko in Zaire, a legacy of Allen and John Foster Dulles, or the Taliban and al-Qaeda, and their closest ally, Pakistan. Rice was only twenty nine year old at the time of Rwanda's Hutu massacre of its Tutsi population. This had taken place in a short one hundred days, from April 7, 1994 to mid-July. During that period, and under the blind eyes and deaf ears of her mentor and then U.N. Ambassador Madeline Albright, seventy percent of the Rwanda Tutsis, twenty percent of the Rwanda population, eight hundred thousand people or so, men, women and children, were murdered by the most inhumane of means. Rice was later interviewed about this, in particular about one of her cold blood quotes that had been widely circulated,

> *"if we call this genocide, and we do not do anything about it, what will the impact be on the upcoming mid-term elections?"*[309]

The journalist who conducted the interview in September 2001, and who chronicled at length this Clinton do-nothing policy, was none other than Samantha Power, who later would become President Obama's U.S. Ambassador to the U.N. When she asked Rice about the quote, her response was

> *"If I said it, it was completely inappropriate, as well as irrelevant."*

Genocide, irrelevant? If there was any doubt about her pivotal role, as well as that of the Clinton Administration, it was all later exposed in confidential documents declassified in 2014 under the Freedom of Information Act[310].

Robin Raphel was excused in 1997, and, to thank her for her twenty plus years of foreign policy service, she was "appointed" Ambassador to Tunisia. Her open support of the Taliban, al-Qaeda, and now-nuclear Pakistan did not sit well with India, which was closer to Russia as a result, Primakov's Doctrine[311] oblige. Susan Rice seemingly got the message and switched sides on Zaire's Mobutu, saying that anything would be better than him – a close paraphrase and one of her lucid moments. Unfortunately she did not stop there and condoned a coalition led by Rwanda's remaining Tutsis, then ruling Rwanda under Paul Kagame, to invade Zaire and remove Mobutu. Ugandan and Rwandan forces installed Laurent-Desire Kabila who self-proclaimed himself President on May 17, 1997. Kabila claimed to be a follower of Patrice Lumumba[312], but he was not the pacifist nationalist Lumumba was. He alienated his former supporters, for one reason or another, and was strangely assassinated in January 2001[313], in the middle of the Second Congo War. Altogether, in what is known as the Great War of Africa, nine African nations and scores of tribal groups were involved, with more than five million casualties, mostly civilians, and counting.

Africa was never an easy puzzle, and Rice was seemingly not very good at puzzles. But she was good at business, and Africa was good business. Zaire, a.k.a. the former Belgian Congo, Congo-Kinshasa, or the Democratic Republic of Congo, not to be confused with the Republic of Congo, a.k.a Congo-Brazzaville, is Africa's third largest country and a wealth, literally, of mineral resources, hence the forever quest for its dominance. When Rice first left Washington in 2001, she went to work for Intellibridge,

> "*a leading provider of international analysis and open-source intelligence for the U.S. national security community and others.*" [emphasis added]

Founded in 1999 by David Rothkopf[314], former managing director of Kissinger Associates, and Anthony Lake, former State Department veteran and National Security Advisor under President Clinton, and her boss during the Rwandan genocide, it was a consulting firm. Underscore "intelligence," as in spook. She worked there until 2002. Rwanda's Kagame was her better known client. The forces he supported had installed Kabila. She may have thought she had it made, but it only lasted for a short while.

Mrs. Rice then joined the Brookings Institution, one of the oldest American Washington think tanks, deemed to be on the left center of the political scale, with a few incursions to the right. While at Brookings, she served as John Kerry's foreign policy advisor during his presidential campaign in 2004, then as Senator Obama's in 2008, advocating his opposition to the war in Iraq. She was rewarded as his first U.S. Ambassador to the United Nations, in a position that he restored to the cabinet level. This soothed her disappointment over Hilary Clinton's nomination as Secretary of State, the seat that Rice had reportedly coveted.

Samantha Power was another of President Obama's weapons. A strident human rights activist, she had authored several books and penned numerous articles, mostly in the liberal press. A young journalist during the genocidal Bosnian War, she then earned a JD from Harvard and, in 1998, became the founding Executive Director of the Carr Center for Human Rights Policy at the Harvard Kennedy School of Government. Her second book, published in 2002, was titled *"A Problem from Hell: America and the Age of Genocide,"* and won her a Pulitzer Prize. In the meantime, one of her famous articles titled *"Bystanders to Genocide"*, which we referred to above, was highly critical of the Clinton Administration's handling of the Rwandan genocide, and singled a few people out, including Susan Rice. Notwithstanding, when Barack Obama was still a U.S. Senator, she worked for his office as a foreign policy fellow, and later joined his Presidential campaign in 2007. She resigned in March 2008 because of a few misplaced statements about Hilary Clinton[315], only to join the transition team right after his election. She was then appointed to the National Security Council as Special Assistant to the President and Senior Director for Multilateral Affairs and Human Rights.

Power's foreign policy doctrine was well-intended – fight for human rights and against genocides. It included military and non-military options. Back in 2002, she had earned an anti-Israel label, considering that Palestinians were on the verge of genocide at the hand of Israel, and that the U.S. should deploy of a "mammoth protection force", widely understood as an invasion of Israel. In 2011, she advocated in unison with Susan Rice and Hilary Clinton – and most say, convinced President Obama – to join a coalition to bomb Libya to save the Libyan opposition from the genocidal hand of Muammar Gaddafi. In 2012, Power and Rice also tried to free Syria's civilian population from Bashir al-Assad's chemical weapons and other murderous attacks. None of these plans worked. Libya gave way to the infamous Benghazi attack in September 2012, and Syria turned into a full-fledged genocide. S.O.S. John Kerry was nowhere in sight[316].

Regardless, Power was unanimously vetted to succeed Rice as U.S. Ambassador to the U.N. on June 5, 2013[317]. Coincidentally, Susan Rice was appointed as National Security Advisor upon Tom Donilon's unexplained resignation.

Donilon was not exactly a newbie. He had been Chief of Staff for Bill Clinton's Secretary of State Warren Christopher. During that period, he was deeply involved in the Bosnian wars. As Obama's second National Security Advisor, he was also deeply involved in the "Arab Spring", the popular revolts that rocked the whole Middle East and North Africa starting in December 2010. And he was a former member of the Steering Committee of the Bilderberg Group, not exactly a powerless entity. Incidentally, his brother Mike was a partner at AKPD Message and Media[318], David Axelrod's kingmaker firm, and counselor to Vice President Joe Biden since 1981, in particular from 2009 to 2013. In a sense, the Donilon Brothers were following the behind-the-scenes footsteps of the Dulles Brothers.

Why Donilan abruptly resigned remains a mystery. Suffice it to say, this paved the way for Susan Rice's appointment as the all-powerful National Security Advisor, a position that did not need Senate confirmation. This was a welcome reprieve for her as she had been under bipartisan criticism for her role in the 2012 Benghazi attack cover-up. Actually, to many, it looked like President Obama was thumbing his nose at her critics.

A quick flash back here. Gaddafi's Libya had fallen in 2011, under the watch of Susan Rice as U.S. Ambassador to the U.N, Hilary Clinton as Secretary of State, and Samantha Power as Senior Foreign Policy Adviser. The plan was less than clear. Gaddafi was killing his own people, threatening European and in particular French and British National Security interests. The United States was reluctant to intervene solely for human rights reasons, despite Samantha Power's credo. Susan Rice had qualified the new National Security Strategy of 2010[319] as a "dramatic departure" from that of the Bush Administration. Of course, she meant this as a positive. Then, it was "strike first, ask questions later; if you are not with us, you are against us". Now, it was "let's ask the other guys first. If we all agree, we will do something, including Climate Change – but we won't fight more than one war at a time; and we certainly won't move without a coalition".

The Bush's had gone to Iraq twice. Bush II had gone there with the hope of nation-building, officially freeing some thirty million people who might conceptually thank the United States after years of oppression and/or massacre. If it worked, the minority-yet-powerful Sunni Arab population would counter balance Shi'a Iran. It would certainly empower the Sunni Kurds and their Peshmerga, potentially rallying their brethren in Syria, Iran, and Turkey, despite their differences. In the process, the United States would rebuild their on-the-ground intelligence in a wildly belligerent country, surrounded by at least six other breeding grounds for most of the world's terrorists. The starting point was regime change, the end game was nation building. Point was, Bush II had a strategy. Whether it would work was a matter of war odds, filled with a multitude of conflicting religious beliefs and unpredictable political outcomes.

When President Obama intervened in Libya, he had no strategy, and no end game. There was a humanitarian reason, but were the consequences that clear? Who would fill the vacuum, the locals as in nation building which had just failed in Iraq? Or some other mercenaries, some other jihadist groups, like in Iraq? National

Security Advisor Tom Donilon, Deputy National Security and chief counterterrorism Advisor John Brennan, and Defense Secretary Robert Gates all disagreed with the plan, but the Women in Power obviously had his Presidential ears[320].

Aside from one war at a time, the only dramatic departure Rice had referred to was that the United States no longer wanted to lead this intervention – or any intervention for that matter. In the case of Libya, Obama waited until the French and the British had formed a coalition under NATO command, and then participated to some Navy extent. It actually took three weeks for then French President Sarkozy to convince Secretary Clinton to join[321]. And it took another week for Obama to address the Nation, while Gaddafi was trampling his people all over[322]. At the United Nations, the only countries to abstain from the Security Council vote for a no-fly zone were Brazil, Russia, India, China and Germany. The BRIC plus the proverbial 1. It passed ten in favor, zero against.

While the country was home to only six million people, it was one of the many which had revolted against hard line regimes in the Middle East and North Africa, the "Arab Spring". With Saddam gone in 2006 and Bin Laden killed in May 2011, there were two delusional tyrants left in the region, al-Assad and Gaddafi[323]. Gaddafi was captured and killed on October 20, 2011.

There was plenty of work left. Libya was one of the most fertile anti-American mujahedeen training ground which, for some reason, the Rice-Power-Clinton trio had overlooked. But Secretary of State Hilary Clinton had a Plan B to deal with the "wrong" rebels. His name was Ambassador J. Christopher Stephens.

Ambassador Stevens was an expert on the Middle East and spoke fluent Arabic. He had served in Israel, Syria, Egypt and Saudi Arabia. In Washington, he had been Director of the Office of Multilateral Nuclear and Security Affairs, and served on the Senate Foreign Relations Committee, on the Iran desk, and in the Bureau of Near

Eastern Affairs. He was the Deputy Chief of Mission in Libya from 2007 to 2009, and Special Representative to the Libyan National Transitional Council from March to November 2011, formed to organize the rebellion's many groups. He was appointed Ambassador to Tripoli in May 2012, at age fifty-two, and was widely believed to be able to play a key role in the stabilization of the "Arab Spring". He exactly knew the terrain, how dangerous the situation could become and he was up to the task, with his own boots on the ground. He was somewhat of a hero in the eyes of the "right" rebels, those yearning for democracy, much like General David Petraeus, former Commanding General of the Multi-National Force in Iraq, of the United States Central Command overseeing military efforts in Afghanistan, Pakistan, Central Asia, the Arabian Peninsula and Egypt, and of the International Security Assistance Force in Afghanistan. General Petraeus, then Director of the CIA, thought he had him covered, with a large presence on the ground whose primary mission was to recover the rockets and missiles of the Gaddafi regime.

11

Benghazi Awry

The sad part was quick to come – sad is a misnomer here. On September 11, 2012, the 11th anniversary of 9/11 and a day remembered by all worldwide, the town of Benghazi on the northern coast of Libya became under attack by what were initially deemed unknown forces. The target of the attack was no other than Ambassador Stevens who gruesomely died in the assault on the U.S. diplomatic and CIA compounds, together with three other American servicemen who came to his rescue – Sean Smith, Glen Doherty and Tyrone Woods. Before they committed the Ultimate Sacrifice, they had helped more than thirty other Americans evacuate.

Ambassador Stevens was the first Ambassador to be killed in office since Arnold Raphel in 1988 in a plane crash in Pakistan. He would be the latest of five Ambassadors to have been killed by mujahedeen. Before Raphel, Ambassador Adolf Dubs in 1979 by the Setami Milli group in Kabul, Afghanistan; Francis Meloy in 1976 by a Palestinian group in Beirut, Lebanon; and Clea Noel Jr. by the PLO "Black September" in 1973 in Khartoum, Sudan. Two other Ambassadors had died in the line of duty, John Gordon Mein in Guatemala, and Laurence A. Steinhardt in Canada. Seven killed in seventy years, five of whom by mujahedeen in the past forty.

Yet, Barack Obama, President, Joe Biden, Vice President, Hilary Clinton, Secretary of State, and General Petraeus, Director of CIA, did not have any substantive public comments to make in reaction to the attack[324]. The only ones to speak out were Jay Carney, Obama's Press Secretary, and Susan Rice, Obama's Ambassador to the U.N.

Jay "The Jester" Carney was expected to act inane[325]. He had been appointed in January 2011 and it was later compiled by Yahoo News that as of June 2013, he had used some version of "I don't have the answer" more than 1,900 times, that he referred the question to someone else 1,383 times, and eluded the question 9,486 times[326]. Clearly, Carney was a man of a few words, but not this time. Two days after the gruesome attack, in his September 14, 2012 press briefing[327], he said:

> "We were not aware of any actionable intelligence indicating that an attack on the U.S. mission in Benghazi was planned or imminent. That report is false. [...] We don't have and did not have concrete evidence to suggest that this was not in reaction to the film".

He was referring to a thirteen minute video that had made it through the internet, alternatively called "Innocence of Muslims", "Innocence of Bin Laden", "Desert Warrior", "The Real Life of Muhammad", or the "Muhammad Movie Trailer". In Cairo, that same anniversary day of September 11, a crowd of some two thousand Muslim Brotherhood sympathizers, emboldened by the recent rise to power of Mohamed Morsi, had rallied in front of the U.S. Embassy in part to protest against this video made by a mysterious U.S. resident[328], Nakoula Basseley Makoula, under the pseudonym "Sam Bacile".

Carney went on to add:

> "We have no information to suggest that it was a preplanned attack. The unrest we've seen around the region has been in reaction to a video that Muslims, many Muslims find offensive. And while the violence is reprehensible and unjustified, it is not a reaction to the 9/11 anniversary that we know of, or to U.S. policy".

Susan Rice, as U.S. Ambassador to the United Nations and a cabinet member, was not supposed to be that idiotic, but she was. So much so that, without her, this book probably would not have been written.

In what was a premeditated attack by a group immediately identified as Ansar al-Sharia in Lybia by the Libyan Prime Minister Mustafa Abushagur and President Mohamed Yousef el-Magariaf themselves, the U.S. compound in Benghazi fell at dusk. The attack started at 2140 local time, 1540 EST. The next target was the CIA annex, one mile away. Within twelve hours, despite repeated calls for help which could have easily been deployed from the U.S. naval base in Sigonella, Sicily, Ambassador Stevens, and Smith, Doherty and Woods were killed by some two hundred men, armed with rocket propelled grenades and armored vehicles – hardly a "spontaneous popular revolt". Ansar al-Sharia was a Yemen-based Salafi organization of jihadists groups, and the leading one in Lybia under the command of Ahmed Abu Khattala, associated with al-Qaeda in the Islamic Maghreb.

Then, five days later, Susan Rice echoed Jay Carney. Not too surprisingly since his wife, Claire Shipman, was a senior correspondent for ABC News, and had been working for Ian Cameron, Susan Rice's husband. They clearly all had the same talking points, as it turned out largely redacted at the request of many of Obama's closest advisors: the State Department spokesperson Victoria "Toria" Nulland[329], the National Security Staff, reporting to National Security advisor Tom Donilon, the Deputy National Security Advisor John Brennan, and the C.I.A. Deputy Director Mike Morell. Only his boss, General Petraeus, strongly disagreed. The reference to a "cable to Cairo", sent on September 10, warning the Embassy of an impending attack, was suppressed, paving the way for the "spontaneous" narrative, and the word "attack" simply became "demonstration". We will probably never find out what General Petraeus meant by:

> "No mention of the cable to Cairo, either? Frankly, I'd just as soon not use this, then… NSS's call, to be sure; however, this is certainly not what Vice Chairman Ruppersberger was hoping to get for unclas. use. Regardless, thx for the great work. [330]"

So, it looked like General Petraeus was not the only one disagreeing with these Talking Points. Vice Chairman Ruppersberger also had a different view, and "Dutch" as he was called, ought to have known. He was the Ranking Democrat on the House Permanent Select Committee on Intelligence.

What they were disagreeing upon was an email from Mike Morell, dated September 15, 2012 at 12:51pm:

> *"Sir, here are the interagency approved points for the Hill. They were worked though the DC this morning and were then shot out for final approval. As mentioned last night, State had voiced strong concerns with the original text due to the criminal investigation. That said, I understand NSS is working on all members briefings this coming week and these are a good starting point. With your concurrence we will get them to our oversight committees and to leadership. [...].*
>
> *[OCA]*
>
> *The currently available information suggests that the demonstrations in Benghazi were spontaneously inspired by the protests at the U.S. embassy in Cairo and evolved into a direct assault against the U.S. diplomatic post in Benghazi and subsequently its annex. There are indications that extremists participated in the violent demonstrations.*
>
> *This assessment may change as additional information is collected and analyzed and as currently information continues to be evaluated.*
>
> *The investigation is on-going, and the U.S. government is working with Libyan authorities to bring to justice those responsible for the deaths of U.S. citizens."*

This exchange followed a September 14 email from Benjamin Rhodes, White House Deputy Strategic Communications Adviser, one in a long series entitled *"PREP CALL with Susan: Saturday at 4:00pm ET"*[331]:

> *"Goals: to convey that the United States is doing everything that we can to protect our people and facilities abroad;* **to underscore that these protests are rooted in an Internet video, and not a broader failure of policy;** *to show that we will resolve in bringing people who harm Americans to justice, and standing steadfast through these protests;* **to reinforce the President and Administration's strength and steadiness in dealing with difficult challenges"**. [emphasis added].

On September 16, our top diplomat was ready to deliver the concocted official version. Speaking on five television Sunday Talk Shows, and despite the assertions to the contrary by the Libyan President and Premier, she vexingly stuck to the redacted narrative:

> *"The currently available information suggests that the demonstrations in Benghazi were spontaneously inspired by the protests at the U.S. Embassy in Cairo and evolved into a direct assault against the U.S. diplomatic post in Benghazi and subsequently its annex. There are indications that extremists participated in the violent demonstrations"*.

There also was a great deal of unanswered questions about Secretary Clinton's involvement, since Ambassador Stephens was in her direct chain of command. The only remarkable statement she would make, in a January 2013 Senate hearing at which she had finally accepted to testify, was:

> *"With all due respect* [Senator Johnson], *the fact is we had four dead Americans. Was it because of a protest or was it because of guys out for a walk one night who decided that they'd go kill some Americans? What difference at this point does it make?*[332]"

While this raised the issue of her competence and of why the cover up, two main questions remained. What had happened to the chain of command? And why the calls that Ambassador Stephens made that night to Gregory Hicks, then deputy chief of mission of the U.S. embassy in Tripoli, which Hicks forwarded for help to the State Department 20 minutes into the attack, were not acted upon from the U.S. naval base in Sicily, less than an hour away[333].

There was also a great deal of controversy as to the role of the National Security Staff. Regardless, John Brennan became C.I.A. Director when the Acting Director, Mike Morell, "retired" on August 9, 2013. By then, it was clear that he bore the lead responsibility of the politically watered down version of the Benghazi Talking Points[334]. Toria Nulland had also left her post, in February 2013 – only to be nominated Assistant Secretary of State for European and Eurasian Affairs in May 2013, and confirmed in September[335].

But what exactly had happened to General Petraeus?

On September 15, 2012, Mike Morell had submitted the "Talking Points" memo to then C.I.A. Director General Petraeus. If he had become C.I.A. Acting Director, and resigned in August 2013, it meant that he had replaced the General at some point in between.

The Benghazi attack occurred less than two months before the 2012 Presidential elections, and an essential part of Obama's platform was withdrawal from Iraq, bin Laden is dead, al-Qaeda has been defeated. Naturally, all gloves were off against anyone standing in the way of the narrative. This sordidly included the only credible member of the group, General Petraeus, who had expressed doubts on how Benghazi had been handled and who was behind the attack. Al-Qaeda was cited in the original Talking Points, and Ansar al-Sharia, of Salafi persuasion, was itself rooted in al-Qaeda's strict Wahhabism. If anyone had doubts, Petraeus had none. Been there, done that. He had reluctantly agreed to the initial politicized version, but he had a job to do, and congressional hearings were coming. Chances were pretty high that he would confirm that al-Qaeda was alive and well, in this case as al-Qaeda in the Islamic Maghreb, and that Ansar al-Sharia in Lybia was an extension of the Yemeni parent organization. Which would kill Ben Rhodes' airbrushed affirmation,

> *"to underscore that these protests are [...] not a broader failure of policy."*

This, in turn, would jeopardize Obama's upcoming reelection. Was that a chance worth taking? The General, like all soldiers, was disposable. Probably the only way to throw him under the bus was to attack his impeccable reputation.

Sordidly, because this became known as the Petraeus Scandal, that of a four-star General who was duly recognized as one of the very best, both from a military and personal standpoint, and of two women, Gilberte "Jill" Khawam Kelley and her twin sister Natalie Khawam Wolfe. Jill Kelley, in particular, was later portrayed by the media as a "Tampa socialite who would entertain high-ranked officers at her home", or alternatively as "volunteer social liaison to the MacDill Air Force Base in Tampa Bay, Florida", or, as her license plate showed, "Honorary Consul General to United States Central Command's Coalition Forces"[336], UNSCOM. It was a mix of sex, lies and videotapes – actually, internet messaging.

The tabloid part was this. Between late 2011 and August 2012, General Petraeus allegedly had an affair with his biographer Paula Broadwell, herself a U.S. Army Intelligence Officer. The affair reportedly ended when the General found out that Broadwell was sending harassing messages to Jill Kelley, a "friend" of the Petraeuses. The nature of these emails is largely undisclosed, but presumably Broadwell was fearing Jill, or Natalie, as "competitors" for the man she nicknamed "Dangerous Dave" or "Peaches". In May 2012, Jill Kelley reported these emails, sent by "KelleyPatrol", to local Tampa F.B.I. agent Frederick Humphries II. This seemed a natural since Agent Humphries was apparently a friend of Kelley, sending her shirtless photos of himself[337]. Whether these photos were goofs, as he later claimed, they dated their friendship back to 2010 so the disclosure was not merely incidental[338].

The Khawam sisters were born in 1975 in Beirut. Thirty seven year old at the time, and fairly attractive from this author's viewpoint, merely looking at their pictures on the internet. Maronites, a must for any Lebanese high official. How they connected to the Lebanese political pyramid is unknown but plausibly played a role in their relationship with UNSCOM, always looking for assets with a Rolodex.

Natalie's husband, Grayson Wolfe, was a lawyer, and former Bush administration official who directed Middle East initiatives and Iraqi reconstruction efforts at the Export-Import Bank. The couple got into a nasty child custody battle and, for some reason, she had the support of Generals Dave Petraeus and John Allen. Four-star Marine General John R. Allen was the Commander of the U.S. Forces in Afghanistan, having succeeded General Petraeus. He also had been nominated to be NATO's Supreme Allied Commander in Europe, pending confirmation by the U.S. Senate. Among her other connections, she counted Senator John Kerry and Senator Sheldon Whitehouse of Rhode Island. She filed for personal bankruptcy in April 2012 and listed $3.6 million in personal debt. $300,000 was owed to her "boyfriend" Gerald Harrington[339], former national vice finance chair[340] for John Kerry's 2004 Presidential run[341].

She also owed $250,000 to Elizabeth Krowne, daughter of Dr. Clifford Krowne, her partner in Fullproof LLC[342]. Dr. Krowne was a physicist at the U.S. Naval Research Laboratory, and an expert in military electromagnetic pulse (EMP) technology[343]. To the uninformed reader, he was just another physicist. Not so. The threat of an EMP attack, first discovered in 1962, was actually so probable and scary that an EMP Commission had been established pursuant to the National Defense Authorization Act for Fiscal Year 2001 (October 2001 to September 2002). It was one of the most secretive U.S. programs, with the threat of the technology spreading worldwide to any country possessing ballistic missile launchers, let alone nuclear weapons. The 2008 208-page report that the Commission released could not have been clearer:

> "*When a nuclear explosion occurs at high altitude, the EMP signal it produces will cover the wide geographic region within the line of sight of the detonation. For example, a nuclear explosion at an altitude of 100 kilometers would expose 4 million square kilometers, about 1.5 million square miles, of Earth beneath the burst to a range of EMP field intensities. This broad band, high amplitude EMP, when coupled into sensitive electronics, has the capability to produce widespread and long lasting disruption and damage to the critical infrastructures that underpin the fabric of U.S. society.*"[344]

Jill Kelley did not have such a long resume. She was simply Natalie's twin sister, and the "Honorary Consul". Sure, the Doctor Kelley Cancer Foundation, on Tampa' Bayshore Boulevard, had gone bankrupt in 2007, but with less than $200,000 in spent assets[345], this was a far cry from Natalie's $3.6 million debt[346].

Throughout the summer of 2012, the FBI uncovered the source of "KelleyPatrol" to be Broadwell, and, in the process, an email account shared by Broadwell and the General confirming the affair. A totally unsecured gmail account. Generally, the FBI shuns from investigating cyber stalking as it is considered a civil matter, unless there is evidence of a national security threat. Furthermore, the fact that Broadwell, a veteran Intelligence Officer, not only had set up a publicly discoverable account, but also shared it with the no less secretive Director of the CIA should have raised flags as to the need for this minimization principle. However, given the "circumstances", and seemingly at the request of Agent Humphrey, the FBI apparently disclosed its findings to Director Robert Mueller and Attorney General Eric Holder[347].

Agent Humphries had not been assigned to the case, but kept pushing. In late October 2012, he called House Republicans Dave Reichert and Eric Cantor, claiming that the Justice Department was covering up the case[348]. His objective was unclear. Take down General Petraeus or take down Obama's DOJ?

This may sound strange but the timeline is there. General Petraeus was the gate keeper on Benghazi and the only real threat to the Administration's narrative, hence to Obama's reelection. By coincidence or by design, Obama's soldiers, led by Robert Mueller, decided to withhold the information until October 21, two weeks before the Election, when the FBI interviewed Paula Broadwell. On October 28, it was General Petraeus' turn. And,

> "On November 6, Election Day, at about 5 p.m., the FBI notifies Director of National Intelligence James Clapper, who oversees the CIA and other intelligence agencies, about Petraeus. Clapper speaks to Petraeus that evening and again Wednesday and advises him to step down."[349]

At that point, the General could no longer do any harm to the Presidency even if he had wanted to.

The Director of National Intelligence (DNI) heads the Intelligence Community (IC) and directly reports to the President. The CIA is one of seventeen IC elements and while the DNI has no management authority over it, it does over its Director. Clapper's suggestion was not a suggestion, it was an offer that could not be refused. Petraeus tendered his resignation to President Obama on November 7, who accepted it a couple of days later.

In the process, Marine General John R. Allen was also found to have exchanged emails deemed explicit with Jill Kelley. He was cleared by the Pentagon inspector general's office, but in the end, he decided to resign instead of taking one of the most coveted military jobs in the world, the NATO Supreme Allied Commander post.

Secretary of Defense Leon Panetta had a more graceful exit, despite his September 27 truism:

> *"It was a terrorist attack. The reason it was clearly a terrorist attack is because it was a group of terrorists who conducted this attack on this facility"*[350].

He retired in February 2013, after an illustrious civil servant career of some forty years. Before being appointed Secretary of Defense in 2011, he had been Director of the CIA since 2009, to be succeeded by General Petraeus. Under his tenure, Osama bin Laden had been located and killed. He knew what he was saying but he too had become a threat.

Obviously, further to his resignation, General Petraeus' voluntary testimony to Congress, scheduled for Thursday November 15, 2012, was abruptly cancelled. However, the bus that would run him over had not yet been invented. On November 16, he testified in a closed door meeting in front of the House and Senate Intelligence Committees. Too late for the election, but better late than never in the story that was unfolding, that of the Middle East in the Grand Game of Go. He confirmed al-Qaeda and other terrorists groups were the Benghazi perpetrators, and that it was not a spontaneous attack. What else he said must have raised some concerns, and five congressional committees started working on Benghazi. Confronted by his colleagues for stonewalling the process, in May 2014, the Speaker of the House John Boehner finally yielded to 178 members of his Republican caucus, and announced the creation of a Select Committee[351].

12

Mid-East Mess - v2

In the meantime, something else had happened in the Middle East, in Egypt, one of the three largest countries in the area, with a population of 84 million[352]. On June 30, 2012, Mohamed Morsi became its first democratically elected President. One would have thought this was a good thing, and that he would last for a while. A year later, on July 3, 2013, he was removed by a popular coup following a massive revolt by an estimated fourteen million protesters taking it to the streets. To put things into prospective, this would equate to some sixty five million people in the United States.

The reason for the protest was fairly obvious, in a country run by secular leaders for the past sixty years, backed by a loyal military. Morsi was Chairman of the Freedom and Justice Party, the political arm of the Muslim Brotherhood. For all of its history since 1928, the Brotherhood had represented the hard liners of Sunni Islam. For most of these years, the Brethren were either imprisoned or outlawed. First during WWII, when its main financial and spiritual supporter, the Grand Mufti of Jerusalem Haj Amin al-Husseini, had to flee to Hitler's Germany. Then by Prime Minister and General Gamal Abdel Nasser, who survived yet another Brotherhood assassination attempt in 1954. Then by President Anwar Sadat after he signed the Camp David Accords and was later assassinated for that. Then by President Hosni Mubarak who was ultimately overthrown in the "Arab Spring" in 2011. At that point, the Brotherhood filled the political vacuum and Morsi was quick to take advantage of the situation. In the early months of his mandate, he revised the Constitution, granted himself unlimited powers, including the power to legislate without judicial oversight in what was to be strict Sharia law, and then some. In his earlier days in Parliament, he had gone on record as a 911 revisionist. As for Israel, Morsi's position was clear:

> "The Zionists have no right to the land of Palestine. There is no place for them on the land of Palestine. [...] By no means do we recognize their Green Line".

And he went on to further call the Israelis "blood-suckers", "warmongers" and "descendants of apes and pigs"[353].

This is who the Muslim Brotherhood Egyptians had elected in 2012, and who the non-Muslim Brotherhood Egyptians fired a year later. His trial included charges of espionage and conspiracy with Hezbollah and Hamas, including the military training of jihadists in Gaza. Morsi, Hamas and the Brotherhood had lost all support, for one reason. Their ultimate Caliphate goal did not sit well with Egypt and Saudi Arabia.

President Obama was not getting it. He had praised Morsi for his election:

> "The United States will continue to support Egypt's transition to democracy and stand by the Egyptian people as they fulfill the promise of their revolution"[354].

Refusing now to listen to the will of the Egyptian people, he then declared:

> "The United States is deeply concerned by the decision of the Egyptian Armed Forces to remove [Morsi] and suspend the Egyptian constitution".

And, to boot:

> "*I now call on the Egyptian military to move quickly and responsibly to return full authority back to a democratically elected civilian government as soon as possible through an inclusive and transparent process, and to avoid any arbitrary arrests of President Morsi and his supporters. Given today's developments, I have also directed the relevant departments and agencies to review the implications under U.S. law for our assistance to the Government of Egypt*"[355].

Not only was he not getting it, he was missing the obvious. General Abdel Fattah el-Sisi, the Defense Minister who deposed Morsi, had been appointed by Morsi himself in August 2012, during the purge of the military, and was previously head of the all-powerful Military Intelligence. He knew what he was doing and had stated his values,

> "*The armed forces' loyalty is to the people and the nation.*"[356]

Then there was Saudi Arabia and the United Arab Emirates, who both supported the General. In July, they pledged $8 billion in cash and loans to restore the Egyptian economy[357], at a time when the International Monetary Fund abandoned the idea of a $4.5 billion loan[358]. In August, when the U.S. and Europe were considering reducing their own aid to Egypt, Saudi Arabia again pledged to make up for any shortfall. This was not just about Egypt, it was about Islamists versus Islamics in the Arabian Peninsula. This was a subtle difference which should not have escaped President Obama, yet it did.

First degree, there was one reason for his tantrum, even if the statement, a call for arms in a foreign democracy, client state to boot, was outrageous. In June 2009, one of his first international speeches, "*New Beginning*", had been delivered in Cairo[359]. Apologetic for everything the United States had done or not done under the sun, he stopped short of taking sides:

> "*I've come here to Cairo to seek a new beginning between the United States and Muslims around the world, one based*

on mutual interest and mutual respect, and one based upon
the truth that America and Islam are not exclusive and need
not be in competition."

He now felt compelled to go all out. Stopping short of calling Morsi's ousting a coup, which would have required the U.S. to cancel all aid to Egypt, he made an alternate wrong choice. He cancelled Operation Bright Star # 14[360], which was to be held in September 2013.

The first Operation Bright Star, a joint military exercise by American and Egyptian forces in Egypt, took place in late 1980 and was rooted in the Camp David Peace Accords. At the time, this had gotten the U.S.S.R. so worried that Brezhnev had deployed his 40th Army in Afghanistan[361]. Since then, another thirteen countries had joined the Operation, the largest of which, in 1999, included seventy thousand participants and an additional thirty three observer nations. According to CENTCOM, Bright Star was DOD's largest recurring military exercise.

So, second degree, were had the Man and his team been, and what were they thinking? Cancelling Bright Star was an open invitation for Russia to waltz into the broader theater via Iran and Syria. The Russo-Islamic Alliance had strange foundations, but it was a reality which Team Obama seemed to ignore. Maybe they had not read Dugin, but they had to know about Primakov. This explicit disdain for the leaders of Egypt and Saudi Arabia, combined with Russia now lurking at the Arabian Sea, was the catalyst for another unexpected Alliance. The time had come for the Kingdom of Saudi Arabia, the United Arab Emirates, and Egypt, to side with Israel and the Iraqi Kurds.

Was Team Obama really ignoring this? Maybe it had miscalculated the Morsi situation in Egypt, a stretch of imagination given the obvious? Or maybe it was closer to Russia than it appeared. At a Nuclear Summit in Seoul, on March 12, 2012, President Obama himself had

had been recorded in a hot mic conversation with outgoing Russian President Medvedev:

> Obama: *"On all these issues, but particularly missile defense, this, this can be solved, but it's important for him to give me space."*
>
> Medvedev: *"Yeah, I understand, I understand your message about space. Space for you..."*
>
> Obama: *"This is my last election. After my election, I have more flexibility."*
>
> Medvedev: *"I understand. I will transmit this information to Vladimir."*[362]

Let's sum it up here, in mid-2013.

On February 1, John Kerry had been appointed Secretary of State, replacing Hilary Clinton and chosen over Susan Rice for their Benghazi fiasco. As noted before, Kerry could turn out to be worse than the devils we knew. In the Seventies, with his sister Peggy, he was a leading figure and spokesman of the Vietnam Veterans Against the War (V.V.A.W.), led by Chicago CPUSA member Abe Feinglass and Ramsey Clark, who would later laud his anti-war foreign policy approach. In the meantime, Kerry would successively support the Castrist Nicaraguan President Daniel Ortega, the Haitian drug lord and Marxist dictatorial President Jean-Bertrand Aristide[363], and later, the Russian-backed and genocidal Syrian President Bashir al-Assad[364]. In 2004, he would oppose the Varela Project, led by Oswaldo Paya against the Castro regime[365]. Simultaneously, he would slap Iayd Allawi, interim prime minister of Iraq, as nothing else than a puppet of the United States[366].

If Kerry thought Allawi was a puppet of the United States, who was he himself a puppet of?

Chuck Hagel was another controversial figure. On February 27, 2013, he had assumed the office of Defense Secretary, replacing Leon Panetta who had largely been MIA during the Benghazi ordeal, except to quickly disavow the Talking Points. Hagel himself was faced with harsh opposition for his advocacy of defense cuts, in the line of Robert Gates[367], and his anti-Israel and pro-Hamas, Hezbollah and Iran views. In a sense, he was not much of a departure from Gates, who repeatedly said that the United States did not get much from Israel in return for the aid it provided her. And much like Gates, he resented the pressure from Saudi Arabia and Israel to suppress the Iranian nuclear initiative, for reasons he never formulated. In the end, Hagel was endorsed by many, and confirmed by the Senate in a contentious filibuster debate[368].

In June 2013, Samantha Power replaced Susan Rice as U.S. Ambassador to the U.N. With no confirmation by the Senate required, i.e. no Benghazi grilling, Susan Rice was appointed National Security Advisor, to succeed Tom Donilan who had resigned for unknown reasons[369].

Then, in August 2013, John Brennan, former Talking Points NSA Deputy, replaced Talking Points Mike Morell as Director of the CIA.

The 2013 deck of cards was not the same than in 2008-2012 but for some reason, our Foreign Policy leaders were following the Russian script. Syria, Iran, OK. Israel, K.S.A.[370], Egypt, not OK. And they certainly were following Susan Rice's National Security "dramatic departure"[371].

Turkey was adding fuel to the fire. Prime Minister Recep Erdogan was playing all sides, keeping in mind the megalomaniac and nostalgic Ottoman Empire words of President Turgut Ozal's,

> "*The next century, the 21st century, will be the century of the Turks*"[372]

and of his successor's, Suleyman Demirel

> *"A Turkic-speaking world from the Adriatic to the Great Wall of China"*[373].

Erdogan's foreign policy was best described as Neo-Ottoman, after the Empire of Suleiman the Magnificent who almost succeeded in conquering Western Europe. Its remnant had been dissolved after the defeat of the Central Powers in WWI. It remained a big player, a country of some eighty million people, secular but eighty percent Muslim, of which three quarters were Sunnis and one quarter Shi'a Alevis[374]. Logistically, it was the sea lock to Russia, with the Black Sea to its North, host to the Black Sea Fleet stationed in Ukraine's Crimea and in Novorossiysk on the Western seaboard of Russia proper. And the gatekeeper of the world's narrowest straits in the Bosporus and the Dardanelles, to the Marmara, Aegean and Mediterranean Seas.

Europeans were not really involved, except through the United Nations. They were economically embroiled in their own growing pains, on and off with the European Collapse scenario[375], and much like Yuri Andropov had predicted[376]. America had changed, for sure. Under Obama's demagogue rule, Republicans were acting as if in puberty. Many real questions, very few practical answers. The major change, from a force projection standpoint, was not where the U.S. was present. It was why she would intervene, and how fast and effective she could be. The new National Security concept was no two wars at the same time, no war without coalition, and no money uselessly spent on Defense. Senator Obama had given the heads-up in his 2004 DNC speech[377]:

> *"Go into the collar counties around Chicago, and people will tell you. They don't want their tax money wasted by a welfare agency or by the Pentagon."*

Tax Money. Since 1999, to pick the year Putin was appointed Vice President by Boris Yeltsin, the United States public finances had greatly deteriorated[378]. The budget deficit had grown from a surplus of 1.3% of GDP to a deficit of 4.1% by year-end 2013[379], and the Federal Debt from $5.8 trillion to $17.1 trillion[380]. For sure, the wars in Iraq and Afghanistan had contributed, and at the end of the Bush Administration, the Debt-to-GDP ratio had gone from 58% to 73%, worrisome but understandable in view of the war on terror and given the 2008 economic and stock market crash. Then, under Obama's tenure, it exploded to 101% by the end of 2013[381].

By many measures, the U.S. was in the weakest financial position it had been in decades, despite a recovering economy. More than never, spending policy had become a political zero-sum game. The country had to choose between what to cut and what not to cut, let alone expand. President Obama, with the support of Pelosi[382], Reid, Gates, Hagel, Clinton, Kerry, Jarrett, Biden, Rice, and Powers, had chosen the European style. Welfare up, Defense down. Were they missing something or were they trying to revision history? Europe had lost its preeminence for the same policies they were now advocating. The Soviet Union had imploded as it tried to live beyond its means on both fronts. Was the New UNanny States, the one calling for "Hope and Change", expecting a different outcome from the same "Experience"?

In the meantime, Russia has replenished its coffers, thanks mainly to its Oil and Gas, and its oligarchs, the Russian equivalent of the much decried U.S. Industrial-Military complex. This was exactly what Aleksandr Dugin had advocated in 1997. In 2011, there were more billionaires in Moscow than in any other city in the world[383].

China had grown in an even more unfathomable fashion. From 1999 to 2013, while Russian GDP had risen from less than $1 trillion to $3 trillion or so, and from some $1,300 to $15,000 on a per capita basis[384], China's went from less than $ 5 trillion to $14 trillion, and from under $1,000 to $8,000 on a per capita basis[385]. If her weakness remained Natural Resources, her strength came from the manufacturing sector, which generated a substantial trade surplus, both with Europe and the U.S. As a result, she was the World's number one creditor, on par with the retired Tiger, Japan[386].

According to the proverb, China was "Sitting atop the mountain and watching the tigers fight". She also was the co-founder of the Shanghai Cooperation Organization, or SCO, and of its predecessor, the Shanghai Five[387]. This was the Who's Who of Eurasia, with the notable exception of Western Europe, the Southern Middle East, and Africa. Not to mention the United States, by definition. In the summit of July 2005, the President of the host country, Kazakhstan's Nursultan Nazarbayev, had summed it up:

> "*The leaders of the states sitting at this negotiation table represent half of humanity.*"

A pretty bold yet accurate statement from the autocrat leader of this strategically important Central Asian country, which also happened to be the world's largest producer of Uranium[388]. Since January 2013, SCO Secretary General was the Russian Dmitry Fedorovich Mezentsev, President of the Centre of Strategic Research in Moscow. In June 2014, the last paragraph of the SCO Mission Statement read as follows:

> "*The SCO member states occupy a territory of around 30 million 189 thousand square kilometers, which makes up three fifths of the Eurasian continent, and have a population of 1.5 billion, which makes up a quarter of the planet's population*[389]."

The key word was Eurasia, as in continent. When asked whether Europe is a continent, nine people out of ten say yes. Same thing about Asia. The fact is, they are not continents, but subcontinents of the Big One, Eurasia. Only Genghis Khan, in the 13th century, came close to conquer it all but to the West, it could not extend past the Arabic Peninsula and what is now known as Western Europe. The question was, who would be the next Gengis Kahn? Russia, China, or the SCO? And what would happen to the Atlantic Alliance...?

Dugin, Primakov, and Brzezinski disagreed on the outcome, but all three had a plan. Team Obama seemingly did not.

In 2014, China's Xi Jinping and Russia's Putin were on the best of terms. On May 21, they signed a $400 billion 30-year gas supply, with Gazprom delivering 1.34 trillion cubic feet of gas annually to China National Petroleum Corporation. Longer term, this may prove to be a double edged sword. Much like in Western Europe, Russia was trying to tie China to its own energy resources. Ukraine was a vivid example of what could go wrong. Xi knew this, but short term came first. And Russia, with its 145 million people, and $2 trillion GDP, had a long way to catch up with China's 1.4 billion population, and $9 trillion GDP.

Putin kept on trying. On May 22, thirty one Chinese were killed and ninety injured in Urumqi, the capital of China's north western Xinjiang region, home to the Islamic Yughur separatists. While Putin's letter of condolence appeared on the website of the Ministry of Foreign Affairs of the PRC[390], there was none from Obama. Only his jester Jay Carney had issued a brief condemnation of the attack[391]. Seemingly, Putin was better at Eurasian diplomacy than the U.S. President, who was exhibiting an acute case of cognitive dissonance. Did he not declare, in November 2009 in Tokyo, that he was America's first Pacific President?

> *"As America's first Pacific President, I promise you that this Pacific nation will strengthen our leadership in this vitally important part of the world.[392]"*

And did he not add, speaking about *"multilateral organizations [that] can advance the security and prosperity of this region,"*

> *"As an Asia Pacific nation, the United States expects to be involved in the discussions that shape the future of this region, and to participate fully in appropriate organizations as they are established and evolve[393],"*

Or maybe he was just keeping a low profile after his March 24 meeting with Xi in The Hague. The Chinese President, on cue with the SCO mantra, had gone to great length to push for the end of U.S. "hegemony". The same website of the PRC Ministry of Foreign Affairs published a long account of the meeting, and quoted Xi as saying:

> "*The Chinese side is willing to work with the U.S. side to always adhere to the right course of establishing a new model of major country relationship and to promote bilateral relations for a constant, sound and stable development. [...] The two sides should adhere to the principles of non-conflict, non-confrontation, mutual respect and win-win cooperation, [...] and effectively manage differences and handle sensitive issues with a more positive attitude and more forceful actions. [...] On the Taiwan issue and Tibet-related issue, the U.S. should abide by its commitment of respecting China's sovereignty and territorial integrity, and no support for activities aimed at splitting China. On the East China issue and the South China Sea issue, the U.S. side should adopt an objective, fair and just attitude, distinguish right from wrong and do more things helpful to promote proper resolutions to the issues and to ease the situation*"[394].

Either way, whatever Russia's plans were, Team Obama was not even trying to disrupt them.

Japan, for itself, once viewed as the emerging contender for world economic supremacy, was not involved either. It was still dealing with the aftermath of its devastating 2011 Fukushima nuclear disaster and, more importantly, its twenty years of deflation and post-WWII syndrome. Thus, while some one hundred thousand American troops and related personnel were still stationed there, flare ups highlighted the precarious nature of the Japanese-American-Chinese relations. In December 2013, when Prime Minister Shinzo Abe paid his respects at the Yasukuni Shrine, the Chinese felt incensed. Not only Japan's wars had been largely of external and imperialistic nature, and incredibly bloody, but some sixteen hundred war criminals who had received some sort of death sentence had been enshrined there, in secret. With its main anti-communist ally in the region in the tank, the United States had to take sides – Japan or China. Dugin had been counting on this as well and, little by little, the animosity between Japan and the U.S. was creeping up, and the relations between Japan and Russia were warming up[395].

In April 2014, a short month after the Xi-Obama meeting in The Hague, the U.S. signed a ten-year military agreement with Philippine President Aquino, the Enhanced Defense Cooperation Agreement, allowing it to use Philippines facilities. First degree, this was the official way to dissuade China from increasing its military presence in the South China Sea.

Second degree, the Philippines had not forgotten December 8, 1941, when Japan invaded it together with Pearl Harbor, destroying much of Luzon, Manila, and then some. The United States was not their favorite Big Brother, but it was the only one they had. This was to remind Japan that the U.S. had other friends in the region.

To the dismay of its Western and Middle Eastern Allies, Obama had botched the much touted "pivot to Asia." He had simply managed to alienate both China and Japan, again leaving the door wide open to Russia, in Asia this time. In a familiar refrain, this was right down Dugin's own Domino Theory. His game plan was simple, and much more ambitious than Primakov's Triangle: the Russia-Germany-Japan-Iran Axis was to topple the United States, Great Britain, China and Turkey. Sooner or later, Russia would annex the Middle East, become the World's Oil and Uranium Kingpin, and the Master of the Route to India. China would have no energy choice but to yield to Russia's blackmail, and the former Axis powers, Japan and Germany, would follow. The Primakov Doctrine on steroids.

Dugin was not alone in his neo-Fascist Ottoman Mongol thinking. In France, his soul mate was Alain de Benoist, leader of the "New

Right." In Belgium, it had been Jean-Francois Thiriart. And in Turkey, Prime Minister Recep Erdogan was lending a very receptive ear to the new Mother Russia strategy. Dugin may have to add it to his Axis, after all.

Putin was following Andropov's script. The deal that Gorbachev and Reagan had made in 1987 was a Russian lure, intended to pause the Cold War which was clearly turning to the Soviet Union's disadvantage at the time. Putin had hit the restart button with Syria and Iran, but needed to distract the world's attention. Anatoliy Golitsyn had it right, this was the sequel to the Perestroika Deception[396].

A year earlier, in 2013, Putin had found his new deception. Ukraine. In his Eurasian strategy, Dugin had labeled it as nothing but a sanitary corridor[397]. Putin pushed its corrupt President Viktor Yanukovych to renege on his commitment to join the European Union, which led to the popular upheaval known as the Euromaidan movement. Yanukovych fled and Putin, "officially" fearing for Russia's naval base in Crimea, annexed it in March 2014. He then turned to the rest of Ukraine, "officially" fearing for the lives of its population of Russian origin, and arming vicious pro-Russian militias to protect it. Within three short months, the fighting was raging, with more than one thousand civilian casualties and three thousand injured in rebel-held territories[398].

Not to minimize the Ukrainian plight, but the deception was working. Putin had achieved two goals. One, to parade his force projection. Two, to divert the world's attention. He was banging on Ukraine's door, and Crimea, the main strategic asset, was a done deal. But the real theater was the Middle East, its oil and access to the rest of Asia. For some reason, Team Obama had suddenly "forgotten" about the Red Lines[399], the two hundred thousand civilian deaths and counting in Syria, the chemical weapons factories, the tsunami of refugees, and Iran's nuclear program. All the timelines "negotiated" with Syria and Iran had expired but the Administration's eyes were now closed – even John Kerry's, who was "negotiating" some more. Joe Biden, with all of his foreign policy experience[400], was once again Missing In Action. Susan Rice had to be the worst – Rwanda, Benghazi, Libya, Ukraine, Crimea, Syria, Iran, Yemen. Etcetera.

In other words, the United States was about to lose the Cold War that never ended. As strange as it seemed, the Man's Administration was abandoning the Truman Doctrine without even putting up a fight. For a flashback, we had to go all the way to Henry Wallace, some eighty years ago.

He had been Franklin Roosevelt's third term Vice President, and, after his death, he stayed on as Harry Truman's Commerce Secretary. A liberal to the extreme left of the Democratic Party, he had turned into a mystic peace activist under the influence of his friend Owen Lattimore. An alleged professor in Chinese Studies at John Hopkins University, Lattimore had been appointed by FDR as advisor to Chiang Kai-Shek. Chiang, while fighting alongside the Allies, had been fighting his own war against communist China for ten years. He did not heed much of Lattimore's soviet-inspired advice. Then, in June 1944, at FDR's request, Wallace and Lattimore visited two Siberian gulag camps in Magadan and Kolyma. Oblivious to reality, Wallace had come back "impressed" with the public relations tour showing the "development" of Siberia and the spirit of the "cities volunteers", which Lattimore described to National Geographic as "strong and well-fed".

Lattimore was later suspected by Joseph McCarthy to be the top Soviet spy in the United States[401]. In the 1948 Presidential Election, Wallace, while running for the left-wing Progressive Party, advocated friendly relations with the Soviet Union and refused to disavow his endorsement by the CPUSA. He was also suspected to have been a KGB agent – in his case, this would have made him a Vice President spy.

Sounds weird? Given Team Obama's trail, and Team Obama's inaction, the parallel was intriguing.

The public, the media, and most scholars had no idea about Russia's Grand Plan. And if they did, they were not talking about it. After all, President Obama's official discourse was replete with sanctions here, sanctions there. This was yet another Red Herring. Beyond his words, he had to know Putin was not a man of sanctions. He was a man of action.

13

Closing In

A year had passed since the Medvedev-Obama mic drop of March 2012, and, in line with the new mantra, the United States was "negotiating". No more pre-emptive strikes. In a fuzzy scheme, everything had to be a coalition, preferably led by NATO or some other friendly entity. The U.S. was negotiating with Syria, which was backed by Iran and Russia. The U.S. was negotiating with Iran, which was also backed by Russia, with Iran turning a blind eye to its atheist regime, and a good ear to the Russo-Islamic Alliance. And the U.S. was hopelessly negotiating with Turkey, Iraq, Afghanistan and Pakistan.

The word "lead" has two homographs. Pronounced "leed", it described John Kerry well, as in lead negotiator and mundane dance partner. Pronounced "led," as in the heaviest of common metals, it was even more fitting. Barack Obama, John Kerry, Susan Rice, Samantha Power, John Brennan, and MIA "Joe" Robinette Biden were sinking deeper by the day.

Russia, to further cajole Iran, had invited it into the Shanghai Cooperation Organization in 2006. Officially, their relationship was about each other's oil and gas. In 2013, Turkey was allowed to join as well, as a "Dialogue Partner". Her bargaining chip was the Black Sea and the Turkish Straits. In 2005, Erdogan, then Prime Minister, had applied for membership into the European Union, but Europe was reluctant to include the Muslim Ottoman leader. Frustrated, he had asked Putin for full membership in his own competing private club. Not only this flew in the face of NATO, but it was a concession to his former rival in the conquest of Central Asia. And it strangely resembled the Yanukovych scenario in Ukraine. In the process, Erdogan severed its former economic, military and diplomatic ties with Israel, and strengthened its anti-Israel, pro- Muslim Brotherhood and pro-Hamas rhetoric.

In short, the U.S. was negotiating with its enemies, to the detriment of its allies, the House of Saud, Egypt, the Kurds, and Israel.

What was worse, negotiating with Syria while Bashar al-Assad was killing his own people, or with Iran which was working on its nuclear weapons program? From a humanitarian standpoint, Syria had to come first. The war had started in the Arab Spring of 2011. By most 2014 estimates, two hundred thousand civilians had been killed, and millions had been displaced. Much like Gaddafi and Saddam Hussein before him, both backed by Russia, al-Assad would resort to any means in order to maintain his power.

Iran was a close second. Soon it would possess forbidden weapons of even larger mass destruction. It did not matter that al-Assad was a Shi'a Alawite[402], or that the Ayatollahs were radical Shi'a Islamists. Russia was their Big Brother too.

It would be simple to leave it at that, but there were three other main Sunni protagonists in the Iraq-Syria theater - the Muslim Brotherhood, al-Qaeda in Iraq (AQI), and Jabhat al-Nusra in Syria. To complicate matters, AQI changed its name to ISI, then to ISIS/ISIL, al-Nusra switched allegiance from ISI to al-Qaeda, and each was fighting for its own turf in the Grand Caliphate Game.

Interestingly, no mention of the Free Syrian Army here. Originally, it was the main armed group opposing the Assad regime, so much so that, in April 2013, the United States had picked General Salim Idriss, its then commander, as the conduit to funnel $123 million in non-lethal aid to the various rebelling factions. Saudi Arabia had decided to do the same for combat aid[403]. However, it had the backing of al-Nusra. While Idriss and John Kerry were confident that this did not matter, by mid-2013, lacking arms and money, the FSA was morphing into it[404]. We were de facto arming an al-Qaeda surrogate. In December, the U.S. suspended the aid, and Idriss was fired in February 2014[405].

It was a very crowded war theater. The Sunni jihadists were Salafi, but some were more Salafi than others. The term refers to the *Salaf*, which describes the first generations of Muhammad's followers, presumed to practice Islam in its purest way. Here is a first distinction. Wahhabism is Salafism but follows the teachings of Muhammad ibn Abd al-Wahhab, a 18th century scholar. As such, it is the official religion of Saudi Arabia and other Salafis do not necessarily agree. For them, al-Wahhab was too remote from the original Salaf to be considered pure. This explains why Saudi Arabia is often at war with traditional Salafi jihadists.

Which is a second distinction. The Salafi jihadists are the extremists, as opposed to the "good" Salafis, and some are more extremists than others. Lastly, while all Salafis are ultimately looking to establish a transnational caliphate, their individual strategy differ. Without getting into details, the Muslim Brotherhood acts as if it respects the nation-states; al-Qaeda, the head office, is after the U.S., the "far enemy" abroad; and AQI is after the "near enemy," i.e. the local apostates. And each have their own ultimate caliphate objective.

Now that we are clear on this, let us go back to the Iraqi and Syrian theaters. The Muslim Brotherhood was created in 1928 in Egypt, and expanded over time into several countries, including the United States[406]. Under cover of Dawah, the Islamic term for volunteer social services, it recruits and finances scores of terrorist organizations[407]. All through the Arab Spring, it fomented chaos, from Tunisia to Egypt to Syria, with one very simple and practical purpose in mind. The worse the chaos, the larger the power vacuum. The larger the vacuum, the easier the Brotherhood would fill it with its Salafi cohorts, led by Hamas in Gaza and the Palestinian Islamic Jihad.

In Syria, where it had a strong presence since the end of the French mandate in the mid-40's, it had been largely wiped out by Hafez al-Assad in the Hama massacre of 1982[408]. The Alawites had always been fearful of the Salafis who were trying to destabilize their regime, and the Ba'ath Party had zero tolerance for dissent. The Arab Spring was the Syrian Brotherhood's chance to try its hand again, under the leadership of Riad al-Shaqfa, and it was at the forefront of the civil war, hidden behind a myriad of front groups: the National Union of Free Syria Students, the Levant Ulema League, the Independent Islamic Democratic Current, the Syrian Ulema League, the Revolution Council for Aleppo and its Countryside, and so on. In November 2012, they tried to make it simpler by regrouping as the National Coalition for Syrian Revolutionary and Opposition Forces, known as the Syrian National Coalition, or SNC, but it soon splintered into smaller groups, again[409]. A mess indeed.

In Iraq, it was operating as the Iraqi Islamic Party since the early 60's. Much like in Syria, it had been repressed forever and banned by Saddam Hussein. His side of the secular Ba'ath Party had less than zero tolerance. With Saddam gone, it had revived to become the largest Sunni political party in Iraq. When the Shi'a Nouri al-Maliki came to power in 2006, it had a double ax to grind.

But it had to contend with "al-Qaeda in Iraq", or AQI. In 2003, Abu Musab al-Zarqawi, a Jordanian who ran a training camp in Afghanistan, had created his own Iraqi jihadist group, Jamaat al-Tawheed wa al-Jihad[410]. Bin Laden was looking for a local affiliate for al-Qaeda and ended up convincing Zarqawi. In 2004, Jamaat al-Tawheed became al-Qaeda in Iraq. Compared to the Muslim Brotherhood, al-Qaeda was bad. Compared to al-Qaeda, Zarqawi was worse. Whereas al-Qaeda's target was the "far enemy," Zarqawi's was the "near enemy," all the local apostates, non-compliant Sunnis, Kurds, Yazidis, and all Dhimmis[411]. Nevertheless, for a while, he had a certain appeal for the tribal Sunni leaders. Al-Qaeda, after all, was Sunni, and they were threatened by the Iraqi Shiite majority. When he was killed in 2006, Abu Ayyub al-Masri took his place, and in October, renamed the group the Islamic State in Iraq, or ISI, with Abu Omar al-Baghdadi as its leader. By then, the local sheikhs in Ramadi, the capital of the largely Sunni Anbar province where AQI had found safe harbor, had had it with al-Zarqawi's methods and were no longer going to cope with ISI. To most, public beheadings, rapes, and other atrocities were simply viewed as Muslims killing Muslims. They decided to cooperate with the coalition but needed more troops to clean up the area. President Bush sent an additional twenty thousand, despite political opposition at home, in what was called the Surge. It worked and by early 2007, the local tribes had regained control of Ramadi. This had dire consequences for ISI. Anbar was on the border of Syria, Jordan, and Saudi Arabia, and the largest province in Iraq, an essential logistical hub. In April 2010, both Abu's were killed, Ayyub al-Masri and Omar al-Baghdadi.

2010 was a bad year for al-Qaeda in Iraq, and President Obama liked that. He could now safely bring our troops home.

2011 was an even worse year for al-Qaeda, the head office in Pakistan. On May 2, Osama bin Laden was located and killed by Seal Team Six. President Obama's first term was shaping up pretty well. He had defeated al-Qaeda and fulfilled his campaign promise to withdraw from Iraq.

Withdraw from Iraq? This was the moment every Salafi jihadist had been waiting for, and Team Obama had telegraphed the timeline. ISI's new leader, Abu Bakr al-Baghdadi (not to be confused with Abu Omar al-Baghdadi who had recently been killed) bore the name of the first caliph of the first caliphate, the Rashidun Caliphate. Abu Bakr, kunya[412] for Abd Allah, was (one of) Muhammad's father-in-law. Coincidence, probably not. Al-Baghdadi's birth name was Ibrahim ibn Awwad ibn Ibrahim ibn Ali ibn Muhammad al-Badri al-Samarrai[413], Abu Bakr was clearly a stretch. In March 2011, when most of the last U.S. troops had been brought home, the Arab Spring sprung, and the Syrian civil war started.

In January 2012, Abu Bakr dispatched his deputy, Abu Muhammad al-Jawlani, to Syria, to establish the Syrian branch of ISI, known as Jabhat al-Nusra. However, ISI was the former al-Qaeda in Iraq, or AQI, and al-Jawlani seemed to prefer his al-Qaeda's ideology. As mentioned earlier, on the extremist scale, al-Qaeda was less bad than ISI, and because more international, more tolerant of other Salafi groups and of the local Muslim population. ISI, to the contrary, was indiscriminate in its killings and targeted every apostate. In April 2013, Abu Bakr tried to pressure al-Jawlani by moving from Iraq to Syria, and declared a fusion between al-Nusra and ISI, to be called the Islamic State in Iraq and Syria, or ISIS (alternatively ISIL, with an L for Levant, or DAESH). Al-Jawlani did not bow and instead, pledged allegiance to al-Qaeda. Ayman al-Zawahiri, the al-Qaeda's Supreme Leader who had taken over after bin Laden, obviously decided in al-Jawlani's favor, and went as far as declaring ISI deviant from al-Qaeda. That did not go too well with al-Baghdadi. In August, ISIS started attacking the other Salafi groups, in Raqqa and Aleppo, including Jabhat al-Nusra, now officially al-Qaeda in Syria. By January 2014, it had taken Raqqa over, declared it the capital of the ISIS caliphate, with al-Baghdadi as Caliph Ibrahim. The next month, al-Qaeda officially severed all ties with ISIS.

That was in Syria. Meanwhile, in Iraq, al-Baghdadi's ISIS, the deviant son of al-Qaeda, was in full swing and had taken back Fallujah, Ramadi and Heet in January 2014. Next would be Tikrit, Saddam Hussein's birthplace, and the all-important town of Mosul, in June. The second largest city in Iraq, it was its industrial hub by reason of the proximity to the Kirkuk oil fields, and controlled the essential Mosul Dam on the Tigris River. There, al-Baghdadi re-affirmed the new Caliphate as simply the Islamic State, or IS, from the Iraqi Kurdistan Diyala province to Syria's Aleppo. All in all, at the end of 2014, IS controlled one-third of Iraq and one-third of Syria, and some nine million people. In the process, while the Peshmerga had saved Kirkuk, it did not try to stop the Yazidi genocide, which highlights how sectarian the war theater was.

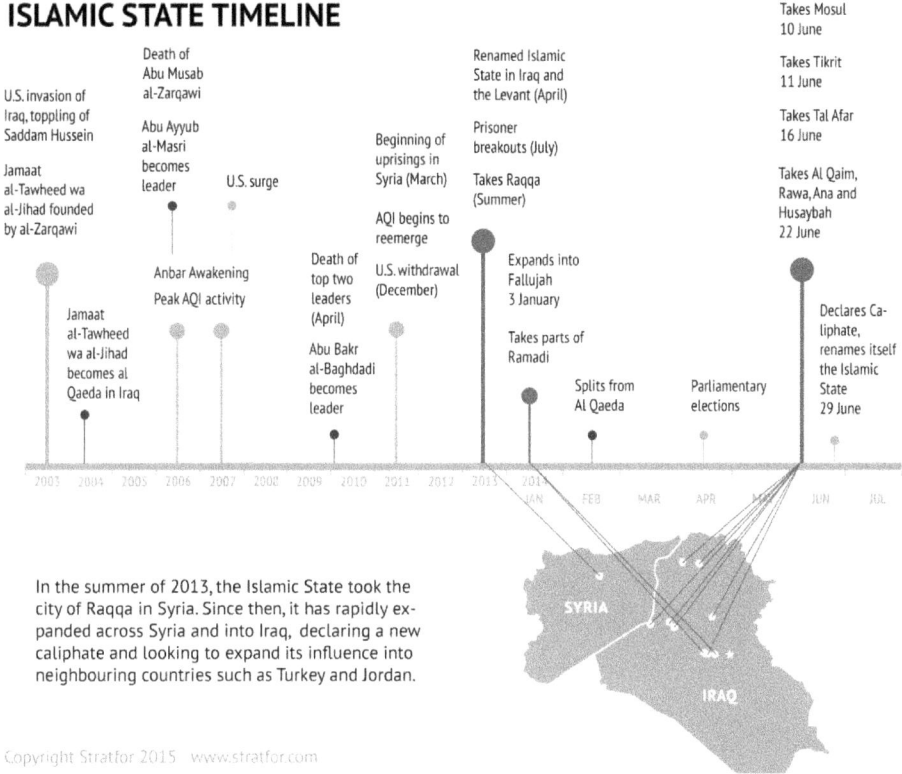

ISLAMIC STATE TIMELINE

Takes Mosul
10 June

Death of
Abu Musab
al-Zarqawi

Renamed Islamic
State in Iraq and
the Levant (April)

Takes Tikrit
11 June

U.S. invasion of
Iraq, toppling of
Saddam Hussein

Abu Ayyub
al-Masri
becomes
leader

U.S. surge

Beginning of
uprisings in
Syria (March)

Prisoner
breakouts (July)

Takes Tal Afar
16 June

Jamaat
al-Tawheed wa
al-Jihad founded
by al-Zarqawi

Takes Raqqa
(Summer)

Takes Al Qaim,
Rawa, Ana and
Husaybah
22 June

AQI begins to
reemerge

Anbar Awakening

Death of
top two
leaders
(April)

U.S. withdrawal
(December)

Expands into
Fallujah
3 January

Declares Ca-
liphate,
renames itself
the Islamic
State
29 June

Jamaat
al-Tawheed
wa al-Jihad
becomes al
Qaeda in Iraq

Peak AQI activity

Takes parts of
Ramadi

Abu Bakr
al-Baghdadi
becomes
leader

Splits from
Al Qaeda

Parliamentary
elections

2003 2004 2005 2006 2007 2008 2009 2010 2011 2012 2013 2014

JAN FEB MAR APR MAY JUN JUL

In the summer of 2013, the Islamic State took the city of Raqqa in Syria. Since then, it has rapidly expanded across Syria and into Iraq, declaring a new caliphate and looking to expand its influence into neighbouring countries such as Turkey and Jordan.

SYRIA

IRAQ

Figure 9 - Islamic State Timeline – Courtesy of Stratfor Worldview, the geopolitical intelligence firm.

Iraq and Syria: ISIL's Reduced Operating Areas as of April 2015

Islamic State of Iraq and the Levant's (ISIL) frontlines in much of northern and central Iraq have been pushed back since August 2014. ISIL can no longer operate freely in roughly 25 to 30 percent of populated areas of Iraqi territory where it once could. These areas translate into approximately 13,000 to 17,000 square kilometers (or 5,000 to 6,500 square miles). However, because of the dynamic nature of the conflict in Iraq and Syria, this estimate could increase or decrease depending on daily fluctuations in the battle lines. ISIL's area of influence in Syria remains largely unchanged, with its gains in As Suwayda', Damascus Countryside, and Homs Provinces offset by losses in Halab and Al Hasakah Provinces.

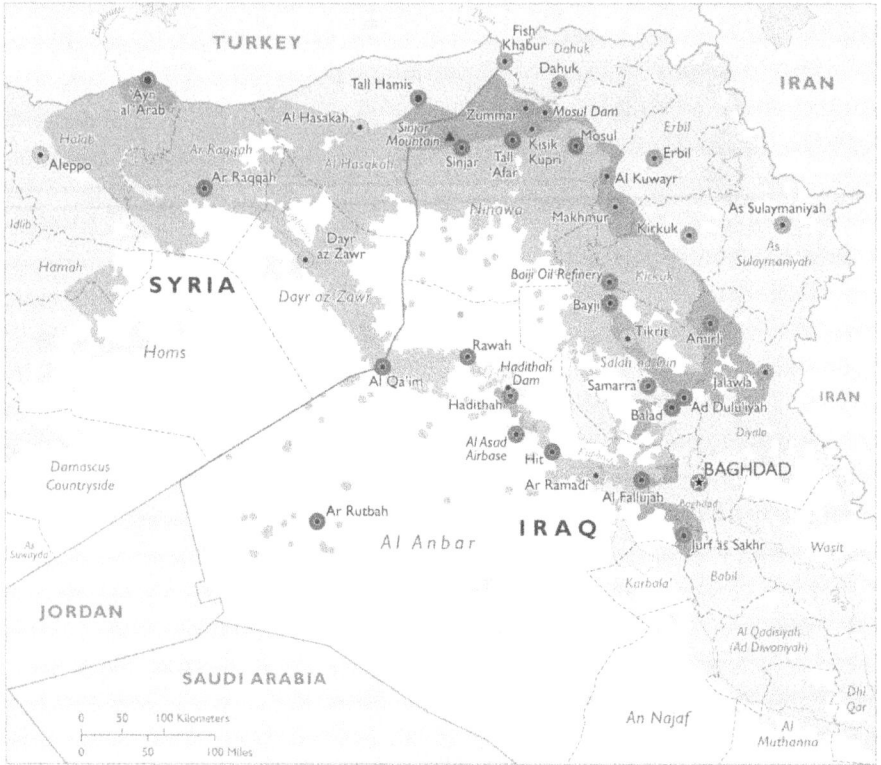

Areas of Influence
- ISIL dominant as of April 2015
- ISIL's territorial losses since August 2014
- Populated area
- Sparsely populated or unpopulated
- --- Administrative boundary

Dominant Group
- ISIL
- Syrian Kurd
- Iraqi Kurdish security forces
- Iraqi Government
- Syrian Government
- Contested city

Note: Our judgment as to which group has dominant influence over a particular city is based on a body of sources that we deem reliable.

Figure 10 - Islamic State - Iraq and Syria – 2014 – April 2015. Source: U.S. Department of Defense.

Things were getting out of hand for al-Maliki, who finally asked for international help. Iranian forces were already covertly in Iraq, but in that June 2014, they made it official. Iran had come to Iraq's rescue. Kata'ib Hezbollah and the Quds Islamic Revolutionary Guards, backed by Russia, avowed enemies of the United States and anything Sunni, were helping the Shi'a Iraqis and the Sunni Peshmerga fend off the bad Sunni Salafis.

In mid-2014, *"Iran had come to Iraq's rescue."* Where was the United States?

To the public at large, Obama had defeated al-Qaeda in 2011, hence Ben Rhodes' memo and the self-serving Benghazi Talking Points[414]. Truth was, he had not, and IS, the new deviant and extreme extremist brand of al-Qaeda, now some fifteen thousand men strong, was filling the vacuum created by his early, unconditional and politically motivated troop withdrawal from Iraq. Not only that, but the Arab Spring, itself a consequence of the 2010 U.S. withdrawal from the Middle East theater, had opened a new front in neighboring Syria, and IS was filling that vacuum as well.

To add insult to injury, there was no more cover from Egypt. In his tantrum response to the ousting of Muslim Brotherhood's Morsi, President Obama had cancelled Operation Bright Star 2013[415], opening the doors to Russia some more.

Team Obama had been in complete denial but had to be consistent. The jihadists had been wiped out of the Middle East in 2011. The Afghan operation would end by December 2014, except for a few thousand troops. No coalition, no boots on the ground for Iraq, we had left in 2010, we were not coming back. It did not matter that the Kirkuk oil fields were threatened, or that Iran could unify Iraq's Shi'a majority, while helping al-Assad maintain his bloody regime.

Until al-Maliki made the call. On June 15, 2014, President Obama whispered a tippy toe order to deploy three hundred Special

Operations advisors, with a clear no-combat troop's caveat, and without giving a name to the operation. By June 30, he had sent a total of eight hundred, mainly in Baghdad. While Russian-backed Iran had no qualms providing weapons to the Peshmerga, to help regain Mosul and its dam and protect Kirkuk, Team Obama was at it again, thinking about it, dropping humanitarian aid, and this time, trying to force al-Maliki out. In itself, this was not be a bad idea but in the meantime, IS was doing inordinate damage. Ultimately, in September-October, an international coalition was formed, which would be called Operation Inherent Resolve. Then everybody was helping the Iraqi Kurds. And by the end of 2014, the U.S. had sent some three thousand no-combat support and training troops. This compared to the twenty thousand President Bush had sent in the 2007 purge, when ISI was not even close to the force IS had become. Iran's President Rouhani could not resist,

> "Had it not been for Iran's timely assistance, many of the Iraqi cities would have fallen to the hands of these vicious terrorists.[…] For us to help the U.S. combat ISIS? Or for them to help us? We've actually been the ones countering terrorism in the region for years.[…] Are Americans afraid of giving casualties on the ground in Iraq? Are they afraid of their soldiers being killed in the fight they claim is against terrorism?"[416]

Russia, of course, loved it. Iran was doing the dirty work to protect her deep strategic interest in the launch pad to the Arabian oil and its sea, and did not want to be disrupted by the Brotherhood or any other Salafi jihadists. Been there done that in Afghanistan, she also remembered her own problems in the Caucasus during its two wars with the hardcore Chechen Islamist rebels. In all cases, al-Qaeda and the likes were the issue, but Putin had found a way to deal with them at home. The Russo-Islamic Alliance was a process, and Putin had been working on it for a while.

Figure 11 - Chechnya, Caucasus, and Central Asia. – Courtesy of the University of Texas Libraries, The University of Texas at Austin.

The first Chechen War had started in 1994, under President Yeltsin's watch. It ended in 1995 in a humiliating fashion for the U.S.S.R., with the infamous Buddyonnovsk hospital hostage crisis[417], seventy miles north of Chechnya, and the re-take of the capital Grozny, in 1996, by the senior Chechen Independence leader Aslan Maskhadov. The first "democratically" elected President of the secessionist and unrecognized Chechen Republic of Ichkeria, Dzhokhar Dudayev, was killed that same year and Maskhadov was elected President in 1997.

This did not improve matters. In 1998, Grozny declared a state of emergency due to political violence, a wave of kidnapping, Islamist terrorism fighting an Islamic unrecognized government, and the emergence of a corrupt system where Russian aid was diverted to various warlords, including the infamous Chechen Mafia.

So the Second Chechen War, brewing since August 1999, officially started in October. Yeltsin was still Russia's President, but Vladimir Putin had just been appointed Prime Minister. It was going to be a different war, even more so when Yeltsin transferred his Presidential powers to Putin on December 31[418]. The difference, simply put, was a stronger Russia and, on the other side, more determined Chechen jihadists, Russia's official target. This led to the gruesome battle of Grozny, from October 1999 to March 2000, which left the capital city in ruins, to be later described by the U.N. as the most destroyed city on Earth. While Russia had re-established its military rule, and Putin had earned himself the telling nickname of "Butcher of Grozny[419]," the violence nevertheless continued.

In a country devastated by war crimes on both sides, some notoriously gross episodes of the times involved civilians. In 2002, The Dubrovka Theater in Moscow was taken over by a leading Chechen Islamist group, the Special Purpose Islamic Regiment. Some forty rebels, with some nine hundred hostages. The Russian Special Forces fumed the theater with an incapacitating substance with turned out to be lethal for some two hundred, including the rebels.

In 2004, worse if there is such a scale, another rebel group took over a school in Beslan, North Ossetia, with eleven hundred hostages, including eight hundred children. Outcome: 331 people dead, including 186 children. In both cases, including the Buddyonnovsk hospital, the terrorist "Emir" Shamil Basayev claimed responsibility in the name of an Islamist Chechnya[420].

To deal with the Chechen jihadists backed by al-Qaeda, without confronting the more tolerable Islamic Sufi separatist movement, Putin went first degree. He simply decided to install a pro-Russian moderate Islamic Sufi President, backed by a local Russian military presence. This was the beginning of Dugin's Russo-Islamic Alliance.

It just so happened that in 1999, such a man, previously militia commander and Chief Mufti of the secessionist Chechen Republic of Ichkeria, had decided to switch sides, and offer his support to the Russian Federal Forces. His name was Akhmad Kadyrov, traditionalist Sufi and staunch anti-Wahhabi[421]. The perfect profile. Naturally, Ichkeria President Maskhadov fired him as Chief Mufti traitor. This did not really bother Kadyrov. When Russia officially took over in 2003, via a "referendum", Putin installed him as President. In 2004, he too was killed by his former associates. Naturally.

His successor, Alu Alkhanov, was also a Russian stooge. Sunni, he promptly suggested that Chechnya be ruled under strict Sharia Law. This was not what Putin and the Sufi population had in mind. In 2007, he brought Alkhanov back to Russia and replaced him with the son of his former foe turned friend, Ramzan Kadyrov, age thirty but already Major General of the Russian Armed Forces, and a recipient of the highest honorary title of Hero of Russia. Somewhat strange for someone whose father was, at some point, a staunch anti-Russian militia commander and Chief Mufti of the rebellion but he was Sufi, and much like his father, not that moderate.

In the meantime, the old separatist guard had been decimated, including former Ichkeria President Maskhadov and rebel leader Shamil Basayev. It sounded like all was calm on the Chechen front. Like in Syria before the Arab Spring.

What you had in Kadyrov was not just the Hero of Russia medalist, it was your run-of-the-mill dictator. He was not hiding his purpose in life: protect Russia, bring down Georgia and Ukraine, kill any jihadist, while at the same time reviving Sufism.

To make sure he was personally protected and feared, he had a five thousand-strong personal guard, the Kadyrovites, composed of his father's former militia when he was on the rebel side. All these mouths had to be fed, and he had his own voracious lifestyle – sports cars, race horses, lavish birthdays, presidential palace[422]. No doubt Uncle Vlad would see to it because short of him or Allah, as Kadyrov once said, he did not have much in terms of personal money. Then again, he did not need a lot. The total Chechen population was a mere 1.3 million and the country's area was a paltry 7,000 square miles, mostly mountains. The size of Hawaii without tourism.

It worked. Within two years, there were officially no more extremists, separatists or jihadists, in Chechnya' streets and mountains.

This was Putin's Russo-Islamic Alliance cornerstone. Officially, Russia no longer was your grandfather's atheist. In Chechnya of all places, previously home to the fiercest anti-Russian Islamist forces, Russia had "proven" it would not only allow but also foster "reasonable" Muslim faith, under Russian law[423]. On one condition, no extremism. Human Rights violations were fine, a bit of Sharia law was a pass, but no Islamists. To Iran, Turkey, Syria, and many in the pan-Arab world, this sounded like a fair mindset. Maybe there was little to fear in a Russo-Islamic Alliance.

And it was real for real, not just in Chechnya. If you did not believe that, in November 2012, the Grand Mufti of Russia, Ravil Gainutdin, confirmed Putin was a friend of Islam and Muslims, actually the best they had in Europe:

> *"While religious freedom is curtailed in Europe, Russia, on the contrary, makes constructive steps to protect believers's rights and feelings. [...] Dozens of mosques, madrasahs, Muslim cultural centers and universities are built an opened in Russia every year."*[424]

This was reminiscent of Hitler's successful efforts to befriend Haj Amin al-Husseini, the Grand Mufti of Jerusalem, president of the Supreme Muslim Council[425], and godfather of the Muslim Brotherhood. A youngster in the Ottoman Army, he was familiar with Germany with whom it had sided during WWI. As a pan-Arab Muslim, he violently opposed Zionism and fathered the concept of a "Judenrein," "clean of Jews," Palestinian State as early as 1933. Music to Hitler's ears, al-Husseini's opposition to Britain grew stronger as it implemented the Balfour Declaration[426]. He had been indicted by the British in 1937 for leading the latest years of revolt but managed to flee to Lebanon and then to Iraq under the cover of his friend Rashid Ali al-Gaylani, former Prime Minister and head of the anti-British Party of National Brotherhood.

Al-Husseini ended up in Berlin in 1941 and his support of the Nazi war effort was unwavering. The Third Reich, realizing his importance in the Muslim world, paid him a fortune of fifty thousand Reichsmarks a month to exhort nationalist Arabs, through Radio Berlin, to kill all Jews and their Palestinian sympathizers. This was the equivalent of twenty thousand dollars a month, in 1941 dollars[427]. He also convinced some twenty thousand Muslims to enlist in the S.S. divisions. And, last but not least, he almost succeeded in giving Hitler what he needed the most: the Kingdom of Iraq, its oil, and access to the Arabian Sea.

If this sounds familiar, it is because history repeats itself. In WWII, Aryans had nothing to do with Arabs, but they had compatible goals. Hitler wanted a New World Order, all the way to Asia. Al-Husseini wanted a pan-Arab world, British free and Judenrein. In 2009, Russians were atheists and disliked Muslims. But Putin also wanted a New World Order, Eurasia, and Iran wanted a pan-Arab world, American free and Judenrein. The enemy of your enemy was your friend, as always.

14

The Beginning Of The End

Logistically, Russia's only naval anchor in the Mediterranean was located in the Syrian port of Tartus, where the material and technical support facility for its Black Sea Fleet was stationed. To understand its strategic importance, a map was worth a thousand words. Tartus was just across from the island of Cyprus, and seventy percent of Russia's Black Sea Fleet was based in Crimea. Not to mention the newer Russian port of Novorossiysk, less than two hundred miles south of Chechnya, where the latest stealth Project 636.3 submarine, the Kolpino, would soon be delivered.

To get to the Mediterranean, presumably to fend off any conflict against either Syria or Iran, or worse, make a run at the Suez Canal, the Russian fleet had to go through the narrowest straights in the world, the Turkish Bosporus, Sea of Marmara, and Dardanelles, and the Aegean Sea. In case of active conflict, it simply could not go back and forth to the Black Sea. Hence the importance of Tartus.

Figure 12 - The Black Sea to the Mediterranean. – Courtesy University of Texas Libraries, The University of Texas at Austin.

So Russia was backing the Assad regime, not only on the ground, but also at the U.N. Security Council where, as Permanent Member, it would veto any sanction against it. To Putin, the Butcher of Grozny[428], al-Assad was to Syria what Kadyrov was to Chechnya.

And Team Obama, despite its new policy of humanitarian intervention was still dancing around the no coalition–no intervention–no two wars at a time rhetoric.

On the Russian side was Foreign Minister Sergei Lavrov, assisted by the largely ineffective U.N. Ambassador Vitaly Churkin. Kerry was seven years older than Lavrov but for all intents and purposes, of the same generation. At the peak of the Viet Nam war, they were on the same side. They were now officially posturing across from each other.

U.S. policy, which had produced no tangible results except for a pinky promise that al-Assad would somehow destroy his chemical weapons by June 2014[429], was slowly being replaced by a bluff so secret that it was all over the media. Kerry and Power were threatening increased military intervention, the key word being threat. A U.N. Security Council Resolution had been signed in September 2013, after al-Assad's chemical weapons killed some fifteen hundred civilians, mostly children, in August in Damascus. A year earlier, President Obama had warned this would be a red line, but had done nothing to enforce it, i.e. retaliate. Now that the 2014 mid-term elections were on deck, with the Benghazi affair alive and disrupting, Team Obama had to find a new offense-is-the-best-defense strategy.

The problem was, the world knew that the offense threat was empty. The Chairman of the Joint Chiefs of Staff, General Martin Dempsey, opposed any intervention for fear of another entangled conflict, a leakage of chemical weapons from Syria to Iran, and to terrorists above and underground. The same went for Defense Secretary Chuck Hagel, even though he was perfectly aware of the situation, if nothing else as chairman of the Atlantic Council. They both felt a military operation was risky, as if any intervention, whether humanitarian or of pre-emptive nature, never was.

But Chuck Hagel, of all people, should have known better. The Atlantic Council was at the core of Atlanticism:

> "Within a few years of the signing of the North Atlantic Treaty in 1949, voluntary organizations emerged in the member countries of the Alliance [...]. In 1961, former Secretaries of State Dean Acheson and Christian Herter, with Will Clayton, William Foster, Theodore Achilles and other distinguished Americans, recommended the consolidation of the U.S. citizens groups supporting the Atlantic Alliance into the Atlantic Council of the United States."[430]

How could he stay silent while Russia was not-so-quietly encircling the Arabian Peninsula, with the stated objective, at least in its upper military circles, to control access to the Arabian Sea, and from there, the whole of Eurasia?

This moronic dialogue between a fake hawkish State Department and a dovish Pentagon, a decisive change indeed from the years before Obama took office, had but one outcome. The Syrian civilian population continued to be killed by all sides, be it by al-Assad, al-Nusra, IS, the Muslim Brotherhood, Hezbollah, et al, with Iran and Russia pulling the strings[431].

Exasperated, the United States Ambassador to Syria, Robert S. Ford, resigned in February 2014:

> *"In February, I resigned as the American Ambassador to Syria, after thirty years of foreign service in Africa and the Middle East. As the situation in Syria deteriorated, I found it ever harder to justify our policy. It was time for me to leave"*[432].

For the same reason, the U.N. Arab League envoy for Syria, Senior Diplomat Lakhmar Brahimi, resigned in May 2014[433].

In August 2014, faced with the same IS quagmire in Iraq, al-Malaki was asked to resign.

Saudi Arabia's frustration with Team Obama's indifference was growing loud. In this dire strengthening of IS transnational Caliphate, the Kingdom was observing the affirmation of America's loss of power in the region, and its zero-sum game consequence, the unchecked expansion of Russia's threatening influence. This was not unnoticed in other Islamist countries. Libya post-Benghazi was just one example. It looked like the U.S. was more fearful of Russia than of doing the right thing, and preferred to watch than to act, Rouhani's motto. What had happened to Susan Rice's memories of Rwanda? How about her talk and no action in Darfur? No remorse? Ambassador Ford and U.N. Arab League Brahimi had vocally resigned, but Samantha Power, the champion of humanitarian-based military intervention, who once advocated pro-Palestinian U.S. intervention against Israel[434], was only venting, if that much.

Egypt took firm action. It was led by its Army whose mandate had long been to protect its borders and its secular regime. Its economy, while recovering after the Morsi year, was still in disrepair. When confronted with extremism, been there done that, it did not blink. On March 4, 2014, a few months after it had banned the Muslim Brotherhood, it banned Hamas. This also meant it would keep a close eye on its twelve kilometers border with Gaza, and on the arms traffic from Iran via Sudan and through the Sinai to Hamas.

On March 24, 2014, in the largest official capital punishment case on record, an Egyptian court sentenced to death five hundred and twenty nine members of the Brotherhood, including Mohamed Badie, its Supreme Guide. This followed the jailing of some sixteen thousand Morsi supporters since he had been overthrown. The "deep concern" expressed by President Obama after Morsi's ouster, was again repeated, this time by Marie Harf, the Deputy State Department spokeswoman, who said that the United States was

> "*deeply concerned, and I would say pretty shocked*" about the mass death sentences. Adding that "*it's an important relationship [that we] don't want to completely cut off*[435]".

"*Completely cut off.*" What did Marie Harf mean by that? Was she threatening a break in relations between the United States and Egypt, and Saudi Arabia with it? Didn't she make the connection between Hamas, the terrorist organization, and the Brotherhood, the other terrorist organization, the Mother of them all?

Hamas, the Arabic acronym for Islamic Resistance Movement, was the name the Muslim Brotherhood took in Gaza in 1987. It had been ruling the Gaza strip since 2007, a concession wrought in violent clashes against Mahmoud Abbas' Fatah. Fatah was historically the leading political faction of the Palestine Liberation Organization (PLO), and included a jihadist military wing of some eight thousand, the al-Aqsa Martyrs Brigade "freedom" fighters. Upon the death of its founder Yasser Arafat, Mahmoud Abbas, a.k.a. Abu Mazen[436], became its leader, and was elected Chairman of the PLO-controlled Palestinian National Authority (PNA or PA)[437] in 2005.

In the 2006 PNA Parliamentary elections, Fatah lost to Hamas but refused to concede power. A civil war ensued and Hamas, self-proclaiming its rule over Gaza, appointed Ismail Haniyeh as "Prime Minister" of the PNA. Mahmoud Abbas' Fatah, relegated to control of the Palestinian Territories' West Bank[438], appointed its own Salam Fayyad instead. Because of continued infighting, the new elections planned for 2010 were not held. As a result, Hamas no longer recognized Abbas as PNA President. In addition, while the PLO had recognized Israel in 1993, and vice versa, Hamas had vowed to never do so. To the contrary, its charter[439] called for her destruction.

When Fatah and Hamas kind of reconciled on April 23, 2014, a few weeks after Egypt had banned Hamas and the Brotherhood, the news was therefore of some importance. Saudi Arabia, for itself, had designated the Brotherhood a terrorist organization on March 7, a statement of extreme significance.

The fate of the newly renamed State of Palestine[440] became even less clear after Abdel Fattah al-Sisi, the Egyptian former Defense Minister and Commander-in-Chief of the Armed Forces, won the May 28, 2014 election. Al-Sisi had previously declared, during his campaign, that he would "finish off"[441] the Muslim Brotherhood. In a turnout of 48%, he had been elected with a 97% landslide of 24 million votes, almost double what Mohamed Morsi, the Brotherhood candidate, had collected two years earlier.

President al-Sisi was clearly determined to combat terrorism, and, like Israel, he too was on the frontline. The statement from the White House Press Secretary was weird, and certainly not as emphatic as when Morsi was elected. Although protocolary, President Obama was still not getting the message about the Brotherhood and Hamas, as strange as it seemed, and was uncannily telling his counterpart, President al-Sisi, what to do, as if he did not know:

> *"We also share concerns raised by observation groups about the restrictive political environment in which this election took place. We have consistently expressed our concerns about limits on freedom of peaceful assembly, association, and expression and call upon the government to ensure these freedoms as well as due process rights for all Egyptians. As Egypt looks toward parliamentary elections later this year, we urge the government to consider the recommendations of the observer groups on ways to improve the administration of future elections"*[442].

Not only was Obama not getting it, maybe he had forgotten that al-Sisi had been Egypt's spymaster, but neither was his Defense Secretary Chuck Hagel. He may not have read Dugin's "Foundations of Geopolitics," or Brzezinsky's "The Grand Chessboard," but he was literate alright. In 2013, after Morsi's ousting, he had sent General al-Sisi a book by Ron Chernow, *"Washington: A Life."* The message was, General George Washington gave up the Presidency to transition to a civilian authority, please consider. Reportedly, he then asked him

> *"Are you going to be the George Washington or are you going to be the Mubarak of Egypt?"*[443]

Aside from the fact that the United States were staunch supporters of Mubarak until Team Obama decided otherwise, Hagel was basically asking al-Sisi not to run and let the Muslim Brotherhood rule. He must have been dismayed when the Egyptian Supreme Council of the Armed Forces convened in January 2014 to nominate the General for President[444].

Hagel must have been further dismayed when King Abdullah bin Abdulaziz al-Saud, "The Custodian of the Two Holy Mosques" heartily congratulated the new President on June 6:

> *"His Excellency, my brother, President Abdulfattah Al-Sisi, may Allah bless him, the President of the sisterly Arab Republic of Egypt [...] in this day of history and in a new stage of the march of Egypt, a country of true Islam and Arabism, I have the pleasure to congratulate you on the kind confidence bestowed on you by the people who entrusted you to cry their hopes, aspirations and dreams for a better future [...] So I call upon all of you Egypt's brothers and friends to organize a donor conference to assist that country to overcome its economic crisis. [...] At the same time, I call on all brothers and friends to refrain from interfering in the internal affairs of Egypt in any form as tampering the affairs of this country is as a violation of Islam and Arabism and at the same time considered an infringement of the Kingdom of Saudi Arabia. It is a non-bargained and non-negotiable principle under any circumstances."[445]*

And he probably fell of his chair when the Israeli leaders chipped in, with Prime Minister Benjamin Netanyahu and President Shimon Peres calling al-Sisi on June 3, 2014, two days before his inauguration, as widely reported by all sides[446]:

> *"Prime Minister Netanyahu noted to the Egyptian president-elect the strategic importance of ties between the countries and in sustaining the peace accords between them. [...] The Prime Minister wished the Egyptian people a future of stability, prosperity and peace. [...] President Sisi thanked President Peres for his kind words."*

The other one who must have clearly felt unnerved was Turkey's Prime Minister, Recep Tayyip Erdogan. Not only was he a staunch supporter of Hamas, but he also had made the forceful point, in

February 2014, that Turkey would not recognize General al-Sisi if elected President[447]. As Turkey's President Abdullah Gul congratulated al-Sisi, he went on to say

> *"I must be honest, this congratulation to me holds no meaning, because it is not possible to offer congratulations to a coup leader."*

In June 2013, Erdogan had hosted Hamas leaders Khaled Mashaal and Ismail Haniyeh. In October 2013, Erdogan had hosted Mashaal again, despite his country's apparent opposition to Hamas[448]. In November 2013, Egypt downgraded its diplomatic ties with Turkey to the Charge d'Affaire level. The split was now evident. Egypt and Saudi Arabia on one side, Turkey on the other.

To put into perspective this infighting among countries of the same faith, we needed to keep the geographical and sectarian map in mind. Egypt's population was around ninety million, Turkey's was around eighty million, both in large majority Sunni. Geopolitically, they complemented each other. Turkey controlled the Turkish Straits, from the Black Sea to the Mediterranean. Egypt controlled the Suez Canal and the upper portion of the Red Sea to the East. Saudi Arabia's population was only around thirty million, but, size wise, it dwarfed both, and controlled access to the Red Sea to the West, from the Suez Canal to the Arabian Sea via the Strait of Bab el-Mandeb, and to the Persian Gulf and the Arabian Sea to the East via the Strait of Hormuz, not to mention its oil riches. At various times since the Prophet Muhammad, each had vied for a Caliphate, and had one for a while. Only Erdogan was still longing for an encore.

Russia was caught in a Bolshoi-like ballet. Its relationship with Egypt had soured after President Sadat signed the Camp David Accords in 1978, and with Mubarak after that. If anything, however, they had one thing in common. They both banned the Muslim Brotherhood, Russia declaring it a terrorist organization in 2003. In 2012, with the election of Mohammed Morsi, Putin tried to schmooze the ban on the Brotherhood[449]. The threat it posed in the Caucasus had been covered by Kadyrov a few years earlier,

> *"Russia has always been and remains the best partner for Islamic states[450]."*

In 2013, now that Morsi was out, he had to switch into reverse again, and deal with al-Sisi and the upcoming King of Saudi Arabia, Crown Prince, Minister of Defense, and Deputy Prime Minister, Salman bin Abdulaziz Al-Saud.

It looked like Putin and Obama were in the same boat, and Egypt and Saudi Arabia were warming up to Israel.

Putin and Obama in the same boat was enough of a riddle, but the facts were there. Under Obama's watch, Putin had been able to snitch Crimea, and expand his sphere of influence, not only to Iran and Syria, but also to Iraq via Iran. And via Iran, he was also looking at Yemen. In other words, he was now positioned to control both the Straits of Hormuz to the East of the Arabian Peninsula, and the Straits of Bab el Mandeb to the West. The next step would be the Arabian Sea and the Indian Ocean to Eurasia. Why did Obama let this happen is the question, but the fact is, it happened.

Letting things happen may or may not require intent. Making things happen does require intent, especially when dealing with a former foe. There was no if or but, Egypt may have once signed a peace accord with Israel, but there was no love between the two. Saudi Arabia was still boycotting her athletes, among many other less mundane Wahhabi rules. And while Egypt had all the financial support it needed from Saudi Arabia, it did not necessarily agree with the means to tackle the Iranian-Syrian situation. So how did Egypt, K.S.A. and Israel converge to the same side of the fence, literally speaking?

The scenario was not unfamiliar, it was the Truman Doctrine deja vu. The withdrawal of U.S. and coalition troops from Iraq was only three years old but these years had been packed with geopolitical turmoil.

First there was the Arab Spring which led to a surging revival of transnational jihadists, each with their own agenda. In Egypt, this had practically destroyed its economy. More importantly, for sovereign countries like Egypt or the Kingdom of Saudi Arabia, the idea of a group of armed fanatics looking to build the next Caliphate was not acceptable, and they had both banned the Muslim Brotherhood, the mother of them all. As to Israel, none of this jihadism was new to her, and she rightfully made no difference between the Brotherhood and Hamas.

The usual premise followed, the enemy of my enemy etc. The Salafis were all bad, but the Islamic State was the worst, having declared its own Caliphate already – even al-Qaeda worried. This was on the local scene. But foremost, on the global scene, there was Iran and its nuclear endeavors. First degree, the Muslim world was seventy five percent Sunni, and Iran was Shiite. More essentially, Iran was Russia's partner in the Russo-Islamic Alliance, and Russia wanted to take over the Arabic Peninsula.

The United States were caught between a rock and several hard places, with Egypt, Saudi Arabia, the Iraqi Kurds, the Syrian Kurds, and Israel on the anti-Russian side, Pakistan, the Taliban, Turkey, the Brotherhood, al-Qaeda and the Islamic State on the Sunni jihadist side, and Syria, Iran, Lebanon, and Hezbollah on the Shi'a jihadist side.

The Palestinian Authority was a hybrid. Hamas was the name the Brotherhood took in Gaza in 1987. Fatah was supposed to be the old Palestine Liberation Organization. Both were Sunni jihadists, so why would Iran finance them? Most observers had overlooked a simple story, which came to light in 2011[451], later confirmed by several official sources including a book written by its own chairman, back in 1984, *"The Other Side: The Secret Relationship Between Nazism and Zionism"*. Mahmoud Abbas, by virtue of the PhD he received in Moscow in 1982, had had very close ties with the Soviet Union, and the KGB. And Russia was now Iran and Abbas' banker.

In the middle of all this stood Afghanistan, about to be left on its own, and Iraq in unstable equilibrium. Russia was gaining hold. China and India were watching.

Let's rewind. In 2010, Susan Rice, then our U.N. Ambassador and now National Security Advisor, had stated that Obama's new National Security Strategy[452] was a dramatic departure from Bush's 2002. Aside from Climate Change, a hoax exposed by many, there was no change in *"the dangers we face"*. Page 4 of the Strategy report read *"violent extremism and insurgency, and stopping the spread of nuclear weapons"*. Four years later, these sounded like empty words but one thing was for sure, the United States would not fight two wars at the same time, policy, combat readiness and budget oblige. The new motto was "coalition". In mid-2013, it looked like someone had picked up on that word, and Hell was about to freeze over.

15

Spy Freeze

Edward Snowden, a twenty nine year-old American, had served in Iraq, worked for the National Security Agency (NSA), then the CIA, and was now a Booz Allen Hamilton employee contracted to the NSA in Hawaii. Close to ten years in the intelligence business, he had developed an animus against spies[453].

Booz Allen Hamilton, was the largest private consulting and intelligence firm – read spook - in the United States, and in the world for that matter[454]. In May 2013, Snowden flew from Hawaii to Hong Kong, China. There he leaked "some" classified information to Glenn Greenwald, an American lawyer and journalist for the reputable and popular British daily The Guardian, to Laura Poitras, an activist American film maker, and to the Washington Post. Most of the information, it seemed, had to do with the NSA Global Surveillance network, Five Eyes[455], PRISM[456], et al, which included many countries. The network had continued to function despite the fact that Congress, in 2003, had defunded its predecessor, the Terrorism Information Awareness Office. While the exact size of Snowden's intelligence leak was unknown, it was believed to include "some" fifteen thousand files from Australia, sixty thousand from Britain, and close to two million from the United States.

Why Snowden chose Hong Kong is a matter of conjecture. According to The Guardian,

> *"He chose the city because they have a spirited commitment to free speech and the right of political dissent."*

A strange opinion of a territory that had been turned over to repressive China in 1997, even considering the Hong-Kong-is-not-China decorum. From a practical standpoint, opinions aside, it was Chinese territory. As a result, he was quickly coined a traitor, an American spying on his own country for the benefit of another, and the question immediately arose. Was he a double, or even a triple agent, reminiscent of the good old Cold War days? As the plot unraveled, his U.S. passport revoked on June 22, the next day he flew from Hong Kong to Moscow with a temporary Ecuadorian travel document. Why Ecuador? Julian Assange was the answer. President Correa denied issuing the document but his stance was in stark contrast with Snowden' thankful words:

> *"The decisive action of your consul in London, Fidel Narvaez, guaranteed my rights would be protected upon departing Hong Kong – I could never have risked travel without that. Now, as a result, and through the continued support of your government, I remain free and able to publish information that serves the public interest"*[457].

Julian Assange was no mystery, and the Correa mishap showed his power. The WikiLeaks' founder[458] and friend of Consul Narvaez had arranged for Snowden's travel to Hong Kong and Moscow[459], all behind Correa's back. Since 2012, Assange had been confined in the Ecuadorian Embassy in London, under political asylum and facing charges from Sweden and the United States. While Correa revoked Snowden's travel document later in June, he allowed Assange to stay in the Embassy.

Aside from China's Hong Kong, and Russia, the only other countries who volunteered asylum for Snowden were Noriega's Nicaragua,

Maduro's Venezuela, and Morales' Bolivia. Assange was not known for a specific political orientation, but what these countries had in common was the pretty obvious color red[460].

The timeline was intriguing. On June 5, 2013 the leaks were exposed by the Press. On June 7, the Guardian revealed the top secret U.S. Presidential Directive 20[461], a list of countries that were potential targets for cyber-attacks, signed by President Obama in October 2012[462]. On June 8, President Obama was meeting with Xi Jinping in Rancho Mirage, California, mainly to discuss cyber security, to include espionage and the use of electromagnetic pulse technology. The U.S. had repeatedly accused China of cyber-attacks. Snowden's revelations effectively pulled the rug from under Obama, hence the idea that Snowden was working for the Chinese.

Pause here for a moment. If Snowden was a Chinese mole, this would drive a wedge between the United States and China, and Russia would ultimately benefit. But, if Snowden was a Russian mole, ending there in permanent asylum, what would we have? China upset at the United States' surveillance, and Russia holding Obama by something more precious than his ears[463]. Sounded like a win-win for Russia.

Snowden was "stranded" in Hong Kong for a month. After been "stranded" at the Moscow airport for another month, he was granted a one-year asylum by Russia. There was a lot a mole could barf in a "stranded" couple of months – actually in much more than that, as Snowden intended to establish himself in Russia permanently.

Anyone remotely familiar with Spying 101, even if just casually reading the press or watching James Bond movies, knew that Intelligence Agencies, worldwide, spy on their citizens. Illegally? That is another question. Spying on other governments was nothing new either, a truism really. Snowden "discovered" the U.S. was going at it all-out. The twenty nine year-old, who had supposedly been ranting for months to no one's interest, appeared to have suddenly awakened with the urge of going public. But spying was not new news per se.

What was news was that Snowden first went to China via Hong Kong, spoke to the British Guardian and to Poitras, who resided in Berlin, then left for Russia. This was a lot of international bean spilling. Instead, he could have chosen to whistle blow to the United States Congress, Fox News, or any other U.S. news organization for that matter. After all, if two "social liaisons" could take down one of the most respected Four-Star General and Director of the CIA[464], and the to-be NATO Supreme Allied Commander, surely the U.S. media and Congress could have taken care of any abuse by the NSA. Even Attorney General Eric Holder agreed, for once.

There had to be more to Snowden's files than eavesdropping. The Australian Attorney General George Brandis, the British Government Communications Headquarters former director Sir David Omand, and the Pentagon were in shock. The leaks were

> *"the biggest theft of U.S. secrets in history", "the most catastrophic loss to British intelligence ever[465]", and "the most serious attack for Western intelligence since WWII".*

So, first degree, this meant traitor. Second degree, this meant whistleblower. Third degree, this meant blackmail. One private conversation kept coming back to mind, that of President Obama and outgoing President Medvedev in March 2012:

> *"On all these issues, but particularly missile defense, this, this can be solved, but it's important for him to give me space. [...] This is my last election. After my election, I have more flexibility."[466]*

Could it be that, at some point, Obama had made some kind of a deal with Putin? Was Snowden somebody's Faustian conscience? His version was less Machiavellian. He was just a freedom hero, who could not,

> *"in good conscience, allow the U.S. government to destroy privacy, internet freedom and basic liberties for people around*

*the world with this massive surveillance machine they're
secretly building.[467]"*

Call it a coincidence, in mid-2013, President Obama and his
Administration went Radio silence. In Iran, the last minute candidate
of the Moderation and Development Party, Hassan Rouhani, was
elected President in an unexpected landslide[468] skillfully engineered
by Ayatollah Ali Khameini. Not only the Kerry-led talks on Iranian
nuclear disarmament went silent, but Team Obama expressed
a concomitant desire to de-escalate economic pressure on the
country[469]. Benefit, Russia. On July 3, in Egypt, Morsi and the
Muslim Brotherhood were ousted and imprisoned. Obama was
chagrined and cancelled Operation Bright Star. Benefit, Russia. And
in Syria, the Kerry-led deal to dismantle al-Assad chemical weapons
factories also went silent, despite the ongoing genocide and the Red
Line. Benefit, Russia.

There was a fourth "Benefit, Russia," maybe the most important.
The Coalition without which Team Obama would not walk the
dog. Snowden had just revealed that the United States was spying
on its partners, notably Germany, and the rest of the world. Shortly
thereafter, in October 2013, Angela Merkel bitterly complained to
President Obama, directly and via his Ambassador, after it was reported
that her mobile phone was tapped[470]. She was quite unhappy, so much
so that on June 4, 2014, "unexpectedly" but with the support of her
government, Germany's federal prosecutor Harald Range announced:

> *"I informed parliament's legal affairs committee that I have
> started a preliminary investigation over tapping of a mobile
> phone of the chancellor* [by the U.S. National Security
> Agency]"[471].

One month later, Germany asked the CIA Station Chief to leave, after
he had recruited an employee of the German Foreign Intelligence
Service.

Brilliant. By coincidence or by design.

Snowden, at first glance, was just one of these things that happen. But beyond his personal vendetta on the government's dark web, he was actually spreading mistrust, in effect dealing a death blow to any American hope of a coalition. If Germany could not trust the U.S., who else in NATO could?

The United Kingdom, the one staunch ally of the U.S., was also on the suspects' list, spying on foreign leaders and several embassies at the G20 Summit it hosted in 2009. So said The Guardian and Snowden[472].

If there was no trust, how could there be a coalition? No coalition, Russia was walking home free. And when there is no trust, there is doubt. Who else was threatened by Snowden's files? The German newspaper Der Spiegel said the NSA targeted one hundred and twenty world leaders[473]. Mission accomplished, silence was deafening.

Only Prime Minister Netanyahu spoke up, at the United Nations General Assembly on October 1, 2013. Rouhani had been propped up as the game changer for Iran, a moderate, a Green Party supporter, maybe even a pacifist, a welcome reprieve from the belligerent and vociferous Mahmoud Ahmadinejad. The West had a new friend, after all[474], judging Rouhani's book by its cover. Then there were those who had not forgotten his role in buying time with the IAEA when the world first discovered Iran's nuclear program[475]. Netanyahu reminded all of his real resume, and the reasons why he was one of the eight candidates selected by the Guardian Council, among the seven hundred whom had registered. Bibi's list was long, and not pretty[476], but it had no echo in Snowden's silence chamber.

Russia also spoke up, in her own opportunistic way, in Ukraine. A E.U. Summit was in the works for the end of November in Vilnius, Lithuania, to take up the admission of Ukraine. Laws needed to be passed by the Parliament in Kiev, in particular concerning the release from jail of Yulia Tymoshenko. She had been a leader of the Orange Revolution in 2004, which ended with a revote for the Presidency, and the upset of the previous winner, Viktor Yanukovych. A Putin puppet, he was replaced by Viktor Yushchenko, in an election which had attracted international interest. Tymoshenko became his Prime Minister from 2007 until 2010, when Yanukovych finally clinched to power. Naturally, she was then jailed and became a symbol of an independent Ukraine, as well as Human Rights abuse. This was the stumbling block for Ukraine's accession to the E.U. In October, it looked like a deal had been struck with Yanukovych. She would be released and leave to Germany for some medical treatment[477]. But on November 21, Yanukovych's party refused to vote the required bills[478], effectively suspending talks with the E.U., and prompting the pro-E.U. Euromaidan protests[479].

On November 24, 2013, a crowd of several thousand, the largest since the Orange Revolution, gathered on the Independence Square in Kiev to the chant of "Ukraine is Europe." Exactly as Dugin had predicted, a quasi-civil war followed, with pro-Russian separatists backed by nasty Russian paramilitaries.

Not only Tymoshenko was on the list of the world's most powerful women, she also was well known for her role in managing the on-going natural gas crisis between Russia and Ukraine. Yet, neither Obama nor Kerry nor Rice nor Powers nor Nulland budged. Neither did the Europeans, as if Ukraine, the largest of the former Soviet Republic after Russia, with its access to the Black Sea, and its gas mainline to Europe, or Tymoshenko, did not matter.

Silence was deafening, indeed, and on that same day, November 24, 2013, in a strange show of unity in the Snowden context, the United States, France, Germany, Britain, China and Russia, i.e. the United Nations Permanent Security Council plus Germany, a.k.a. P5 +1, agreed to a deal with Iran, and a big deal at that[480]. The Joint Plan of Action, as it was called, included Iran's access to its previously frozen foreign reserves, and a best behavior lifting of sanctions on oil trade, among others, worth some $11 billion in all. In exchange, the group obtained some nebulous promise that Iran would limit its nuclear program for ten years, and that it would intercede with al-Assad and his chemical weapons, deadline mid-2014.

It did not smell right. The Israeli government called it an "historical mistake", and even the moderate Yair Lapid, Israel's Finance Minister, confirmed:

> *"We are not comfortable but this warning needs to be done. We have six months until there is (hopefully) a better agreement. [...] I want to clarify that Israel will not let Iran develop nuclear military capability."*[481]

Saudi Arabia could not agree more. Prince Mohammed bin Nawaf bin Abdulaziz[482] put it clearly:

> *"We are not going to sit idly by and receive a threat there and not think seriously how we can best defend our country and our region."*[483]

John Kerry and President Obama did not seem to care[484], they were happy with yet another save-facing delay which met Russian approval. Iran's Rouhani, for himself, was laughing all the way to the bank. Bad smell, blackmail, it happened. $11 billion[485]. His sixteen years as secretary of the Supreme Security Council were finally paying off.

Foreign Minister Lavrov and President Putin were happy too. The Iran deal had been struck, and Putin, blowing smoke up everybody's map of Eurasia, was toying with Ukraine and took Crimea over in March 2014[486]. Maybe Snowden was just a 29-year old computer geek who did not like spies, but he sure was conveniently eating borscht in Moscow.

With Team Obama thinking about it, Israel was now on her own to combat what was shaping up as the inevitable scenario – her destruction by a Russian-backed nuclear Iran which would ultimately team up with Syria, Lebanon, Iraq and Yemen to go after Saudi Arabia and Egypt. Fortunately, Israel was a formidable war machine, and so was the House of Saud. Egypt, reborn, had its own socio-economic problems to deal with, but was on board.

This was Putin's and Obama's main mistake. They were underestimating the will of a Nation which had no alternative but to survive, Israel, that of a Dynasty which had no option but to maintain its Islamic supremacy and extreme wealth, Saudi Arabia, and that of a Country whose army and people had fought hard to bring it back from the brink, Egypt. All knew their history book, and their essential place in the geopolitical Grand Game of Go.

President Obama, his Secretary of State John Kerry, his Secretary of Defense Chuck Hagel, his Assistant Secretary of European and Eurasian Affairs Victoria Nulland, his National Security Adviser Susan Rice, his Ambassador to the U.N. Samantha Power, his C.I.A. director John Brennan, and their predecessors in the Obama Administrations, all had put their eggs in the same rotten basket. In supporting Morsi's Muslim Brotherhood, they had chosen the wrong side of Sunni Islam. On the Shi'a side, in negotiating with Iran's Ayatollahs, Syria's Bashir al-Assad and Iraq's Nouri al-Maliki, they were paying lip service to the will of their own Client States and of Israel, the U.S. anchor in the Middle East. Under President Obama and his advisers' blind eye, the balance of power in the Middle East was inexorably shifting away from the Truman Doctrine, and in Russia's favor. For some reason.

The other mistake they made was to ignore the Iraqi Kurds. In the autonomous region of Iraqi Kurdistan, KRG President Masoud Barzani, his Peshmerga fighters, with the Kirkuk oil field containing the world's sixth largest reserves, was Israel's unofficial but powerful ally. Mostly Sunni, the six million Iraqi Kurds had a large Christian population and maintained excellent relations with Israel. In the Seventies, they had fought Saddam Hussein who destroyed some six hundred of their villages and displaced some two hundred thousand Kurds. Later, in the Iran-Iraq war of the Eighties, Hussein had waged another genocidal campaign against them, this time killing tens of thousands civilians with chemical weapons[487], and destroying about eighty percent of their five thousand villages. Al-Maliki did not sound much better to them, a Shi'a with strong relations in Damascus and

Tehran, overtones of corruption, and Hezbollah support. Not only that, but when ISIS emerged as the jihadist caliphate by excellence, its fight against al-Maliki extended to all apostate-sembling, certainly the Iraqi Kurds[488]. As expected, Al-Maliki did not lift a finger. Barzani was asking for U.S. assistance, but Obama and his team were still thinking about it, in mid-2014, when Abu Bakr al-Baghadi took over Mosul, and declared the Islamic State Caliphate.

How short sighted could one be? The Iraqi chaos was an overture of choice for the Kurds, they finally had a shot at real independence. The Kurdish Regional Government (KRG) was considered the second safe place after Israel and attracted scores of immigrants of all faiths. More importantly, independence from Iraq could lead to a much larger thirty to forty million people Kurdistan, to include the Iranian Kurds to the East, the Turkish Kurds to the North, the Syrian Kurds to the West, and the overall Kurdish diaspora, despite their differences.

Russia had a long and good relation with the KRG. If reunification was to happen, it would have to choose, Kurdistan and its oil on one hand, Iraq, Iran, Syria and Turkey on the other. Smartly, Iran started to arm the Peshmerga while Team Obama was still thinking.

The United States also had a long and good relationship with the Kurdish people, and should have had no dilemma. Egypt, Saudi Arabia, the UAE and Israel on one side, Russia, Dugin and Snowden on the other. Yet, it missed another real opportunity to create a formidable wedge against Russian interference in the region. A big mistake, indeed.

On May 30, 2014, the White House Press Secretary, Jay "The Jester" Carney, resigned from his post. The official role of the Press Secretary is to inform the Press, and the public at large, of what the President is saying, or thinking. In this case, it was to deflect criticism about what the President was not saying, or thinking. Carney was very good at that[489] so, surely, something must have broken his camel back for him to leave the stage. His boss had just signed an historical "peace" agreement with Iran, yet he was getting flack for it, and for Ukraine, and for Crimea, and for some other blunders. Or maybe Jay knew too much about Russia's intentions– he had been Time's Moscow correspondent in Putin's early days.

He was replaced by Josh Earnest. Aptly named, as President Obama pointed out when appointing him, Josh was nevertheless as good as Carney at fudging, with one major difference. The Press Corps liked him. He had been in Obama's wings in the 2008 campaign, and his Deputy Communications Director since then. His boss at the time was David Axelrod, whom we have spoken at length about, and he had worked for Democratic big wigs such as the unsavory Terry McAuliffe and the odd ball Howard Dean. He also had been Principal Deputy Press Secretary and Jay Carney's Chief of Staff. So there was another major difference between "The Jester" Carney and "Earnest" Earnest. One was a simple journalist, if that much, the other was a Machine official.

This was all President Obama needed, a political mouth piece to help him establish his legacy, as he would be a lame duck after the November 2014 midterm elections. There was a good chance he lose his current majority of 53-47 in the Senate, and probably also see the Republicans maintain control of the House, so the bloom was off the rose. Actually, with approval ratings in the low 40's and disapproval ratings in the mid 50's, the rose was wilting. The list of blunders was long.

In 2011, Operation Fast & Furious, the secret Department of Justice gun-running scheme to identify Mexican drug cartels, was discovered upon the shooting of border patrol agent Brian Terry and ICE Agent Jaime Zapata. In 2012, President Obama had cited executive privilege allowing the Department of Justice to stonewall Congress. As a result, Attorney General Eric Holder, Obama's unwavering faithful, was the first cabinet member ever to be held in contempt of Congress on both felony and civil charges, in a 255-67 vote by the House. In September 2014, under the threat of impeachment[490], Holder finally resigned but continued to serve until his successor, Loretta Lynch, was confirmed in April 2015.

In another blunder, in 2013, the IRS targeting of conservative groups for political purposes was also revealed. Director Lois Lerner repeatedly pleaded the Fifth and was placed on paid administrative leave before retiring in September.

Then there was the failing $1.4 trillion healthcare plan that the President had shoved down Congress' throat in 2010, under the leadership of Nancy Pelosi[491] and Harry Reid. At first, when Healthcare.org was launched in mid-2013, the website simply did not work. Yet, close to $300Mn had been spent to build it. While logic had it that it would be an American top software company who did the job, it was not. It was the Montreal-based CGI Group. After becoming a laughing stock, Human and Health Services Secretary Kathleen Sebellius finally resigned in April 2014. In the meantime, to offset the Welfare budget, the Defense budget had been cut to pre-WWII levels.

Snowden and the NSA were of particular importance to the younger generation. My own computer technician, in his early thirties, insisted that I remove my Skype camera for fear I would be spied on, "like anyone else." And the Benghazi cover-up was still under investigation, with some 58% of Americans believing President Obama, his Administration, and former Secretary Hilary Clinton, were hiding information.

As a likely 2016 Presidential hopeful, Hilary Clinton was not helping Obama's cause either. Her Secretary of State memoirs, "Hard Choices", leaked in May 2014, offered but a poor political denial of her own Benghazi responsibility, which Americans disapproved 50 to 35. A couple of weeks after the book's public release, she was on track to reach some 300,000 copies, far short of the one million copies publisher Simon & Schuster had shipped to bookstores on consignment, and way short of the 1.4 million copies her 2003 First Lady memoir, "Living History", had sold. Needless to say, way short also of the dollar advance she had received from Simon & Schuster, rumored to be some $14 million. This spoke volume to her loss of credibility, from First Lady to Secretary of State, but she did not refund the publisher.

Then came the Veterans Affairs' healthcare scandal, another blow to Obama's government model of running healthcare. In November 2013, a VA secret wait list of prioritized patients was disclosed by the press, as well as the fact that many Veterans may be dying because of delays, all for the sake of performance bonuses. The result was surprisingly quick for an Administration who had relied on denial as its primary defense. It only took VA Secretary General Eric Shinseki six months to resign, on May 30, 2014.

In the meantime, Obama's dealings with the Crimean-Ukrainian and the Israel-Hamas crisis[492] were tanking his ratings on Foreign Policy below 40%, on their way to the mid-30%[493]. Apparently, most people thought he should stop talking and do something else than play golf. Very few knew about the real Game of Go, Russia, Eurasia and the Middle East.

This was the background when White House Press Secretary Jay Carney's decided to resign, on the same day as Secretary Shinseki, without even waiting for President al-Sisi to take office in Egypt, to the chagrin ot the Obama Administration. At least, he would not have to fudge about this one. He had been the Man's faithful Jester but apparently decided he could no longer give the Press the runaround, or worse. Instead, he passed the potato to Josh Earnest, and later took a job at CNN, a natural for a Time magazine veteran[494].

And, as if pressure would not abate, President Obama committed a blunder which came under harsh bipartisan critic, a Washington oddity. The next day, on May 31, 2014, he approved the exchange of Army Sergeant Bowe Bergdahl, held for five years as a prisoner of war by the Taliban, against five key Taliban Commanders held in Guantanamo Bay. The decision caused so much stir in public opinion that a welcome celebration in his hometown of Hailey, Idaho, with a population of only eight thousand, had to be cancelled for fear of protests. There were many reasons for that. One, it was not clear whether or not Sgt. Bergdahl had actually deserted his unit while in Afghanistan. Several of his colleagues thought he did, adding that six of his unit members were killed trying to find him.

Two, the Administration was to give a thirty-day notice to Congress prior to any prisoner's release from Guantanamo. It did not, which prompted Secretary Hagel, in a testimony to Congress on June 11, to say

"We could have done a better job of keeping you informed"[495].

It was later revealed that some ninety people in the Administration knew about the deal beforehand, but not Congress. This may have been another reason why Carney resigned, he had to know.

In the same testimony, Hagel was asked whether the Administration had violated U.S. policy to not negotiate with terrorists, to which he replied he had not, that the negotiations were conducted with the Emirate of Qatar, clearly not what Congress wanted to hear. Qatar was a known supporter of anything extremist, from the Muslim Brotherhood to Hamas to Hezbollah, and home to the news network Al Jazeera, funded by the House of Thani, Qatar's ruling family. It also funded the Libyan Islamic Fighting Group, Al-Nusra, Ansar Dine and the Movement for Unity and Jihad in West Africa, all linked to al-Qaeda, and the extremist Egyptian cleric Yusuf al-Qaradawi, one of the spiritual leaders of the Muslim Brotherhood. Even Chechen President Razman Kadyrov, of all people, thought he was off the wall – he had called Russia "an enemy of Islam":

> *"The Muslims of Russia hope that Qaradawi will once again think about his statement, make a critical assessment of it, and realize the erroneous and destructive character of such statements And – which particularly important – ask himself who would benefit from representing the Islamic world and Russia as standing in contrast to each other. We call on him to do so"*[496].

Suffice it to say, al-Jazeera was the reason why the UAE, Saudi Arabia and Bahrain recalled their ambassadors to Qatar in March 2014. And the U.S. was negotiating with Qatar, not a terrorist country? Clearly, the Bush Doctrine had been flushed down the drain.

Congress, and the public, did not want to hear either that if any of the five released Guantanamo detainees were to go back to lead terrorist operations, more American lives would be put at risk, and that such a deal would naturally encourage more American hostage taking.

To understand the public opinion backlash of what seemed to be, at first, a post mortem Talking Point to the Benghazi fiasco, i.e. "we do not leave anyone behind", a cursory review of the detainees' resume helped[497].

Khair Ulla Said Wali Khairkhwa was directly associated with Bin Laden, a friend of the same tribe as Afghan President Hamid Karzai, and a major opium drug lord.

Mullah Mohammad Fazi was wanted by the United Nations in connection with the massacre of thousands of Afghan Shiites during the Taliban's rule, and assessed as having high intelligence value.

Mullah Norullah Noori was governor of the Balkh province in the Taliban regime, and was assessed high risk and high intelligence value.

Abdul Haq Wassiq was the deputy chief of the Taliban's intelligence regime.

Mohammad Nabi Omari was the Taliban's chief of communications.

According to Senator John McCain, they were "the hardest of the hard-core". Senator Lindsay Graham simply called them a "Taliban Dream Team". Yet, the Man, President Obama himself, had this to say on the day after the exchange:

> "*I make absolutely no apologies for making sure we get a young man back to his parents [...]. We had a prisoner*

of war whose health had deteriorated and [...] we saw an opportunity and we seized it, and I make no apologies for that.[...] I'm never surprised by controversies that are whipped up in Washington [...] We do not leave anybody wearing the American uniform behind".

Naturally, these pseudo Benghazi Talking Points were immediately endorsed by National Security Adviser Susan Rice, who added

"we have a sacred obligation to bring that person back".

These were the same who were watching some movie during the Benghazi attack. And while the Man and Susan Rice's official intent was to reunite Sgt. Bergdahl with his parents, Jani and Bob, he actually refused to do so. Somehow, they had gotten the story wrong but it made for a great photo op in the Rose Garden[498].

Trying to sort it out, once again, a number of things did not make sense. One, it had to have taken more than a few days to get ninety people in the Administration involved.

Two, when Sgt. Bergdahl finally made it home on June 13, after a couple of weeks in the Landstuhl Medical Center in Germany, he was looking in good health – maybe not mentally, but physically. Yet, his release had been "validated" by claims of his rapidly deteriorating health, with YouTube videos "evidence". Had our intelligence failed, or did we blindly trust Qatar, the mediator? Susan Rice and the Man seemingly had no problem either way. Even Nancy Pelosi trusted Qatar's word when it came to jihadists:

"We have to confer with the Qataris, who have told me over and over again that Hamas is a humanitarian organization", prefacing her remarks with a penetrating view of the obvious, *"War is a deadly thing"*[499].

Naturally, al-Jazeera, financed by the ruling al-Thani family, pitched in:

> "*Qatar is a key U.S. ally and was instrumental in completing the deal that gained the May 31 release of army sergeant Bowe Bergdahl, who was held for five years by the Taliban, in exchange for the release by the U.S. of five Taliban commanders imprisoned at Guantanamo Bay, Cuba.*"[500]

Undoubtedly, many must have been surprised to learn that Qatar was a key ally of the United States, even though it maintained a token military base there, in al-Udeid, a legacy of Sadam's invasion of Kuwait in 1990-1991.

Plus, an $11 billion arms deal was in the works, except it was not public knowledge.

An $11 billion arms deal with Qatar, who harbored and financed terrorists groups, where Hamas leader Khaled Mashaal had his primary residence, with whom the UAE, Saudi Arabia and Bahrain had severed diplomatic relations, and who had helped the Muslim Brotherhood and Mohamed Morsi come to power in Egypt? Military base or not, this sounded like a stretch.

Three, didn't we leave men behind in Benghazi? Why the sudden rush, after five years, to "liberate" Sgt. Bergdahl? Certainly, the idea of exchanging these detainees was nothing new. It dated back to 2010, and had been turned down by then Defense Secretary Robert Gates and his successor, Leon Panetta. Could it be that President Obama, and his National Security Advisor, Susan Rice, were trying to spruce back the Administration's image in time for the 2014 midterms, despite the Benghazi scandal? In the Rose Garden, President Obama declared:

> "*an ironclad commitment to bring our Prisoners of War home. That's who we are as Americans.*" A photo op, or a photo farce?

Four, weren't we debating how to squelch the rise of al-Qaeda and its deviant surrogate, IS? How long would it take for this "Dream Team" to surreptitiously leave Qatar and get back to business?

The answers to these four questions were yes, yes, yes, and not long. The commitment was one year, which Taliban Leader Mullah Omar, naturally, chanted in victory:

> *"I extend my heartfelt congratulations to the entire Afghan Muslim nation, all the mujahedeen and to families and relatives of the prisoners for this big victory."*[501]

This is where we were in June 2014, in the Grand Game of Go. Russia was not-so-quietly expanding its Middle East territory, en route to the Arabian Sea and the gates of Asia. It had Crimea to the North, hosting its Black Sea Fleet. It was destabilizing Europe to the West, through Ukraine. It was eyeing Turkey, on the South side of the Black Sea, and its outlet to the Mediterranean. It was consolidating that access point through Syria, and the port of Tartus, sitting right above the Suez Canal in Egypt. Which it threatened, third hand, via Iran which was feeding Hamas in Gaza. And while Egypt was too remote for a frontal challenge, Russia was playing footsie with the countries to the West of the Red Sea - Sudan, its southern genocidal neighbor and arms conduit to Hamas, Eritrea next to it, and Ethiopia and Somalia in the Horn of Africa, on the West side of the Straits of Bab el-Mandeb. Iran, of course, was the piece of resistance. To its West, it controlled the Persian Gulf and the Strait of Hormuz to the Arabian Sea. It also threatened Iraq, ensconced between Syria and Iran. And through its support of the Houthis, it controlled Yemen, on the East side of the Strait of Bab el-Mandeb.

In short, Russia had encircled Saudi Arabia, the United Arab Emirates, Egypt, and Israel, with Iraq still in the balance, and Turkey on the verge. And Kurds were being killed everywhere, dashing any hope of reunification.

This is what Team Obama had allowed to happen. We were now at The Tipping Point of the Atlantic Alliance. One more step by Russia through any of its proxies, most likely Iran, and at some point Turkey, Putin would have succeeded where Stalin had failed, and Hitler before him. Just like Dugin said, and one step beyond what Golitsyn had predicted[502].

But Israel, Saudi Arabia, Egypt, the UAE and the Iraqi Kurds were busy writing the next chapter. This was in mid-2014.

Figure 13 - Eurasia – Source: Getty Images

Maps And Tables

Endnotes

Foreword:

1   The Game of Go, invented in China some 2500 years ago, is a board game for two players in which the aim is to surround more territory than the opponent [Wikipedia]. No computer has ever won against a human.

2   Author of many neo-fascist, neo-Bolshevik, neo-Eurasian political "science" books, most importantly "Foundations of Geopolitics," published in 1997 and only available in Russian, destined for the Russian Military. A useless computer translation is now available on Amazon.

3   Communist Party of the United States.

4   "The Fourth Political Theory," page 193, http://www.4pt.su/

The End:

5   Al Jazeera had started broadcasting in the United States in August 2013.

6   Parchin is a military site subject to specific inspections. "Nuclear Deal Silent on Iran's Parchin Military Plant, Bushehr," The Washington Free Beacon, July 14, 2015, http://freebeacon.com/national-security/nuclear-deal-silent-on-irans-parchin-military-plant-bushehr/

7   "Oil trade off Yemen coast grew by 20% to 4.7 million barrels per day in 2014," U.S. Energy Information Administration, April 23, 2015, https://www.eia.gov/todayinenergy/detail.php?id=20932

Yuri's Trojan Horse:

8   "Ex-KGB Chief Says Andropov Supported Purges," The New York Times, June 15, 1989, http://www.nytimes.com/1989/06/15/world/ex-kgb-chief-says-andropov-supported-purges.html

9   Yuri Andropov was head of the KGB between 1965 and 1982. He became General Secretary of the Communist Party in November 1982 and Chairman of the Presidium of the Supreme Soviet in June 1983 to his death.

[10] Allegedly, in the fall of 1960, Khrushchev took off his shoe and waived it in protestation at the 902nd Plenary Meeting of the UN General Assembly. What is clear, Khrushchev was upset to find out that the Eisenhower Administration had resumed its U-2 spy planes missions.

[11] Ronald Reagan's speech to the National Association of Evangelicals in Orlando, Florida, March 8, 1983, http://chnm.gmu.edu/1989/archive/files/reagan-evil-empire-3-8-83_8727d7fa45.pdf .

[12] It was later revealed that Stasi, the powerful East German Secret Police, had compiled a 9,000-page file on Helmut Kohl, which ultimately led to his resignation as Chairman of the West German Christian Democrat Union (CDU) in 2000.

[13] "Stasi: The Untold Story of the East German Secret Police", by John O. Koehler.

[14] Anatoliy Golitsyn, "The Perestroika Deception", 1995, and "New Lies For Old", 1984.

[15] See Chapter 3.

[16] Full text of "Anatoliy Golitsyn Perestroika Deception, https://archive.org/stream/AnatoliyGolitsyn/Golitsyn-ThePerestroikaDeception-TheWorldsSlideTowardsTheSecondOctoberRevolution1995_djvu.txt

[17] Anatoliy Golitsyn had it right, but failed to see the scope, which he confined to "Europe from the Atlantic to the Urals". The Urals is the mountainous region of eastern Russia which is considered the natural but fictitious boundary between Europe and Asia. Dugin took it all the way to Eurasia.

[18] Russian President Boris Yeltsin's shock resignation speech came in an address on Russian television on 31 December 1999, http://news.bbc.co.uk/2/hi/europe/6584973.stm

[19] "Russia test fires intercontinental missiles", by cctvupload channel, October 12, 2008, YouTube http://youtu.be/uxXAjXKwxjQ

[20] The Nye Committee, named after Republican Senator Nye from North Dakota, was formed in 1934 and held ninety three hearings until 1936. It investigated the relationships between banking interests and what became known as the military-industrial complex, leading to the Neutrality Acts of the late 1930's. Interestingly, the legal assistant was no other than Alger Hiss, later identified by Whittaker Chambers, in 1948, as a Soviet spy. Chambers was himself a reformed member of the USCPA and former Soviet spy.

[21] "Caught on open mike, Obama tells Medvedev he needs "space" on missile defense," The Washington Post, March 26, 2012, https://www.washingtonpost.com/politics/obama-tells-medvedev-solution-on-missile-defense-is-unlikely-before-elections/2012/03/26/gIQASoblbS_story.html?noredirect=on&utm_term=.c5f060c60c3f . See Chapter 12.

22 "The Truman Doctrine," Yale Law School, The Avalon Project, "President Harry S. Truman Address Before a Joint Session of Congress, March 12, 1947, http://avalon.law.yale.edu/20th_century/trudoc.asp

23 U.S.S.R stands for Union of Socialist Soviet Republics. Readers should note that in Soviet ideology, communism and socialism are synonyms.

24 See Chapter 2.

25 Nikita Khrushchev Reference Archive, Speech to the 20th Congress of the Central Committee of the Communist Party of the Soviet Union, February 24-25, 1956," Marxist.org, https://www.marxists.org/archive/khrushchev/1956/02/24.htm

26 "Stalin Denounced by Nikita Khrushchev," History Today, Volume 56, Issue 2, February 2006, https://www.historytoday.com/richard-cavendish/stalin-denounced-nikita-khrushchev

27 Most people do not know how prevalent the communist party was in the U.S. in the 1920-1960 period, even though the word McCartism may ring a bell. Most people today also think the words communism and socialism have different meanings. In the Soviet era, they were one and the same. Hence this walk down memory lane.

28 "Nikita Khrushchev goes to Hollywood," Smithsonian.com, July 2009, https://www.smithsonianmag.com/history/nikita-khrushchev-goes-to-hollywood-30668979/

29 "Belgian Colonial Education Policy," The Ultimate History Project, http://ultimatehistoryproject.com/belgian-congo.html

30 https://www.globaldashboard.org/2011/12/06/how-big-is-the-congo-very-big/

31 Stephen Kinzer, "The Brothers – John Foster Dulles, Allen Dulles, and Their Secret World War", p. 268.

32 See Chapter 4.

33 Allen Dulles was one of the seven members of the Warren Commission, which investigated President Kennedy's assassination. Another sulfurous member of the commission was John McCloy, mostly known as former President of the World Bank. Before that, McCloy was a Cravath lawyer and as such a close friend of the Dulles brothers. He had also been the counsel to I.G. Farben, the German industrial best known as Hitler's war machine, and owner of I.G. Auschwitz. His edifying biography was written by Kai Bird, "The Chairman John McCloy."

34 "Nkrumah and Ghana's independence struggle," Workers World, October 4, 2009, https://www.workers.org/2009/world/nkrumah_1008/

35 Minutes of the Second Congress of Comintern, August 4, 1920. http://www.marxists.org/history/international/comintern/2nd-congress/ch10a.htm

[36] Not to be confused with William Dudley "Big Bill" Haywood, another quite active U.S. Marxist during the early Twentieth century, founding member of the violent Chicago-based Industrial Workers of the World, and sentenced to twenty years under the Espionage Act of 1917. He fled to seek Stalin's asylum in 1921.

[37] www.CPUSA.org

[38] "Harry Haywood Archive," The Marxist Leninist, https://marxistleninist. wordpress.com/harry-haywood-archive/, Marxists Internet Archive, https://www.marxists.org/archive/haywood/index.htm

[39] The Quaker population in Kenya accounts for roughly half of the worldwide total, and double that of the U.S., https://www.friendsjournal. org/new-worldwide-quaker-released/

[40] "Malinowski: Odyssey of an Anthropologist, 1884-1920", by Michael W. Young, 2004.

[41] "Ralph Bunche: An American Odyssey" by Brian Urquhart, 1998, and "Ralph Bunche: Model Negro Or American Other?" by Charles P. Henry.

[42] "Pan-African History: Political Figures from Africa and the Diaspora since 1787", by Hakim Adi and Marika Sherwood.

[43] "Nkrumah and Ghana's independence struggle," Workers World, October 4, 2009, https://www.workers.org/2009/world/nkrumah_1008/

[44] « Letter from W.E.B. Du Bois to Communist Party of the U.S.A., October 1, 1961 », http://credo.library.umass.edu/view/full/mums312-b153-i071

The Red Web:

[45] "Winston Churchill's Iron Curtain Speech, titled "The Sinews of Peace," WinstonChurchill.org, March 5, 1946, https://winstonchurchill.org/ resources/speeches/1946-1963-elder-statesman/the-sinews-of-peace/

[46] Office of Strategic Services, https://www.cia.gov/about-cia/history-of-the-cia

[47] http://en.wikipedia.org/wiki/History_of_Soviet_and_Russian_ espionage_in_the_United_States

[48] So named as they had been recruited by Soviet spy Arnold Deutsch on the campus of Britain's world famed Cambridge University. The International Spy Museum, Washington D.C., "The Cambridge Five" by Thomas Boghardt, http://www.spymuseum.org/education-programs/ spy-resources/background-briefings/the-cambridge-five/

[49] "Kim Philby, Double Agent, Dies," The New York Times 1988 Archives, https://www.nytimes.com/1988/05/12/obituaries/kim-philby-double-agent-dies.html

[50] "Philby of Arabia: St. John Philby," 1973, by Elizabeth Monroe.

[51] Loftus and Aarons, "The Secret War Against The Jews", chapter II and III. Also "The Arab Concession – The World that Frank Holmes

Made," Penn State Department of Earth and Mineral Engineering, https://www.e-education.psu.edu/egee120/node/241

52   The role of al-Husseini is essential to understand these dynamics of the region. Ask me for details.

53   "My Silent War: The Autobiography of a Spy," Kim Philby, written from Moscow in 1967.

54   Stephen Kinzer, "The Brothers", p. 99.

55   See Chapter 2.

56   Seabee comes from the initials CB, for Construction Battalions.

57   OSS – Office of Strategic Services, which morphed into the CIA in 1947.

58   Wisner was later diagnosed with psychotic mania and committed suicide at age fifty six.

59   Walter Isaacson and Evan Thomas, "The Wise Men: Six Friends and the World They Made"

60   U.S. Department of State, Office of the Historian, document 292, https://history.state.gov/historicaldocuments/frus1945-50Intel/d292

61   "Obituary: Mary Bancroft" by Godfrey Hodgson, 2/17, 1997, http://www.independent.co.uk/news/people/obituary-mary-bancroft-1279184.html

62   According to McCloy's biography by Kai Bird, Lew Douglas had this to say about Morgenthau: "*The Administration has lost real ability in Acheson… and has acquired stupidity and Hebraic arrogance and conceit in [Secretary of Treasury Henry] Morgenthau.*""The Chairman," p. 100.

63   The NKVD was the abbreviation for the People's Commissariat for Internal Affairs, i.e. the interior ministry of the Soviet Union.

64   "Witness", by Whittaker Chambers, 1952.

65   "The Case against Harry Dexter White: Still Not Proven", IMF Working Paper from the Secretary's Department, prepared by James M. Boughton, August 2000, http://www.imf.org/external/pubs/ft/wp/2000/wp00149.pdf

66   "Bush/Nazi Link Continued," The New Hampshire Gazette, Vol. 248, No. 3, November 7, 2003, http://www.nhgazette.com/the-bushnazi-stories/bushnazi-link-continued/

67   "Phillips Nuremberg Trials Collection: Trial 5 – Flick Case," Alexander Campbell King Law Library, University of Georgia, http://libguides.law.uga.edu/c.php?g=177170&p=1164752

68   "Auschwitz: 60 Year Anniversary – the Role of IG Farben-Bayer," Alliance for Human Research Foundation, January 27, 2005, http://ahrp.org/auschwitz60-year-anniversary-the-role-of-ig-farben-bayer/

69   Kai Bird, "The Chairman," p. 320.

70   Ibid, p. 365.

71   CIA archives, "Nazi War Crimes Disclosure Act", declassified in 2001, http://www2.gwu.edu/~nsarchiv/NSAEBB/NSAEBB138/CIA%20 Information%20Act%20-%20Reinhard%20Gehlen.pdf

72   Glenn Yeadon, "The Nazi Hydra in America" Suppressed Story of a Century", "The Gehlen Network", p. 374.

73   "Nomination of John Foster Dulles Secretary of State-Designate, Hearing before the Committee on Foreign Relations, United States Senate, Eighty-Third Congress, First Session [...], January 15, 1953," page 6, The Library of Regents of The University of Minnesota, Y4.F76(2):D88, https://babel. hathitrust.org/cgi/pt?id=umn.31951d02094773i;view=1up;seq=2

74   Stephen Kinzer, "The Brothers – John Foster Dulles, Allen Dulles, and Their Secret War", p. 121 and 146.

75   Ibid, p. 119-120, 124.

76   Don Fulsom, Crime Magazine, "Gerald Ford's role in the JFK Assassination Cover-up", http://www.crimemagazine.com/gerald-fords-role-jfk-assassination-cover

77   Kai, Bird, "The Chairman: John J. McCloy: The Making of the American Establishment".

78   See Chapter 2.

79   "Aleksandr Dugin: A Russian Version of the European Radical Right?," Marlene Laruelle, Woodrow Wilson International Center for Scholars, Kennan Institute, Occasional Paper # 294, https://www.wilsoncenter.org/ sites/default/files/OP294.pdf

80   John B. Dunlop, "Aleksandr Dugin's Foundations of Geopolitics", http://www.4pt.su/en/content/aleksandr-dugin%E2%80%99s-foundations-geopolitics. John B. Dunlop is Senior Fellow, Emeritus, at the Hoover Institution at Stanford University.

81   Marlene Laruelle, "Aleksandr Dugin: A Russian Version of the European Radical Right?", Woodrow Wilson International Center for Scholars, Kennan Institute, Occasional Paper # 294, http://www.wilsoncenter.org/ sites/default/files/OP294.pdf

82   "Kenyatta jailed for Mau Mua uprising," History.com, 2010, https://www. history.com/this-day-in-history/kenyatta-jailed-for-mau-mau-uprising

83   On March 10, 2013, his son Uhuru Kenyatta, one of Africa's richest men, became President whilst facing trial in The Hague-based International Criminal Court for crimes against humanity.

84   http://www.wnd.com/2010/02/125349/

85   See Chapter 3.

86   "Christian A. Herter: The American Secretaries of State and their Diplomacy, XVIII," George Bernard Noble, Rowman & Littlefield, 1970

87   https://www.pratt.edu/the-institute/history

88   The Middle East Institute, http://www.mei.edu/mission, not to be confused with the Middle East Institute at Columbia University, http://www.mei.columbia.edu/

89   Not to be confounded with W.E.B. Du Bois' World Peace Council.

90   The W.E.B. DuBois School of Marxists Studies was created in 1972.

91   "Eisenhower and Nixon Are Renominated [...]," The New York Times, August 23, 1956, https://archive.nytimes.com/www.nytimes.com/library/politics/camp/560823convention-gop-ra.html

92   "The Other Barack: The Bold and Reckless Life of President Obama's Father," Sally H. Jacobs, 2011, page 86.

93   "Barack Hussein Obama Sr. Immigration File," obtained via Freedom of Information Act request, https://www.scribd.com/doc/54015762/Barack-Hussein-Obama-Sr-Immigration-File

94   Dr. Frank Laubach, known as "The Apostle to the Illiterates," was a missionary, deemed mystic by some accounts, whose mission was to teach the poor and the oppressed how to read so that they could rise and fight for their freedom, in particular in the colonial world.

95   "The Other Barack," Sally H. Jacobs, p.70.

96   Ibid.

97   "The Case Against Barack Obama, Sr.," The American Thinker, November 7, 2011, https://www.americanthinker.com/articles/2011/11/the_case_against_barack_obama_sr.html

98   See Chapter 3.

99   Later confirmed in a 1995 video published by 22-CityView – Cambridge Public Library, MA, under the YouTube title "From the Vault – Barack Obama – SEP 1995," at minute 8:45 to 8:59, https://youtu.be/w5JlqDnoqlo

100   "Writers of the Black Chicago Renaissance" by Steven C. Tracy

101   Vernon Jarrett was to become, in 1983, the father-in-law of Valerie Jarrett who, in 1991, hired the Obama's wife and became his closest advisor.

102   Robert Taylor was Valerie Jarrett's grandfather. He had been chairman of the Chicago Housing Authority and the son of Robert Robinson Taylor, who worked with the revered Booker T. Washington, father of the Civil Rights Movement.

103   See Chapter 4.

104   Not to be mistaken with the conservative World Peace Foundation.

105   In 1987, Chicago Mayor Harold Washington hired David Axelrod as campaign consultant. Don Rose was the Mayor's advisor.

106   http://www.hawaii.edu/uhwo/clear/HonoluluRecord1/frankblog1949.html

107   The CIO and the less radical American Federation of Labor merged in 1955 to create the AFL-CIO.

108   "Sex Rebel: Black" by Bob Greene, a.k.a. Frank Marshal Davis, 1968.

[109] Later, in 1956, Davis was subpoenaed by the Senate Subcommittee on Un-American Activities, and pleaded the Fifth.

[110] According to "The Communist: Frank Marshall Davis, The Untold Story", by Dr. Paul Kengor, the FBI had a 600-page file on Frank Davis, CPUSA member 47544.

[111] "Frank-ly Speaking," University of Hawaii, Compilation of Frank Marshall Davis' editorials in the Honolulu Record, 1949-1950, http://www.hawaii.edu/uhwo/clear/HonoluluRecord1/frankblog1949.html

[112] "The Other Barack: The Bold and Reckless Life of President Obama's Father," Sally H. Jacobs, 2011, p. 91.

[113] Ibid, p. 114.

[114] Today, in Hawaii, African Americans still comprise only 1.5% of the student population.

[115] "East-West Center Origins," https://www.eastwestcenter.org/about-ewc/origins

[116] See Chapter 2.

[117] "The Other Barack: The Bold and Reckless Life [...], Sally H. Jacobs, PublicAffairs, 2011, p. 107.

[118] Ibid, p. 114-115.

[119] Ibid, p. 121-124.

[120] "Barack Hussein Obama Sr. Immigration File," obtained pursuant to a Freedom of Information Act Request by the weekly Arizona Independent, https://www.npr.org/sections/thetwo-way/2011/04/27/135770919/immigration-files-of-obamas-father-paint-unflattering-picture, and SCRIBD, https://www.scribd.com/doc/54015762/Barack-Hussein-Obama-Sr-Immigration-File

[121] "College, Graduate Schools Will Raise Tuition in 1964," The Harvard Crimson, May 21, 1963, https://www.thecrimson.com/article/1963/5/21/college-graduate-schools-will-raise-tuition/

[122] Letter from Harvard University to Barack H. Obama (Sr.), May 27, 1964, INS File obtained by Sally H. Jacobs under FOIA, https://www.scribd.com/doc/54015762/Barack-Hussein-Obama-Sr-Immigration-File

[123] Barack's "half-uncle" was subject to deportation from the U.S. as an illegal immigrant in 1989, and his trial, heard on December 3, 2013, allowed him to remain in the US and be issued a green card. http://www.nydailynews.com/news/politics/president-obama-uncle-new-immigration-hearing-article-1.1536067

[124] "The Other Barack: The Bold and Reckless Life of President Obama's Father," Sally H. Jacobs, PublicAffairs, 2011, p. 151.

125 "A Look in the Mirror," National Association of Independent Schools, Winter 2014, https://www.nais.org/magazine/independent-school/winter-2014/a-look-in-the-mirror/

126 "Sally H. Jacobs," Pulitzer Center, https://pulitzercenter.org/people/sally-h-jacobs

127 "The Making of the Book That Made Obama," Politico, January 27, 2009, https://www.thedailybeast.com/the-making-of-the-book-that-made-obama

128 HistoryLink.org, The Free Online Encyclopedia of Washington State History, "Stanley Ann Dunham, mother of Barack Obama, graduates from Mercer Island High School in 1960, Essay 8897, by Phil Dougherty, January 22, 2009, http://www.historylink.org/index.cfm?DisplayPage=output.cfm&file_id=8897

129 "Obama's mother known here as "uncommon"," The Seattle Times, April 8, 2008, https://www.seattletimes.com/seattle-news/politics/obamas-mother-known-here-as-uncommon/

130 "The Unitarian Church and Obama's Religious Upbringing," American Thinker, December 27, 2008, https://www.americanthinker.com/articles/2008/12/obama_from_unitarian_to_libera_1.html

131 131 Investigation of communist activities in the Seattle, Wash., area, -Part 2, Hearings before the Committee on Un-American Activities House of Representatives, March 18 and 19, 1955. p.443 to 466, http://depts.washington.edu/labhist/cpproject/images/hearings/HUAC/Seattle-HUAC%201955%20Part%202.pdf

132 "Obama's mother known here as "uncommon"," The Seattle Times, April 8, 2008, https://www.seattletimes.com/seattle-news/politics/obamas-mother-known-here-as-uncommon/

133 The reason for the separation is the subject of much controversy, some authors stating the couple was madly in love but had to for financial and INS reasons, some saying that their marriage was never recorded and a matter of convenience for a young girl getting pregnant.

134 The Post & Email, August 22, 2010, https://www.thepostemail.com/2010/08/22/confirmed-stanley-ann-dunham-began-studies-in-september-1961-not-august/

135 "Communism in Washington State," http://depts.washington.edu/labhist/cpproject/index.shtml

136 Stephen Kinzer, "The Brothers," p.241-242.

137 The University records say she received both, which seems quite unlikely.

138 In 2015, Punahou tuition, all inclusive, was about $22,000 per year.

139 In Barack's memoirs, "Dreams," he notes "Nobody seemed to mind [...] that I was the only eleven- or twelve-year-old.], page 77. This would place the story in 1972-1973. He makes one timeline mistake though. On page

76, he talks about meeting *"a poet named Frank,""But by the time I met Frank he must have been pushing eighty [...]."* Frank Marshall Davis was born in 1905, so he was sixty seven or sixty eight at the time. He died when he was eighty one.

[140] Ibid,*"Don't tell your grandmother,"* page 77.
[141] Today, 1.6% of Hawaii's population is Black or African American, https://www.to-hawaii.com/ethnicity.php
[142] Barack Obama, "Dreams from my father," p. 58.
[143] Ibid.
[144] Ibid, page 75.

Red Herrings From Chicago:

[145] In 2015, Occidental College tuition, all inclusive, was about $50,000 per year.
[146] The Fulbright Scholarship program is administered by the State Department. Neither Barack Obama nor Barry Soetoro are listed as notable alumnus. Bureau of Educational And Cultural Affairs, "The Fulbright Program, Heads of State/Government," https://eca.state.gov/fulbright/fulbright-alumni/notable-fulbrighters/heads-stategovernment
[147] Bureau Of Educational And Cultural Affairs, U.S. Department of State, https://eca.state.gov/fulbright/fulbright-alumni/notable-fulbrighters/nobel-laureates President Obama received the Nobel Peace Prize in 2009.
[148] John M. (Mike) McConnell bio as Vice Chairman of the Carlyle Group, November 2011. http://www.boozallen.com/about/leadership/executive-leadership/McConnell . McConnell was Director of the National Security agency form 1992 to 1996, and Director of National Intelligence from 2007 to 2009.
[149] "Booz Allen, the World's Most Profitable Spy Organization," Bloomberg Businessweek, June 21, 2013, http://www.bloomberg.com/news/articles/2013-06-20/booz-allen-the-worlds-most-profitable-spy-organization
[150] www.USPIRG.org
[151] http://wtpotus.wordpress.com/2012/08/21/taking-care-of-business-international-obamas-co-workers/
[152] David Remnick, "The Bridge: The Life and Rise of Barack Obama," January 2011.
[153] PBS Frontline, The Choice 2008, John Gilmore, July 24, 2008: http://www.pbs.org/wgbh/pages/frontline/government-elections-politics/choice-2012/the-frontline-interview-gerald-kellman/
[154] http://harvardlawreview.org/about/

155 University of Illinois Springfield, archives of Illinois Issues, http://illinoisissues.uis.edu/archives/2008/09/whyorg.html and http://www.gatherthepeople.org/Downloads/WHY_ORGANIZE.pdf

156 "The Gamaliel Foundation," Capital Research Center, July 16, 2010, https://capitalresearch.org/article/the-gamaliel-foundation-alinsky-inspired-group-uses-stealth-tactics-to-manipulate-church-congregations/

157 http://www.americanthinker.com/2008/10/who_wrote_dreams_from_my_fathe_1.html and http://desip.igc.org/desip/ObamasDreams.html

158 http://stpete.patch.com/groups/opinion/p/8a9acc4c-81b7-4d41-a0df-ea09755c28d5

159 Library of Congress Name Authority File, http://id.loc.gov/authorities/names/n82031474.html

160 http://docslide.us/documents/vernon-jarrett-will-arabs-back-ties-to-blacks-with-cash-november-6-1979-article-st-petersburg-evening-independent.html

161 Books by Khalid al-Mansour: "The lost Books of Africa Rediscovered – We Charge Genocide", "Challenges of Spreading Islam in America and Other Essays", "The Seven African Arabian Wonders of the World: The Black Man's Guide to the Middle East", etc.

162 Several videos of Percy Sutton about Barack Obama and Khalid al-Mansour http://www.bing.com/videos/search?q=Khalid+Al+Mansour+Percy+Sutton&Form=VQFRVP#view=detail&mid=22783797440378CD2DC022783797440378CD2DC0

163 Politico, Sept. 4, 2008, http://www.politico.com/blogs/ben-smith/2008/09/obama-camp-denies-sutton-story-011581, American Thinker, Dec. 27, 2009, http://www.americanthinker.com/blog/2009/12/percy_sutton_dies_his_obama_re.html

164 https://www.sourcewatch.org/index.php/Khalid_Al-Mansour

165 "Renowned Global Speaker Khalid Al-Mansour to deliver lecture at UTech, September 13, 2012, http://go-jamaica.com/pressrelease/item.php?id=1081

166 "Giuliani rejects $10 million from Saudi prince," CNN.com, October 12, 2001, http://www.cnn.com/2001/US/10/11/rec.giuliani.prince/index.html

167 Alternatively known as the National Liberation Front for South Vietnam, operating both in South Vietnam and Cambodia, Viet Cong was mainly an insurgent army, created in 1954, whose name is the contraction of "Communist traitor to Vietnam" in Vietnamese. It is distinct from the Viet Minh, which was a political organization created in 1941 to fight for Vietnam independence, then under French occupation.

168 "Eisenhower gives famous "domino theory" speech," History.com, https://www.history.com/this-day-in-history/eisenhower-gives-famous-domino-theory-speech

169 "America's Stake in Vietnam, American Friends of Vietnam, Washington, DC, 1 June 1956," JFK Presidential Library and Museum, https://www.jfklibrary.org/Asset-Viewer/Archives/JFKSEN-0895-014.aspx

170 Bill Ayers was a prolific writer. Among many other books, he authored "A Simple Justice: The Challenge of Small Schools". This was his field of expertise. Published in 2000, his co-author was the leader of the New Communist Party, Mike Klonsky.

171 "An historical analysis of the Chicago Public Schools Policy [...], 2010", Siobhan Marie Cafferty, page 79 to 90. https://ecommons.luc.edu/ cgi/viewcontent.cgi?referer=http://www.google.com/url?sa=t&rct=j&q =&esrc=s&source=web&cd=1&ved=0ahUKEwjGppOo1uLaAh UR0FMKHagvBXEQFggnMAA&url=http%3A%2F%2Fecommons. luc.edu%2Fcgi%2Fviewcontent.cgi%3Farticle%3D1059%26context% 3Dluc_diss&usg=AOvVaw3-LGJOxg4_CgRtvTS8PrL2&httpsredir= 1&article=1059&context=luc_diss

172 "Why The Ayers Family Helped Obama," WND, March 31, 2012, http://www.wnd.com/2012/03/why-the-ayers-family-helped-obama/

173 "Radical-In-Chief: Barack Obama and the Untold Story of American Socialism," Stanley Kurtz, October 2012, Threshold Editions, page 119 to 124.

174 On April 16th, 2008, during a Presidential debate, co-moderator ABC's George Stephanopoulos had asked Obama *"On this issue, general themes of patriotism, in your relationships. A gentleman named William Ayers. [...] Can you explain that relationship for the voters and explain to the Democrats why it won't be a problem?"*, to which he answered *"This is a guy who lives in my neighborhood, who's a professor of English in Chicago who I know and who I have not received some official endorsement from. He's not somebody who I exchange ideas from on a regular basis"*, *"He lied about Bill Ayers?"*, FactCheck. org, https://www.factcheck.org/2008/10/he-lied-about-bill-ayers/. And "William Ayers GMA Interview About Obama – November 14, 2008,"several videos at http://www.bing.com/videos/search?q=obama+stephanopo ulos+ayers+2008&&view=detail&mid=B85982C8605000E58CB6B 85982C8605000E58CB6&&FORM=VRDGAR,

175 "Ayers and Obama crossed paths on boards, records show," CNN Politics, October 7, 2008, http://www.cnn.com/2008/POLITICS/10/07/obama. ayers/

176 "Obama and the Woods Fund of Chicago," American Thinker, July 7, 2008, https://www.americanthinker.com/articles/2008/07/ obama_and_the_woods_fund_of_ch.html

177 "About the Foundation," Woods Fund Chicago, http://www.woodsfund. org/about-foundation/history-of-the-fund

178 "The President's Utility: Crony capitalism in Chicago turns "green" into greenbacks," Capital Research Center, September 10, 2013, https:// capitalresearch.org/article/14995/

179 "Obama and the Woods Fund of Chicago," American Thinker, July 7, 2008, https://www.americanthinker.com/articles/2008/07/ obama_and_the_woods_fund_of_ch.html

180 "Khalidi of the PLO," Sandbox, October 30, 2008, http://martinkramer. org/sandbox/2008/10/khalidi-of-the-plo/

181 "The L.A. Times Suppresses Obama's Khalidi Bash Tape," National Review, October 27, 2008, https://www.nationalreview.com/2008/10/ la-times-suppresses-obamas-khalidi-bash-tape-andrew-c-mccarthy/

182 "Target of FBI terro-support raid visited W.H." Politico, October 1, 2010, https://www.politico.com/blogs/under-the-radar/2010/10/target-of-fb i-terror-support-raid-visited-wh-029665

183 U.S. House of Representatives, Subcommittee on Un-American Activities, July 12. 1962, p. 1672 to 1698, http://www.channelingreality.com/ Documents/History/1962_unAmerican_Activities_Hearing.pdf

184 Obituary, Chicago Tribune, August 29, 2004, http://articles. chicagotribune.com/2004-08-29/news/0408290011_1_mr-canter-chicag o-politicians-mayor-washington

185 "Hatchet Man: The Rise of David Axelrod," Chicago Magazine, December 1, 1987, http://www.chicagomag.com/Chicago-Magazine/ December-1987/Hatchet-Man-The-Rise-of-David-Axelrod/

186 See Endnote # 139.

187 "How Mayor Washington Influenced Barack Obama," Chicago 5 Ward Room, November 26, 2012, https://www.nbcchicago.com/blogs/ward-room/How-Mayor-Washington-Led-To-President-Obama-180845381.html

188 See Chapter 5.

189 "Former ComEd CEO," Chicago Sun Times Obituary, June 12, 2007, https://www.pressreader.com/usa/chicago-sun-times/20070612/ 282385510094182

190 "Mike Klonsky's Blog," http://michaelklonsky.blogspot.com/

191 "FBI Files Document Communism in Valerie Jarrett's Family," Judicial Watch, June 22, 2015, https://www.judicialwatch.org/blog/2015/06/ communism-in-jarretts-family/

192 "Crossed Paths: Chicago's Jacksons and Obamas," The New York Times, Jodi Kantor, February 24, 2013, https://www.nytimes.com/2013/02/25/ us/politics/crossed-paths-chicagos-jacksons-and-obamas.html

[193] The record shows that Bernardine left Sidley & Austin in 1987, while Michele joined in 1988. So, the exact date of their acquaintance is not set, but they did get acquainted, for sure. Not only Ayers and Dohrn later baby sat for the Obama couple, they also stumped for him in 1995.

[194] "Black History in America", http://www.myblackhistory.net/Michelle_Obama.htm

[195] Reverend Wright baptized both Malia in 1998 and Natasha "Sasha" in 2001.

[196] "Crossed Paths: Chicago's Jacksons and Obamas," The New York Times, February 24, 2013: http://www.nytimes.com/2013/02/25/us/politics/crossed-paths-chicagos-jacksons-and-obamas.html?pagewanted=all&_r=0

[197] PUSH was the acronym for People United to Save Humanity, founded in 1971 by Jesse Jackson. He also founded the National Rainbow Coalition in 1984, and merged them into Rainbow/PUSH in 1996.

[198] "Vernon Jarrett, 84; Journalist, Crusader," Obituary, Washington Post, May 4, 2004, http://www.washingtonpost.com/wp-dyn/articles/A53239-2004May24.html

[199] Alice Palmer had formally announced Obama's candidacy for the Illinois Senate on September 19. 1995 at the Ramada In in Lakeshore, in the same room where Harold Washington had announced his candidacy for Mayor some twenty years earlier.

[200] "Showing his bare knuckles; In first campaign, Obama revealed hard-edged, uncompromising sid […]," Chicago Tribune, April 4, 2007, http://articles.chicagotribune.com/2007-04-04/news/0704030881_1_petitions-voter-rights-candidates/2

[201] In 1992, Obama organized a voter registration campaign called Project Vote, deemed to be associated with the now barred ACORN.

[202] "Obama Kick-Back Cronyism, Part 1 […]," Forbes, October 25, 2011, https://www.forbes.com/sites/larrybell/2011/10/25/obama-kick-back-cronyism-part-1-stimulating-green-energy-the-chicago-way/#27a53791632c

[203] "Pragmatic Politics, Forged on the South Side", The New York Times, May 11, 2008, page 5 of 7., https://www.nytimes.com/2008/05/11/us/politics/11chicago.html

[204] Google was launched in 1998, and Wikipedia in 2001.

[205] "Obama's ghost writer fesses up!," Salon, October 7, 2009, https://www.salon.com/2009/10/07/ayers_2/

[206] "Who Wrote Dreams From My Father?" American Thinker, Jack Cashill, October 9, 2008, https://www.americanthinker.com/articles/2008/10/who_wrote_dreams_from_my_fathe_1.html

207 "Who Wrote Audacity of Hope?," American Thinker, Jack Cashill, July 12, 2009, https://www.americanthinker.com/articles/2009/07/who_wrote_audacity_of_hope_1.html

208 Unclassified Memorandum from Brzezinski to President Carter, The White House, December 26, 1979, https://nsarchive2.gwu.edu/carterbrezhnev/docs_intervention_in_afghanistan_and_the_fall_of_detente/doc73.pdf

209 "The Wise Men: Six Friends and the World They Made", by Walter Isaacson and Evan Thomas, 1986, which describes the architects of the containment policy of the Communist Bloc during the Cold War. They were John McCloy, later dubbed "The Chairman of the Establishment," Robert Lovett, George Kennan, Averell Harriman, Charles Bohlen, and Dean Acheson.

210 Counterpunch, "Who supported the Khmer Rouge?" Gregory Elich, October 16, 2014, https://www.counterpunch.org/2014/10/16/who-supported-the-khmer-rouge/. This may sound strange but here is a quick refresher. Historically, Vietnam was China and Cambodia's enemy. But when it came to fight the French colonialists, or the U.S. Imperialists, they would unite, in this case with the Soviet Union. However, the Soviet Union and China had their own problem, not only in terms of communist ideology, but mainly, like all other countries, in terms of border disputes. In the 60's, while they were on the same side of the Vietnam War, the Sino-Soviet relationship deteriorated, leading to an armed clash on Zhenbao Island in 1969. Hanoi had to choose and chose the Soviet side. Mao withdrew all personnel from North Vietnam, and, playing on the historical fear that Cambodia had of Vietnamese hegemony, started to arm the Cambodian rebels, the Khmer Rouge, led by the Maoist Pol Pot. At the same time, the United States under President Nixon decided to help Prince Norodom Sihanouk, officially non-aligned but alternating between China, the U.S.S.R., and the U.S. This led to the Cambodian Civil War, and to the surge in Khmer Rouge power. After the fall of Saigon in South Vietnam, and of Pnom Penh in Cambodia, both in April 1975, the Khmer Rouge, now in charge of Cambodia renamed Democratic Kampuchea, started to raid Vietnam territories. This led to the Kampuchea-Vietnam War, ending with Vietnamese occupation in 1979, as the People's Republic of Kampuchea. The story does not end here, but for all intents and purposes, this is when Zbigniew Brzezinski was supporting Pol Pot's regime: he was fighting the Vietnamese, who were armed and financed by the Soviet Union... Under Pol Pot, between 1975 and 1979, between 1.5 to 3 million civilians were killed by the Khmer Rouge, out of a population of 8 million.

211 "India," Country Studies /Area Handbook Series, sponsored by the U.S. Department of Army, Library of Congress, http://countrystudies.us/india/133.htm

212 "Despite Criticism, Obama Stands By Adviser Brzezinski," The New York Sun, September 13, 2007, https://www.nysun.com/national/despite-criticism-obama-stands-by-adviser/62534/

213 Afghanistan, "Introduction,", The World Factbook, CIA, https://www.cia.gov/library/publications/the-world-factbook/geos/af.html

214 "Durand Line: The Future Time Bomb," Daily Afghanistan Outlook," January 15, 2012, http://outlookafghanistan.net/topics.php?post_id=3124

215 "Britain and France conclude Sykes-Picot agreement," History.com, 2009, https://www.history.com/this-day-in-history/britain-and-france-conclude-sykes-picot-agreement

216 The weaker faction of the PPDA was the Parcham.

217 See Chapter 12.

218 See Chapter 4.

219 Kai Bird, "The Chairman", p. 650.

220 See Chapter 3.

221 See Chapter 1.

222 On October 6, 1981, President Sadat was assassinated during a military parade by a group of Islamists soldiers.

223 "The Skin That Burns," A film by Narges Bajoghli, 2012, https://www.theskinthatburns.com/

224 Eastern Iranian and southern Afghanistan people, speaking Pashto. Peshawar is the capital of the Peshawar District in Pakistan, on the Northwestern border with Afghanistan.

225 https://www.investigativeproject.org/document/28-treasury-department-designaton-of-global-relief

226 "Land mines: Hidden killers," The State of the World's Children 1996, UNICEF, https://www.unicef.org/sowc96pk/hidekill.htm

227 The game of Go originated in China 2,500 years ago or so. According to Wikipedia, It is a "zero-sum, perfect-information, partisan, deterministic strategy game", much like chess, checkers or Othello. However, because it is played with 181 black stones against 180 white stones, no computer has been able to beat a human at the professional level.

228 When Robin Raphel retired from her 30-year career with the State Department in 2005, she joined the firm of Cassidy & Associates as a lobbyist for Pakistan.

229 "President Clinton's Address to Joints Chief an Pentagon Staff, February 17, 1998, http://www.cnn.com/ALLPOLITICS/1998/02/17/transcripts/clinton.iraq/

230 Congress Republican majority won in 1994 in the Gingrich Revolution. See p. 68.

231 H. Res. 611, "Impeaching William Jefferson Clinton, President of the United States, for high crimes and misdemeanors," https://www.congress. gov/bill/105th-congress/house-resolution/611

232 "Bin Laden Family Evacuated," CBS News, September 20, 2001, https://www.cbsnews.com/news/bin-laden-family-evacuated/

233 Declassified State document # 157813 [Version 1], Cable, "Deputy Secretary Armitage's Meeting with Pakistan Intel Chief Mahmud: You're Either With Us or You're Not," September 13, 2001, https://nsarchive2. gwu.edu/NSAEBB/NSAEBB358a/doc03-1.pdf

234 "Coalition of The Willing," term coined by President George W. Bush at a NATO summit in 2002, later used to list countries actively involved in the 2003 Iraq invasion.

235 "President Bush Outlines Iraqi Threat," The White House, October 7, 2002, https://nsarchive2.gwu.edu/NSAEBB/NSAEBB80/new/doc%2012/ President%20Bush%20Outlines%20Iraqi%20Threat.htm

236 Organization for the Prohibition of Chemical Weapons, http://multiple. kcvs.ca/site/pdf/English_Version_4_papers.pdf

237 "Why we stuck with Maliki – and lost Iraq," The Washington Post, July 3, 2014, https://www.washingtonpost.com/opinions/why-we-stuck-with-maliki--and-lost-iraq/2014/07/03/0dd6a8a4-f7ec-11e3-a606-946fd632f9f1_story.html?utm_term=.a46cd4efc584

238 See Chapter 3 and "People's Friendship University of Russia turns 50," RT video, https://youtu.be/bN_oEJEp9Ro

239 "The "Primakov Doctrine": Russia's Zero-Sum Game with the United States," Ariel Cohen, The Heritage Foundation, No. 167, December 15, 1997, http://s3.amazonaws.com/thf_media/1997/pdf/fyi167.pdf

240 Mr. Zafarjadeh's National Council of Resistance of Iran has been associated with the Mujahedin-e Khalq (MEK), listed as a terrorist organization by the U.S. State Department from 2003 to 2012."The Mujahedin-e Khalq in Iraq – A Policy Conundrum,"Rand Corporation, https://www.rand.org/pubs/monographs/MG871.html . Khalq in Pashtun means "masses," or "people," as in communism. Be it as it may, the IAEA acted on Mr. Jafarzadeh's information, and corroborated it – as well as further information provided by NCRI.

241 "Treaty on the Non-Proliferation of Nuclear Weapons (NPT), 1968" U.S. Department of State, https://www.state.gov/t/isn/trty/16281.htm

242 "Egypt's Muslim Brotherhood and Iran," The Washington Institute, February 12, 2009, www.washingtoninstitute.org/policy-analysis/view/ egypts-muslim-brotherhood-and-iran"

243 "Obama's Missing Thesis," The Weekly Standard, July 25, 2008, https://www.weeklystandard.com/jaime-sneider/obamas-missing-thesis

244 "Barack Obama," Christianity Today, https://www.christianitytoday.com/ct/topics/o/barack-obama/

245 See Chapter 6.

246 In Backgammon, a back-game is when your opponent seems to be winning and has cornered you in the back of your board. You must wait for the opponent to make a mistake. The odds are longer but if you win, you usually win bigger than in a normal game, called hit-and-run.

247 While some media reports say that he was a Professor of Law, he never really was. The University states that he first was lecturer, then senior lecturer, and as such was "regarded as professor, although not full-time or tenure-track." No student seem to have come forward to claim attendance. Source: The Law School at the University of Chicago, media inquiries, "Statement Regarding Barack Obama," http://www.law.uchicago.edu/media

248 See page 36.

249 "Rezko role bigger than admitted," Politico, March 14, 2008, https://www.politico.com/story/2008/03/rezko-role-bigger-than-admitted-009049

250 "Chicago Straight," Chicago Magazine, Politics & City Life, May 18, 2009, http://www.chicagomag.com/Chicago-Magazine/June-2009/Chicago-Straight/

251 After working for the Tribune from 1970 to 1983, Jarrett had left for the Sun-Times and retired in 1995. He passed away in May 2004.

252 "Jon Favreau," The New York Times, January 20, 2008, https://www.nytimes.com/2008/01/20/fashion/20speechwriter.html

253 Pat Buchanan on DNC keynote address by State Senator Obama, YouTube, https://youtu.be/QEzrJ-k9vH0

254 "Barack Obama: Keynote Address at the 2004 Democratic National Convention," The American Presidency Project, July 27, 2004, http://www.presidency.ucsb.edu/ws/?pid=76988

255 David Axelrod's website, www.Akpdmedia.com

256 "Ryan's ex-wife signs on to keep divorce files sealed," Chicago Tribune, May 11, 2004, http://articles.chicagotribune.com/2004-05-11/news/0405110233_1_divorce-records-sealed-jack-ryan

257 "Obama's signature move: unsealing private records," Ann Coulter Letter, Humanevents. Com, August 1, 2012, http://humanevents.com/2012/08/01/ann-coulter-obamas-signature-move-unsealing-private-records/

258 "Media averts eyes from subpoenas to Obama top staff," American Thinker, January 25, 2009, https://www.americanthinker.com/blog/2009/01/media_averts_eyes_from_subpoen.html

[259] "Barack Obama, Keynote Address at the 2004 Democratic National Convention," The American Presidency Project, The University of California, July 27, 2004, http://www.presidency.ucsb.edu/ws/?pid=76988

[260] "The Other Barack: The Bold and Reckless Life of President Obama's Father," Sally Jacobs, PublicAffairs, 2011, page 2.

[261] Republicans had picked up four seats for a fifty five to forty four majority, and one Independent.

[262] "Russia tied to Iraq's missing arms," The Washington Times, October 28, 2004, https://www.washingtontimes.com/news/2004/oct/28/20041028-122637-6257r/

[263] Howard Dean never recouped his lead but the former outspoken Governor of Vermont, an innovator in terms of campaign fund raising, was rewarded with the chairmanship of the Democratic National Committee, an office he held from 2005 to 2009.

[264] See Chapter 5.

[265] Al-Zarqawi had founded Jamaat al-Tawheed wa al-Jihad in 2003, then agreed with bin Laden to rename it al-Qaeda in Iraq in 2004. They were competing but they needed each other. http://www.stratfor.com/sites/default/files/main/images/IS-timeline-dec.png .

[266] "Kazakhstan country profile," BBC News, https://www.bbc.com/news/world-asia-pacific-15263826

[267] Brookings Institute, Opinion paper by Gill Bates, May 4th, 2001, "Shanghai Five: An Attempt to Counter U.S. Influence in Asia?", http://www.brookings.edu/research/opinions/2001/05/04china-gill

[268] "Russia and the Middle East: The Primakov Era," Dr. Robert O. Freedman, Middle East Review of International Affairs Vol. 2, No. 2, May 1998, http://www.rubincenter.org/meria/1998/05/freedman.pdf

[269] By ChrisnHouston - File:Control of the U.S. Senate.PNGFile:Control of the U.S. House of Representatives.PNG, CC BY-SA 3.0, https://commons.wikimedia.org/w/index.php?curid=28885585

On To The White House:

[270] AIG stock price had peaked at $100 or so in 2001 and was then worth $1.50.

[271] Franck Prissert, "Anatomy of the Meltdown – 1998-2008 – The Worst Decade in Stock Investing, or Was It?", p. 133.

[272] The Federal Reserve Board, "Remarks by Governor Ben. S. Bernanke", November 21, 2002, http://www.federalreserve.gov/boarddocs/speeches/2002/20021121/default.htm

[273] On September 2008, before the $350 billion bail-outs or so, the Congressional Budget Office was projecting a $407 billion deficit in Fiscal 2008, ending in September. This was twice the 2007 amount.

274 "Iraqi surge exceeded expectations, Obama says,"NBC News, September 4, 2008, http://www.nbcnews.com/id/26550764/ns/politics-decision_08/t/iraqi-surge-exceeded-expectations-obama-says/#.WxxWAzO0Wpo

275 Axelrod's daughter suffers from epilepsy, and Hilary Clinton had been quite active in Axelrod's Foundation "Citizens United for Research in Epilepsy, a.k.a. as C.U.R.E.

276 The title "Audacity of Hope" was in reference to a sermon delivered by Obama's highly controversial pastor, Jeremiah Wright, and the title of his 2004 speech at the Democratic Convention. The sermon was titled "Audacity to Hope." Later on, Obama would distance himself from Wright.

277 See Chapter 5.

278 See Chapter 6.

279 Democrats in the House, 57 plus 2 Independents in the Senate.

280 A well-established reference to Adam Smith's "Wealth of Nations," to explain the markets' tendency towards equilibrium. In plain English, a term to describe the ability for the market to act on information that is not yet known, the opposite of the Efficient Market Theory advocated by Nobel Prize Eugene Fama, father of the skeptic Random Walk Theory of the mid Sixties.

281 ARRA was introduced in the House on January 26, 2009, but had been in the works before President Obama took office. It was signed into law on February 17, 2009. The Congressional Budget Office estimated it would cost $831 billion over ten years. http://www.cbo.gov/sites/default/files/cbofiles/attachments/02-22-ARRA.pdf

282 In Q4, 2008 and Q1, 2009, the U.S. GDP did decline by 6% in both quarters.

283 http://group30.org/members

284 Fiat money refers to money created with no other collateral than the confidence in the issuer.

285 Otherwise known as fractional money creation. You deposit $100, the bank can now lend $90 (the difference is called reserve). The $90 loan, when deposited, becomes another $81 loan. Ultimately, the money created is the initial amount divided by the reserve requirement. In this case where the RR is 10% and the initial deposit is $100, the money created is $1000.

286 In 2005, Salazar had voted against increasing fuel-efficiency standards for cars and trucks, and against the repeal of tax breaks for major oil companies. In 2006, he voted to allow offshore drilling in Florida. In 2007, he voted against a Global Warming bill.

287 Dr. Chu's studies on how to cool and trap atoms with laser light won him a 1997 Nobel Prize, and he was a fervent advocate of renewable energy, in particular glucose-based, and nuclear power.

[288] "The Next Solar Mirage: Crescent Dunes, or Solyndra v2": http://seekingalpha.com/author/the-other-street/instablog/3.

[289] Alamosa Concentrated Solar Project, https://www.energy.gov/lpo/alamosa

[290] For background, "Anatomy of the Meltdown", Franck Prissert, Chapter 4 b), "Anthropogenic Climate Change – And Ethanol."

[291] "5 Big Wins in Clean Energy from the Loan Program Office," Department of Energy, February 17, 2016, https://www.energy.gov/articles/5-big-wins-clean-energy-loan-programs-office

[292] "Portfolio Projects," Department of Energy, Loan Program Office, https://www.energy.gov/lpo/portfolio/portfolio-projects

[293] http://www.solarreserve.com/what-we-do/csp-projects/crescent-dunes/

[294] Consumers buy KWh, or KiloWatt per hours, and a MegaWatt, or MW, is just a thousand KiloWatt, or KW.

[295] "Top Obama doner George Kaiser says he didn't play politics to win government loan," The Washington Post, September 2, 2011, https://www.washingtonpost.com/politics/solyndra-closure-affects-foundation-linked-to-obama-donor/2011/09/02/gIQAkjF4wJ_story.html?utm_term=.79cc29edcf98

[296] "The Solyndra Mess Gets Messier," National Review, September 29, 2011, https://www.nationalreview.com/corner/solyndra-mess-gets-messier-andrew-stiles/

[297] "The Next Solar Mirage: Crescent Dunes, or Solyndra v2," The Other Street's Blog, September 29, 2011, https://seekingalpha.com/instablog/475623-the-other-street/221767-the-next-solar-mirage-crescent-dunes-or-solyndra-v2

[298] "Anatomy of the Meltdown – 1998-2008," Franck Prissert, 2009-2011, Chapter 4b, "Anthropogenic Climate Change – and Ethanol."

[299] STORM' 1994 Manifesto, "Reclaiming Revolution", page 20. Source: The Internet Archive, www.archive.org

[300] "Timing of Protest is Suspect / Mumia supports disrupt youth event," SFGate, October 9, 1999 https://www.sfgate.com/bayarea/johnson/article/Timing-Of-Protest-Is-Suspect-Mumia-supporters-2903851.php

[301] The Ella Baker Center for Human Rights, "People Of Color Groups To Stand In Solidarity With Arab Americans and to Mourn the East Coast Dead", press release dated 11-01 calling for a "Solidarity Meeting" on September 12, 2001 in Oakland and including "9/11 Attacks: STORM's Four Main Points in Response to the bombings of the World Trade Center and the U.S. Pentagon."

[302] www.answercoalition.org and www.discoverthenetworks.org

[303] Robert Chandler, 2008, "Shadow World: Resurgent Russia, the Global New Left, and Radical Islam", page 273.

304 The NASSCO3 trio's defense lawyer was Leonard Weinglass, who later defended Mumia Abu-Jamal, the same who Van Jones organized support for. https://www.marxists.org/history/erol/ncm-5/cwp-nassco-5.htm

305 "Ahmadinejad Meets With U.S. Peace and Black Activists," Black Agenda report, September 29, 2010, https://www.blackagendareport.com/content/ahmadinejad-meets-us-peace-and-black-activists

306 http://www.mirror.co.uk/news/world-news/syria-bashar-al-assad-john-kerry-2246874

307 Ian Cameron left ABC in November 2010. He had worked with George Stephanopoulos, President Clinton press secretary, and Christiane Amampour, the renowned ABC and CNN journalist who is married to James Rubin, former Assistant Secretary of State during the Clinton Administration, and adviser to former Secretary of State Hilary Clinton and to President Obama. Ian Cameron has since disappeared from the public scene.

308 See Chapter 7.

309 Samantha Power, "Bystanders to Genocide", Chapter VII "Genocide? What Genocide", The Atlantic, September 2001, http://www.theatlantic.com/magazine/archive/2001/09/bystanders-to-genocide/304571/?single_page=true

310 "#Rwanda20yrs," The National Security Archive at George Washington University, https://nsarchive2.gwu.edu/NSAEBB/NSAEBB511/ and "Declassified U.N. Cables Reveal Turning Point in Rwanda Crisis of 1994," The New York Times, June 3, 2014, https://www.nytimes.com/2014/06/04/world/africa/un-cables-reveal-a-turning-point-in-rwanda-crisis.html

311 Primakov was a Soviet apparatchik, then Minister of Foreign Affairs for President Yeltsin, and a proponent of multipolarism to weaken what he called the U.S. unilateralism post-WWII. He advocated a Russia-India-China axis.

312 See Chapter 3.

313 "Laurent Kabila," Obituary, The Guardian, January 18, 2001, https://www.theguardian.com/news/2001/jan/19/guardianobituaries1

314 David Rothkopf, sold Intellibridge, now CEO and editor of Foreign Policy, previously owned by the Washington Post.

315 "After "Monster" Remark, Aide to Obama [Samantha Power] Resigns," http://thecaucus.blogs.nytimes.com/2008/03/07/obama-aide-apologizes-for-calling-clinton-a-monster/?_r=0

316 Kerry and al-Assad having dinner with their wives in Damascus in February 2009, http://www.mirror.co.uk/news/world-news/syria-bashar-al-assad-john-kerry-2246874

317 In May 2014, Mrs. Power was getting frustrated with the Administration policy – read Rice, Hagel, Dempsey and Obama – to not intervene in the Syrian genocide. But she was not resigning, just venting. http://www.bloombergview.com/articles/2014-05-06/did-samantha-power-just-rebuke-obama-on-syria

318 Mike Donilon's bio on David Axelrod's AKPD website, http://akpdmedia.com/team/mike-donilon/

319 National Security Strategy 2010, http://nssarchive.us/NSSR/2010.pdf

320 Pun intended. Barack Obama is known to have large ears.

321 "As France takes the rein on Libya […]," LA Times, March 20, 2011, http://articles.latimes.com/2011/mar/20/world/la-fg-libya-sarkozy-20110320

322 The White House, Office of the Press Secretary, March 28, 2011, https://obamawhitehouse.archives.gov/the-press-office/2011/03/28/remarks-president-address-nation-libya

323 This is purely subjective. Other local names that come to mind: Recep Erdogan in Turkey, Mahmoud Ahmadinejad in Iran.

324 According to files obtained in April 2014 by Judicial Watch, under the Freedom of Information Act, Secretary Clinton did issue a short press release the next day, simply stating *"Some have thought to justify this vicious behavior as a response to inflammatory material posted on the internet"*. For his part, General Petraeus did not agree with the official account of events.

325 In this author's opinion, one of the worse choices in the Obama's staff were his Press Secretaries, Robert Gibbs first, then Jay Carney. In stark contrast with President Bush's Ari Fleischer, Scott McClellan, Tony Snow and certainly Dana Perino.

326 The Ticket, Yahoo News, "The top 9,486 ways Jay Carney won't answer your questions (interactive)", by Rachel Rose Hartman and Chris Wilson, June 21, 2013.

327 The White House, Office of the Press Secretary, September 14, 2012, Press Briefing by Press Secretary Jay Carney, http://www.whitehouse.gov/the-press-office/2012/09/14/press-briefing-press-secretary-jay-carney-9142012

328 "Egypt Protesters Attack U.S. Embassy in Cairo," Huffington Post, September 11, 2012, https://www.huffingtonpost.com/2012/09/11/egypt-protesters-us-embassy_n_1874247.html

329 "Benghazi Talking Points Had 12 Versions," ABC News, May 10, 2013, http://abcnews.go.com/politics/t/blogEntry?id=19149119

330 Email exchange between Michael J. Morell, Deputy CIA Director (MichaelJM), and David H. Petraeus (DAVIDHP74) dated Saturday September 15, 2012, posted by Ryan Lizza, CNN investigative reporter, on Twitter. https://twitter.com/RyanLizza/status/334797365368197120/photo/1

331 Also obtained in April 2014 by Judicial Watch as a result of a June 2013 Freedom of Information Act lawsuit, http://www.judicialwatch.org/press-room/press-releases/judicial-watch-benghazi-documents-point-whit e-house-misleading-talking-points/

332 "Hilary Clinton testifies before House committee on Benghazi – live," The Guardian, January 23, 2013, https://www.theguardian.com/world/2013/jan/23/clinton-testifies-congress-benghazi-live

333 "Benghazi whistle-blowers testify at House hearing," USA Today, May 8, 2013, https://www.usatoday.com/story/news/world/2013/05/08/benghazi-hearing-whistleblowers/2143813/

334 "Document: White House records on Benghazi talking points," Politico, May 16, 2013, https://www.documentcloud.org/documents/70122 4-130516-wh-benghazi-document-ap.html

335 The word Eurasian had been added in 2001 by President Bush and S.O.S. Colin Powell.

336 "Jill Kelley requested "diplomatic protection," MyFox Tampa Bay, November 12, 2012, by FOX 13 Tampa Bay Staff Bio, "in 911 call, http://www.myfoxtampabay.com/story/20087394/2012/11/13/jill-kelley-911-calls

337 The New York Times, November 14, 2012, Veteran F.B.I. Agent Helped Start Petraeus E-Mail Inquiry", by Michael Schmidt. Scott Shane and Alain Delaqueriere, http://www.nytimes.com/2012/11/15/us/frederic k-humphries-fbi-agent-in-petraeus-case.html?pagewanted=all&_r=0

338 "Shirtless FBI agent unmasked," UPI, November 15, 2012, https://www.upi.com/blog/2012/11/15/Shirtless-FBI-agent-unmasked-PHOTO/6291353014900/?st_rec=98521353052800

339 Huffington Post, November 15, 2012, "Natalie Khawam Got Hefty Loan From Defense Department Lobbyist, by Christina Wilkie and Jason Cherkis, http://www.huffingtonpost.com/2012/11/15/natalie-khawam-loan-lobbyist_n_2141022.html?utm_hp_ref=politics

340 https://www.capitolcitygrp.com/about

341 CBSNews, November 16, 2012, "Beyond two generals: The political ties of Jill Kelley and her sister", by Sharyl Attkisson, http://www.cbsnews.com/news/beyond-two-generals-the-political-ties-of-jill-kelley-and-her-sister/

342 "Natalie Khawam Business Partner Builds Top-Secret Weapons for U.S. Military," The Huffington Post, November 19, 2012, https://www.huffingtonpost.com/2012/11/19/natalie-khawam-clifford-krowne_n_2161685.html

343 Electronics and Physics of Left-Handed Materials and Circuits, NRL Review 2004, by C.M. Krowne, Electronics Science and Techology Division, U.S. Naval Research Lab, http://www.nrl.navy.mil/research/nrl-review/2004/simulation-computing-modeling/krowne/

[344] 2008 Report of the Commission to Assess the Threat to the United States from Electromagnetic Pulse (EMP) Attack, page vi, http://www.empcommission.org/docs/A2473-EMP_Commission-7MB.pdf . A 62-page executive report on the same subject was issued in 2004, and largely ignored.

[345] "More Dirt: Kelley and Her Cancer Charity," Non Profit Quarterly, November 15, 2012, https://nonprofitquarterly.org/2012/11/15/more-dirt-kelley-and-her-cancer-charity/

[346] "The 10 strangest details of the David Petraeus Affair [Updated]," The Week, November 20, 2012, http://theweek.com/articles/470462/10-strangest-details-david-petraeus-affair-updated

[347] The Denver Post, November 19, 2012, "FBI detoured from usual path in investigating Broadwell e-mails", by Richard Lerner, the Associated Press, http://www.denverpost.com/ci_22023520/fbi-detoured-from-usual-path-investigating-broadwell-e?source=infinite

[348] http://www.seattletimes.com/seattle-news/politics/timeline-of-events-in-generals-scandal/

[349] "Timeline of events surrounding CIA Director Petraeus' resignation," Reuters, November 11, 2012, https://www.reuters.com/article/us-cia-petraeus-timeline/timeline-of-events-surrounding-cia-director-petraeus-resignation-idUSBRE8AB01G20121112

[350] CNN World, Barbara Starr and Adam Levine, September 27th, 2012, "Panetta: Terrorists "clearly" planned Benghazi attack", http://www.cnn.com/2012/09/27/world/africa/libya-consulate-attack/

[351] Press release from the office of the Speaker of the House dated May 2nd, 2014, http://www.speaker.gov/press-release/boehner-establish-select-committee-benghazi

[352] In 2012, Egypt's population was 84Mn, followed by Turkey's 80Mn, Iran's 78Mn, Afghanistan's 33Mn, Iraq's 31Mn, and Saudi Arabia's 26Mn. https://www.indexmundi.com/

[353] The Middle East Media Research Institute archives, "Morsi in 2010", http://www.memri.org/clip_transcript/en/3702.htm

[354] The White House Office of the Press Secretary, June 24, 2012, "Readout of the President's Call with President-Elect Morsi of Egypt", http://www.whitehouse.gov/the-press-office/2012/06/24/readout-president-s-call-president-elect-morsi-egypt

[355] The White House Office of the Press Secretary, July 3, 2013, "Statement by President Barack Obama on Egypt", http://www.whitehouse.gov/the-press-office/2013/07/03/statement-president-barack-obama-egypt

[356] "Army chief El Sisi emerges as Egypt's new strongman after Morsi's ouster," Reuters News, July 4, 2013, https://www.thenational.ae/world/mena/army-chief-el-sisi-emerges-as-egypt-s-new-strongman-after-morsi-s-ouster-1.646867

357 UAE offers Egypt $3 billion support, Saudis $5 billion," Reuters, July 9, 2013, https://www.reuters.com/article/us-egypt-protests-loan-idUSBRE9680H020130709

358 "IMF abandons plan to provide $4.8 billion loan to Egypt," July 25, 2013, https://www.rt.com/news/egypt-imf-loan-talks-596/

359 "Remarks by the President at Cairo University, 6-04-09," The White House Office of the Press Secretary, https://obamawhitehouse.archives.gov/the-press-office/remarks-president-cairo-university-6-04-09

360 http://www.globalsecurity.org/military/ops/bright-star.htm

361 See Chapter 12

362 "Caught on Open Mic [...]," Washington Post, March 26, 2012, https://www.washingtonpost.com/politics/obama-tells-medvedev-solution-on-missile-defense-is-unlikely-before-elections/2012/03/26/gIQASoblbS_story.html?utm_term=.f3ebf04f833c and "Obama's Medvedev Hot Mic Gaffe", WSJ, March 27, 2012, https://www.wsj.com/video/obama-medvedev-hot-mic-gaffe/5F7CF09D-CFD5-4805-A72C-3378D5F8371E.html

363 "AIM Report: John Kerry's Marxist Bedfellows – April A," Accuracy in Media, April 16, 2004, https://www.aim.org/aim-report/aim-report-john-kerrys-marxist-bedfellows-april-a/

364 "John Kerry and Bashar al-Assad dined in Damascus," The Telegraph, September 3, 2013, https://www.telegraph.co.uk/news/worldnews/middleeast/syria/10283045/John-Kerry-and-Bashar-al-Assad-dined-in-Damascus.html

365 "Kerry's Cruel Realism," The New York Times, June 19, 2004, https://www.nytimes.com/2004/06/19/opinion/kerry-s-cruel-realism.html

366 "Bush slams Kerry over "brave" Iraqi," The Washington Times, September 25, 2004, https://www.washingtontimes.com/news/2004/sep/25/20040925-121237-3283r/

367 In January 2011, during Obama's first term and when he was Secretary of Defense, Robert Gates announced his plan to save $100 billion off the $700 billion Pentagon budget, and to cut an additional $78 billion. The cuts would reduce the Marine Corps by some 20,000 people, i.e. 10 percent, and the Army active duty personnel by some 50,000 soldiers, i.e. 5 percent. His successor Chuck Hagel, in early 2014, announced plans to cut another $113 billion, to the lowest since before WWII.

368 Ten Ridiculous Questions From Chuck Hagel's Confirmation Hearing," The Nation, January 31, 2013, https://www.thenation.com/article/ten-ridiculous-questions-chuck-hagels-confirmation-hearing/

369 Ibid.

370 K.S.A. stands for Kingdom of Saudi Arabia.

371 See Chapter 10.

372 "Reflections on Europe," Dennis L. Bark, Hoover Institution Press, Stanford University, 1997, p. 96.

373 "Turkey's Diplomacy: A Double-Edged Sword," Stratfor Worldview, December 15, 1999, https://worldview.stratfor.com/article/turkeys-diplomacy-double-edged-sword

374 Turkish Alevis are not the same as Syrian Alawites. "Are Syrian Alawites and Turkish Alevis the same?", CNN World, April 17, 2012, http://globalpublicsquare.blogs.cnn.com/2012/04/17/are-syrian-alawites-and-turkish-alevis-the-same/

375 In the aftermath of the European Debt Crisis of 2010, best described by the unfortuname acronym PIIGS, for Portugal, Ireland, Italy, Greece and Spain.

376 See Chapter 2.

377 PBS NewsHour, July 27, 2004, http://www.pbs.org/newshour/bb/politics-july-dec04-obama-keynote-dnc/

378 See Chapter 9.

379 "Federal Surplus or Deficit as a Percent of Gross Domestic Product," Economic Research Federal Reserve Bank of St. Louis, https://fred.stlouisfed.org/series/FYFSGDA188S

380 "Federal Debt: Total Public Debt," Economic Research Federal Reserve Bank of St. Louis, https://fred.stlouisfed.org/series/GFDEBTN

381 "Federal Debt: Total Public Debt as Percent of Gross Domestic Product," Economic Research Federal Reserve Bank of St.Louis, https://fred.stlouisfed.org/series/GFDEGDQ188S

382 In the November 2010 mid-term elections, Republicans regained control of the House. Nancy Pelosi was no longer Speaker but she still was a loud voice in the Democratic caucus.

383 "Moscow Leads Cities With Most Billionaires," Forbes, May 17, 2011, https://www.forbes.com/2011/05/17/cities-with-most-billionaires/

384 CIA World Factbook, https://www.cia.gov/library/publications/the-world-factbook/geos/rs.html

385 In terms of Purchasing Power Parity, CIA World Factbook, https://www.cia.gov/library/publications/the-world-factbook/geos/ch.html.

386 This has always sounded alarmist. In reality, China and Japan are the largest foreign holders of U.S. Treasuries, but the amount they each own is about $1 trillion. Certainly a big number in financial markets terms, but not that big in the grand scheme of Federal Debt things.

387 See Chapter 9 and SCO's website, http://www.sectsco.org/EN123 .

388 In 2005, Nazarbayev was the first in a series of dominoes which led Russia to later own 20% of U.S. Uranium production, a deal that involved

Bill Clinton at the time, and Hilary Clinton in 2010-2011, known as Uranium One. "The Clinton Foundation received millions from investors as Putin took over 20% of U.S. uranium deposits," Business Insider, April 23, 2015, http://www.businessinsider.com/the-clintons-putin-and-uranium-2015-4

389 SCO. This excludes the Observer States and the Dialogue Partners.

390 *"President Vladimir Putin of Russia Sends Letter of Condolence to Xi Jinping over the Violent and Terrorist Incident in Urumqi"*, http://www.fmprc.gov.cn/mfa_eng/zxxx_662805/t1159019.shtml, May 22nd, 2014.

391 "U.S. condemns terrorist attack in China," UPI, May 22, 2014, https://www.upi.com/Top_News/World-News/2014/05/22/US-condemns-terrorist-attack-in-China/7151400783784/

392 "Barack Obama: First Pacific President? Not exactly," Time, November 14, 2009, http://swampland.time.com/2009/11/14/barack-obama-first-pacific-president-not-exactly/

393 "America's fisrt Pacific president," Politico, November 13, 2009, https://www.politico.com/story/2009/11/americas-first-pacific-president-029511

394 www.fmprc.gov.cn, or if you prefer to read in English, http://www.fmprc.gov.cn/mfa_eng/topics_665678/xjpzxcxdsjhaqhfbfwhlfgdgblshlhgjkezzzbomzb_666590/t1140973.shtml

395 https://www.stratfor.com/analysis/russia-japan-ideal-time-warm-relations

396 See Chapter 2.

397 See Chapter 4.

398 This book ends sometime in the summer of 2014. As I was editing the book for publication, I added the word "vicious" when describing the pro-Russian rebels. On July 17th, 2014, they downed Malaysian Airline Flight MH17, going from Amsterdam to Kuala Lumpur, killing all 298 passengers and crew on board. Later, they land mined the site to prevent access by international organizations and inspectors. Whether this event would prove pivotal in rallying world public and official opinion was yet unclear.

399 On August 20, 2012, President Obama had declared *"We have been very clear to the Assad regime – but also to other players on the ground – that a red line for us is we start seeing a whole bunch of chemical weapons moving around or being utilized."* CNN, https://www.cnn.com/2012/08/20/world/meast/syria-unrest/index.html

400 Robert Gates, in his memoirs "Duty: Memoirs of a Secretary at War", had this to say about Joe Biden's experience: *"I think he has been wrong on nearly every major foreign policy and national security issue over the past four decade".* Gates had been President Bush' Defense Secretary from 2006 to 2008, and Obama's from 2008 to 2011.

401 "Joseph McCarthy: Reexamining the Life and Legacy of America's Most Hated Senator," Arthur Herman, The Free Press, 2000, p. 121-128.

402 "What does it mean to be Alawite, and why does it matter in Syria?," Los Angeles Times, February 7, 2012, http://latimesblogs. latimes.com/world_now/2012/02/syrian-president-alawite-wha t-does-that-mean-and-why-does-it-matter.html

403 "Syrian rebel leader Salim Idriss admits difficulty of unifying fighters," McClatchy, May 7, 2013, https://www.mcclatchydc.com/news/nation-world/world/article24748906.html

404 "Free Syrian Army rebels defect to Islamist group Jabhat al-Nusra," The Guardian, May 8, 2013, https://www.theguardian.com/world/2013/ may/08/free-syrian-army-rebels-defect-islamist-group

405 "Free Syrian Army replaces chief-of-staff Salim Idriss," BBC News, February 17, 2014, https://www.bbc.co.uk/news/world-middle-east-26224498

406 The most notable Brotherhood affiliate in the U.S. is the Council on American Islamic Relations, known as CAIR. "US group CAIR named terrorist organization by United Arab Emirates," Fox News, November 17, 2014, http://www.foxnews.com/us/2014/11/17/us-group-cair-adde d-to-terror-list-by-united-arab-emirates.html

407 "Politics or piety." Brookings, https://www.brookings.edu/research/ politics-or-piety-why-the-muslim-brotherhood-engages-in-social -service-provision-a-conversation/

408 "Breaking the silence over Hama atrocities," al-Jazeera, February 2, 2012, https://www.aljazeera.com/indepth/features/2012/02/201222321 55715210.html

409 "How the Muslim Brotherhood Hijacked Syria's Revolution," ForeignPolicy, March 13, 2013, https://foreignpolicy.com/2013/03/13/ how-the-muslim-brotherhood-hijacked-syrias-revolution/

410 "Who is Jamaat al-Tawid and Jihad," Stratfor, September 20, 2004, https://worldview.stratfor.com/article/who-jamaat-al-tawhid-and-jihad

411 Dhimmis: Non Muslims.

412 A kunya is a nickname or a war name. Abu means Father, followed by first born or symbolic name.

413 "What ISIS' Leader Really Wants," The New Republic, September 1, 2014, https://newrepublic.com/article/119259/isis-history-islamic-states-new-caliphate-syria-and-iraq

The Beginning Of The End:

414 See Chapter 11.

415 See Chapter 12.

416 "Iran's Leaders on Iraq Crisis and ISIS," United States Institute of Peace, October 16, 2014, http://iranprimer.usip.org/blog/2014/oct/16/iran s-leaders-iraq-crisis-and-isis

[417] "Remembering Budyonnovsk," OpenDemocracy, June 15, 2015, https://www.opendemocracy.net/svetlana-bolotnikova/remembering-budyonnovsk

[418] See Chapter 2.

[419] "West praises Putin, the butcher of Grozny," Socialist Worker, January 6, 2000, https://socialistworker.co.uk/art/36645/West+praises+Putin%2C+the+butcher+of+Grozny

[420] "Shamil Basayev," The Economist, July 13, 2006, https://www.economist.com/node/7160644

[421] "The Battle Against Wahhabism in Chechnya," Islamoblog, December 2008, http://islamoblog.blogspot.com/2008/12/battle-against-wahhabism-in-chechnya.html

[422] "Sanctions against Russia hit Chechen leader's prize-winning racehorses," The Guardian, October 17, 2014, https://www.theguardian.com/world/2014/oct/17/russia-sanctions-hit-chechen-leaders-racehorses

[423] "Chechen leader raps Qaradawi for calling Russia "enemy of Islam," Interfax-Religion, November 12, 2012, http://www.interfax-religion.com/?act=news&div=10080

[424] "Russia is not an enemy of Islam – senior Muslim cleric," RT, November 21, 2012, https://www.rt.com/politics/islam-muslim-enemy-mufti-220/

[425] See Chapter 4.

[426] The November 2, 1917 letter from Foreign Secretary Lord Balfour to Lord Rothschild, announcing support for the establishment of home for the Jewish people in Palestine.

[427] In today's terms, this would be worth between $80,000 and $100,000 per month.

[428] "Russians in Grozny bloodbath," The Guardian, December 15, 1999, https://www.theguardian.com/world/1999/dec/16/russia.chechnya

[429] United Nations Security Council Resolution 2118, signed September 27th, 2013. By mid-June 2014, the Syrian regime was still holding onto at least twelve chemical weapons plants, five of which were underground, and was regularly using them against its people.

[430] http://www.atlanticcouncil.org/about/history

[431] The sectarian nature of Syrian rebels is well documented in this BBC article, "Guide to Syrian Rebels," BBC News, December 13, 2013, https://www.bbc.com/news/world-middle-east-24403003

[432] Robert S. Ford, op-ed in The York Times, June 10th, 2014, http://www.nytimes.com/2014/06/11/opinion/ford-arm-syrias-opposition.html?hp&rref=opinion&_r=1

433 UN announcement of Lakhdar Brahimi's resignation, May 13, 2014, https://www.un.org/sg/en/content/sg/speeches/2014-05-13/announcement-lakhdar-brahimis-resignation-united-nations-and-arab

434 http://www.timesofisrael.com/anti-israel-statement-from-2002-may -haunt-powers-un-envoy-bid/

435 "Egyptian court sentences 529 Brotherhood members to death," Reuters, March 24, 2014, https://www.reuters.com/article/us-egypt-brotherhood-courts/egyptian-court-sentences-529-brotherhood-members-to-death-idUSBREA2N0BT20140324

436 Abu Mazen is Mahmoud Abbas' kunya, i.e. his war name.

437 The PNA is the body which administers the Palestinian territories, to include the West Bank and the Gaza strip which Israel had annexed after its decisive win against Egypt, Jordan and Syria in the 1967 Six-Day War. It was created in the framework of the Oslo accords, signed in 1993-95 after the PLO and Israel had recognized each other's right to exist. The Oslo accords, however, omitted to provide for the creation of a Palestinian state.

438 Excluding East Jerusalem and its suburbs, which Israel had annexed after the Six-Day War in 1967.

439 "Hamas Covenant 1988," The Avalon Project, Yale Law School, http://avalon.law.yale.edu/20th_century/hamas.asp

440 When the United Nations recognized Palestine as a non-member UN observer state (November 29th, 2012), the PNA changed its official name to the State of Palestine.

441 "Egypt's El-Sisi Vows to FINISH OFF The Muslim Brotherhood," YouTube, CNN, https://youtu.be/ssE8fqofSlI

442 "Statement by the Press Secretary on the Presidential Elections in Egypt", June 4, 2014, http://www.whitehouse.gov/the-press-office/2014/06/04/statement-press-secretary-presidential-election-egypt

443 Politico Magazine, January 12th, 2014, "Hey General, It's Me, Chuck. Again.", by Shadi Hamid. http://www.politico.com/magazine/story/2014/01/chuck-hagel-al-sissi-egypt-102068_Page2.html#.U71gKtMg85s

444 Jerusalem Post, January 3rd, 2014, "US pressuring Egyptian army not to back al-Sisi in presidential election", by Ariel Ben Salomon, http://www.jpost.com/Middle-East/US-pressuring-Egyptian-army-not-to-back-al-Sisi-in-presidential-election-336975

445 Saudi Press Agency, June 3, 2014, "Saudi Reaction to Al-Sisi Victory in Presidential Election", http://susris.com/2014/06/06/saudi-reaction-to-al-sisi-victory-in-presidential-election/

446 In particular by the pro-Hezbollah Lebanese daily Al Akhbar and the liberal-left Israeli daily Haaretz.

447 MEMO, The Middle East Monitor, February 13, 2014, "Erdogan: Turkey will not recognize Al-Sisi if elected President", https://www.middleeastmonitor. com/news/europe/9726-erdogan-turkey-will-not-recognise-al-sisi-if-ele cted-president

448 The Jerusalem Post, October 8th, 2013, "Turkish PM Erdogan hosts increasingly isolated Hamas leader Mashaal in Ankara", http://www.jpost. com/Diplomacy-and-Politics/Turkish-PM-Erdogan-hosts-increasingly-isolated-Hamas-leader-Mashaal-in-Ankara-328176

449 "Presidents of Russia, Egypt meet for second time," Russia Beyond, April 23, 2013, https://www.rbth.com/international/2013/04/23/ presidents_of_russia_egypt_meet_for_second_time_25317.html

450 "Chechen leader raps Qaradawi for calling Russia "enemy of Islam," November 12, 2012, Interfax-Religion, http://www.interfax-religion. com/?act=news&div=10080

451 "Abbas's Thesis That Zionists Worked with the Nazis: Taught in Palestinian Schools," Israel Resource Review, April 30, 2011, http://israelbehindthenews.com/abbass-thesis-that-zionists-worked-with-the-nazis-taught-in-palestinian-schools/7159/

452 "National Security Strategy – May 2010," http://nssarchive.us/NSSR/2010.pdf

Spy Freeze:

453 "Edward Snowden: the whistleblower behind the NSA surveillance revelations," The Guardian, June 11. 2013, https://www.theguardian.com/ world/2013/jun/09/edward-snowden-nsa-whistleblower-surveillance

454 "Booz Allen, the World's Most Profitable Spy Organization," Bloomberg Businessweek, June 21, 2013, http://www.bloomberg. com/news/articles/2013-06-20/booz-allen-the-worlds-most-profitable-spy-organization

455 Five Eyes is the code name for the United Kingdom-United States of America Agreement, or UKUSA, an Intelligence alliance comprised of Australia, Canada, New Zealand, the United Kingdom and the United States, which dates back to the Atlantic Charter of 1941, which itself defined the Allied goals for WWII and after.

456 PRISM is an NSA system that gathers intelligence from the largest Internet companies, Microsoft, Google, Facebook, Yahoo and others. "Here is everything we know about PRISM to date," The Washington Post, June 12, 2013, https://www.washingtonpost.com/ news/wonk/wp/2013/06/12/heres-everything-we-know-about-prism-to-date/?utm_term=.9e28860ba211

457 Rory Caroll, The Guardian, July 1st, 2013, http://www.businessinsider.com/ correa-we-helped-snowden-by-mistake-2013-7

458 WikiLeaks, founded in 2006, is a major online publisher of "secret" information, news leaks and classified media from "anonymous" sources.

459 "Incredible strain in relations between Ecuador and Wikileaks founder Julian Assange over his involvement in Edward Snowden NSA whistleblower affair," The Independent, July 1, 2013, https://www.independent.co.uk/ news/world/politics/exclusive-incredible-strain-in-relations-between -ecuador-and-wikileaks-founder-julian-assange-over-8681776.html

460 "Edward Snowden and the NSA files – timeline," The Guardian, August 21, 2013, https://www.theguardian.com/world/2013/jun/23/ edward-snowden-nsa-files-timeline

461 https://fas.org/irp/offdocs/ppd/ppd-20-fs.pdf

462 "Obama orders US to draw up overseas target list for cyber-attacks," June 7, 2013, https://www.theguardian.com/world/2013/jun/07/obama- china-targets-cyber-overseas

463 Easy pun. Obama's ears were oversized, by press accounts.

464 The Khawam sisters and General Petraeus affair, See Chapter 11.

465 The Telegraph, October 11, 2013, https://www.telegraph.co.uk/news/ uknews/terrorism-in-the-uk/10371541/Sir-David-Omand-Snowden-lea k-is-most-catastrophic-loss-to-British-intelligence-ever.html

466 See Chapter 12.

467 "Edward Snowden: the whistleblower behind the NSA surveillance revelations," The Guardian, June 11, 2013, https://www.theguardian.com/ world/2013/jun/09/edward-snowden-nsa-whistleblower-surveillance

468 The elections were to be held on June 14, 2013. Rouhani announced his candidacy on March 11, and registered on May 7. He won with 51% of the votes. https://www.rand.org/content/dam/rand/pubs/perspectives/ PE100/PE109/RAND_PE109.pdf

469 "Obama hold historic phone call with Rouhani and hints at end to sanctions," The Guardian, September 28, 2013, https://www.theguardian. com/world/2013/sep/27/obama-phone-call-iranian-president-rouhani

470 "Angela Merkel's call to Obama: are you bugging my mobile phone?," The Guardian, October 24, 2013, https://www.theguardian.com/world/2013/ oct/23/us-monitored-angela-merkel-german

471 "Germany to probe alleged NSA snooping of Chancellor Merkel's phone", June 4, 2014, http://on.rt.com/t11cgk

472 "GCHQ intercepted foreign politicians' communications at G10 summits," The Guardian, June 17, 2013, https://www.theguardian.com/uk/2013/ jun/16/gchq-intercepted-communications-g20-summits

473 "GCHQ and NSA Targeted Private German Companies and Merkel,", Spiegel Online, March 29, 2014, http://www.spiegel.de/international/germany/ gchq-and-nsa-targeted-private-german-companies-a-961444.html

[474] "Obama holds historic phone call with Rouhani and hints at end to sanctions," The Guardian, September 28, 2013, https://www.theguardian.com/world/2013/sep/27/obama-phone-call-iranian-president-rouhani

[475] "The Geneva deal and Iran's Nuclear Ambitions," Fathom, Winter 2014, http://fathomjournal.org/the-geneva-deal-and-irans-nuclear-ambitions/

[476] "Prime Minister says the world must not be fooled by the new face of the Iranian Regime," Full text of Netanyahu's 2013 speech to the UN General assembly, October 1, 2013, https://www.timesofisrael.com/full-text-netanyahus-2013-speech-to-the-un-general-assembly/

[477] "Ukraine' Tymoshenko should be free in a month: daughter," Reuters World News, October 17, 2013, https://www.reuters.com/article/us-ukraine-tymoshenko-idUSBRE99G0EG20131017

[478] "Ukraine fails to pass bills freeing Yulia Tymoshenko before EU summit," The Guardian, November 21, 2013, https://www.theguardian.com/world/2013/nov/21/yulia-tymoshenko-ukraine-fails-pass-bills

[479] See Chapter 12.

[480] "Sanctions Relief: What Did Iran Get?", Roubini Global Economics, http://www.defenddemocracy.org/content/uploads/general/Roubini FDDReport.pdf

[481] USA Today, November 24th, 2013, "Israel calls Iran nuclear deal a "historic mistake", by Michele Chabin, http://www.usatoday.com/story/news/world/2013/11/24/iran-nuclear-deal-israel-reactions/3690161/

[482] Prince Mohammed bin Nawwaf bin Abdulaziz was Saudi Arabia's Ambassador to the U.K. since 2005.

[483] Time, November 26th, 2013, Aryn Baker, "Saudi Arabia Considers Nuclear Weapons After Iran's Geneva Deal", http://world.time.com/2013/11/26/saudi-arabia-considers-nuclear-weapons-after-irans-geneva-deal/

[484] John Kerry, paraphrasing Ronald Reagan: "You don't have to trust the people you're dealing with, you have to have a mechanism put in place whereby you know exactly what you're getting and you know exactly what they're doing." https://www.politico.com/blogs/politico-now/2013/11/kerry-on-iran-its-not-based-on-trust-178235

[485] Iran Deal, November 2013. The official State Department estimate was $7 billion.

[486] See Chapter 12 and Al Jazeera "Timeline: Ukraine's political crisis," September 20, 2014, https://www.aljazeera.com/news/europe/2014/03/timeline-ukraine-political-crisis-201431143722854652.html

[487] The al-Anfal campaign, including the Halabja Massacre of March 16th, 1988.

[488] An important note here about the Yazidis in Iraqi Kurdistan. The Yazidi genocide was perpetrated by the Islamic State and started on August 3, 2014. On that morning, the KRG Peshmerga withdrew for Yazidi land,

the Shingal, or Sinjar, Mountains. Why is a difficult question for the KRG, suffice it to say that many Yazidis were viewing the settlement of Sunni Iraqi Kurds inn Shingal as "Kurdification," a way to include it in the Greater Kurdistan.

489 See Chapter 11.
490 H. Res. 411 (113th Congress): Impeaching Eric H. Holder, Jr., Attorney General of the United States, for high crimes and misdemeanors," https://www.govtrack.us/congress/bills/113/hres411
491 Nancy Pelosi's 2010 quote about the vote on the Affordable Care Act is now famous: "we have to pass the bill so that you can find out what is in it […]"
492 Israel had launched a massive operation called Protective Edge in Gaza to stop Hamas rocket fire, which had increased after the kidnapping and murder of three Israeli teens and the IDF reprisal.
493 Associated Press-GfK Poll: Ukraine crisis sinks Obama's already-low approval rating, but sanctions draw support", March 26, 2014, http://ap-gfkpoll.com/featured/our-latest-story-4, and "Crises Undercut Support for Obama's long game in Foreign Policy", Wall Street Journal Online, August 6, 2014, https://www.wsj.com/articles/crises-undercut-support-for-obamas-long-game-in-foreign-policy-1407369041
494 Time Warner owns CNN.
495 "Hagel: Bergdahl deal was "imperfect" but right decision," CNN, June 11, 2014, http://www.cnn.com/2014/06/11/politics/bowe-bergdahl-release/index.html
496 "Chechen leader raps Qaradawi for calling Russia "enemy of Islam," November 12, 2012, Interfax Religion, http://www.interfax-religion.com/?act=news&div=10080
497 CNN U.S. May 31st, 2014, "The Gitmo detainees swapped for Bergdahl: Who are they?": http://www.cnn.com/2014/05/31/us/bergdahl-transferred-guantanamo-detainees/index.html
498 "Obama, Parents give Thanks for Bergdahl's Freedom", U.S. Department of Defense, DoD News, May 31, 2014, http://archive.defense.gov/news/newsarticle.aspx?id=122377 .
499 July 27, 2014, Nancy Pelosi's interview by CNN's Candy Crowley. https://youtu.be/CaonAORDP-A .
500 Al Jazeera, "US strikes $11bn arms deal with Qatar. Agreement to provide Apache attack helicopters and air-defence systems thought to be biggest US arms deal this year", July 15, 2014, http://www.aljazeera.com/news/middleeast/2014/07/us-strikes-11bn-arms-deal-with-qatar-2014714223825417442.html

[501] Al Jazeera, "Taliban five arrive in Qatar after swap deal", June 1, 2014, http://www.aljazeera.com/news/middleeast/2014/06/taliban-five-arrive-qatar-after-swap-deal-20146113536748321.html

[502] See Chapter 2.

Index

B

About the Author

Franck was born and raised in France, went to Columbia University a long time ago, and became an American citizen in 1993. His grandfather Sroul had to leave Poland in the Twenties, then Germany in the Thirties, but did not have the papers for the steamboat. He stayed on the Riviera, while his trunk landed somewhere in New Jersey, at the baker's daughter he was supposed to marry. From these memories, Franck has nurtured a passion for liberty, freedom, and the pursuit of happiness. He is an engineer by education, an investment and real estate advisor by trade, and an amateur historian when things get out of whack in his world. He writes for his sons, and for all the young adults and older folks who are curious to know, "what happened, really?"

His first book was about the worst decade on Wall Street, 1998 - 2008. Drawing on his thirty years of salt mine experience, first at Brown Brothers Harriman & co, then with his own boutique Capital Max known as The Other Street, he illustrated how the market's decline was about as bad as it gets, yet why the following decade should be spectacularly good. Luckily it was, Schumpeter on steroids. This book is different, a mix of historical facts and hypotheticals, a non-fiction fiction book, but it follows the same principle - we all focus on recent events while losing track of how they developed. Hopefully, Franck got the ending wrong this time. If all goes well, Israel may not have to nuke Iran.

Sroul's trunk is likely gone by now, or maybe in an attic somewhere, but Franck found a meme which he keeps in his sons' quarters – so that the memories live on. He dedicates this book to his wife Sally, and his sons Maxime, Sasha-Raphael, Gabriel, and Noah, who are his oxygen.

And to his father without whom he and his family would have never made it Home. To America.

www.ingramcontent.com/pod-product-compliance
Lightning Source LLC
Chambersburg PA
CBHW060330100426
42812CB00003B/937